Lac la Biche, Alberta

Baptisms, Marriages and Burial

1853 - 1884

Gail Morin

Second Edition

2016

Special Recognition: Geoff Burtsonshaw

Lac la Biche Baptisms, Marriages and Burials 1853-1884

..., Abraham and Genevieve Duquette: M-2, Abraham, adult son of Eyostwaskamikutew and Catherine Gladu, married 20 January 1870, Genevieve Duquette, widow of Frank Johnston, Witnesses: Joseph Duquette, father of Genevieve, and Angelique Sauve, M. R. Remas priest o.m.i. (page 110)

..., Benoit : B-269, Benoit ..., baptized 1 November 1862, age 7 months, son of Joseph ... and Catherine Gibott, Godmother: Agathe Auger, Tissot Jn. priest o.m.i. (page 50)

..., Cecile and Silvy: B-35 and 36, Cecile, age one month, and Silvy, age about 3 years, baptized 15 May 1854, the names of the parents unknown, M. R. Remas p.o.m.i. (page 7)

..., Emilie: S-9, Emilie, buried 19 October 1874, wife of Jean-Baptiste Kakikekamik, Present: J. Bte. Kakikekamik and Charles Houle, H. Leduc priest o.m.i. (page 146-147)

..., Emilie; See Jean-Baptiste Kakikekamik and Emilie

..., Honorine-Marie: B-7, Honorine-Marie, baptized 18 March 1877, age about 2 months, born of the legitimate marriage of Henriand Christine, Godfather: Francois Cardinal, Godmother: Adele Mustatip, H. Leduc priest o.m.i. (page 167-168)

..., Jany: B-11, Jany, baptized 1 March 1878, age one month, legitimate daughter of Hubert and Catherine of Lac Castor, Godmother: Rosalie, E. Grouard priest o.m.i. (page 176)

..., Joseph: B-8, Joseph, baptized 31 March 1878, age three months, legitimate son of the deceased Joseph (of Lac Castor) and Marie Anne Okimawiskam, Godfather: Guillaume Villebrun, E. Grouard priest o.m.i. (page 176)

..., Judith: B-24, Judith, baptized 11 July 1880, born 7 July 1880, of the legitimate marriage of Pascal and Angele, Godmother: Marie, E. Grouard priest o.m.i. (page 198)

..., Marguerite: B-35, Marguerite, baptized 24 October 1877, age about 15 days, legitimate daughter of Pierre and Rosalie (of Lac Castor), Godmother: Isabelle, E. Grouard priest o.m.i. (page 173)

..., Marie: B-11, Marie, baptized 19 February 1881, age about 80 years, the priest served as godfather, Collignon o.m.i. p. (page 204)

..., Marie-Luce: B-13, Marie-Luce, baptized 29 April 1878, legitimate daughter of Jean-Baptiste (son of the deceased Louison) and Josephine Mesaskiw, Godmother: Marie-Luce, E. Grouard priest o.m.i. (page 178)

..., Mary: B-28, Mary, baptized 20 August 1877, legitimate daughter of Jean-Pierre and Judith (Montagnais), Godmother: Sophie, E. Grouard, priest o.m.i. (page 172)

..., Melanie; See Pierre Gladu and Melanie

..., Therese: B-26, Therese ..., baptized 11 October 1882, age about 3 months, legitimate daughter of Jean-Baptiste and ___, Godmother: Marie, wife of Antoine, E. Grouard priest o.m.i. (page 221)

1

Lac la Biche Baptisms, Marriages and Burials 1853-1884

..., Therese; See Joseph Nipiteham and Therese

...., Veronique: S-2 Veronique, wife of Paul Desjarlais, buried 15 February 1873, died 4 days, age about 35 years, Present: Jules Desjarlais and Jean-Baptiste Cardinal, V. Vegreville priest o.m.i. (page 134)

**** B-363, ... missing..... Leblanc, Godmother: Bethsy Branconnier, V. Vegreville priest o.m.i. (page 71)

**** Missing entries: page 70, B-358, B-359, B-360, B-361, B-362, B-363 (1st part), in 1865

Adam, Bethsy: B-130, Bethsy Adam, baptized 17 May 1857, age 9 months, daughter of George Adam and Angelique Dejarlais, Godfather: Louis Desrochers, Godmother: .. Baudry, Tissot priest (page 25)

Adam, Isabelle; See Jean-Baptiste Belcourt and Isabelle Adam

Akamiyesiw, Marie: B-45, Marie Akamiyesiw, baptized 10 May 1854, age 7 years, Godmother: Margueritte Pepamwewitam, M. R. Remas p.o.m.i. (page 8)

Alexandre Gladu dit Janvier, baptized 13 July 1871, age 5 months, son of Pierre Gladu dit Janvier and Melanie Naali, Godmother: Victoire Naali, + Henri Ev. D'Anomour o.m.i. (page 121)

Alexis, Emilia: B-33, Emilia Alexis, baptized 18 September 1869, age 15 days, legitimate daughter of Alexis (Cris) and Isabelle Watsekan, Godmother: Julie McGillis, V. Vegreville p.m.a.o.m.i. (page 107)

Amiskiyinisis, Jean Bapatiste: B-291, Jean-Baptiste Amiskiyinisis, baptized 8 December 1863, born yesterday, of the legitimate marriage of Jean-Baptiste Amiskiyinisis and Nannecy Quintal, Godfather: Augustin Auger, Godmother: Esther Bruneau, Tissot Jn. priest o.m.i. (page 55)

Amiskuiyinis, Jean Baptiste: B-189, Jean Baptiste Amiskuiyinis, baptized 12 June 1859, age about 25 years, Godfather: Joseph Ladouceur, Tissot Jn. priest o.m.i. (page 34-35)

Amiskuiyinisis, Monique: B-227, Monique Amiskuiyinisis, baptized 9 June 1861, born today, of the legitimate marriage of Baptiste Amiskuiynisis and Nancy Quintal, Godmother: Isabelle Quintal, Tissot Jn. priest o.m.i. (page 42)

Amiskuiynisis, Jean Baptiste and Nancy Quintal: M-20, Jean-Baptiste Amiskuiynisis married 26 June 1860 Nancy Quintal, Present: Maisonneuve and Salasse, Tissot Jn priest o.m.i. (page 38)

Amiskweiyinishwew, Madeleine: S-12, Madeleine Amiskweiyinishwew, buried 7 November 1860, age about 50 years, Witnesses: Isidore Decoin and George Cook, Maisonneuve, A. priest o.m.i. (page 39-40)

Amiskweiyinishwew, Magdeleine: B-214, Magdeleine Amiskweiyinishwew, baptized 3 November 1860, age about 50 years, Godmother: Agathe Ladouceur, Tissot Jn priest o.m.i. (page 39)

Amiskwiyinisis, Angele: B-394, Angele Amiskwiyinisis, baptized 12 December 1866, born the same day, legitimate daughter of Jean-Baptiste Amiskwiyinisis and Nancy Quintal, Godmother: Catherine Ladouceur, V. Vegreville, priest mis. o.m.i. (page 77-78)

Lac la Biche Baptisms, Marriages and Burials 1853-1884

Amiskwiyinisis, Sophie: B-32, Sophie Amiskwiyinisis, baptized 12 December 1870, age 8 days, legitimate daughter of Jean-Baptiste Amiskwiyinisis and Nancy Quintal, Godfather: Francois Amiskwiyinisis, Godmother: Philomene Cardinal, V. Vegreville priest o.m.i. (page 116)

Ancy, Suzane: B-71, Suzane Ancy, baptized 17 May 1855, age 6 months, daughter of Ancy, Godmother: Suzanne Laurent, M. R. Remas p.o.m.i. (page 13)

Aniskwewin, Isabelle: See Joseph Bruno and Isabelle Aniskwewin

Anonis, Brigitte: B-203, Brigitte Anonis, baptized 21 April 1860, age 8 years, daughter of Anonis, Tissot Jn priest (page 37-38)

Anpit, Sophie: B-22, Sophie Anpit, baptized 9 November 1873, age one month, daughter of Anpit and Yatcakwan, Godmother: Sophie St.Sauveur, E. Petitot priest o.m.i. (page 139)

Antoine, Lettor (Narebrin); See Jean-Marie Gladu (dit Janvier) and Lettor Antoine (Narebrin)

Apitsiskwesis, Angelique: B-216, Angelique Apitsiskwesis, baptized 30 November 1860, age about 25 years, Godmother: Marguerite Kitimakis, Tissot Jn. priest o.m.i. (page 40)

Apitsiskwesis, Angelique; See Pierre Cardinal and Angelique Apitsiskwesis

Aputsan, Moyse: B-8, Moyse Apuitsan, baptized 18 March 1883, age 20 days, illegitimate son of Aputson Sowisis and Honorine Lapoudre, Godfather: Moyse Decoine, Godmother: Christine Bews (Hughes), Collignon o.m.i.p. (page 225)

Aputsan, Thomas and Honorine Lapoudre: M-3, Thomas Aputsan married 26 August 1883 Honroine Lapoudre, Present: Isidore Decoine (x) and C. Racette (signed), Collignon o.m.i.p. (page 230)

Aputsan, Thomas Sosisis: B-28, Thomas Sosisis Aputsan, baptized 26 August 1883, age about 21 years, son of Sosisis and Kowigutiw, Godfather: Isidore Decoine, Collignon o.m.i.p. (page 230)

Arcan, Caroline: B-41, Caroline Arcan, baptized 29 September 1869, age 9 months, daughter of Abraham Arcan and Kwesesis, Godfather: Julien Genereux, Godmother: Marie Tastawits, V. Vegreville p.m.a.o.m.i. (page 108)

Arkan, Antoine: B-128, Antoine Arkan, baptized 17 May 1857, age 2 years, son of Pierre Arkan and Magdeleine Beaudry, Godfather: Edouard Genereux, Godmother: Marianne Beaudry, Tissot Jn. priest o.m.i. (page 24)

Arkan, Louis: B-132, Louis Arkan, baptized 23 September 1857 (Fort Carlton), age 3 months, son of Pierre Arkan and Magdeleine Crise, Godfather: Louis Leveillee, Godmother: Marguerite Desjarlais, Tissot priest (page 25)

Asteaganis, Marguerite: B-177, Marguerite Asteaganis, baptized 19 Defc 1858, age about 5 years, daughter of Asteaganis and Marguerite Mustuskpeyakut, Godmother: Marie Mustuskpeyakut, Maisonneuve A. priest o.m.i. (page 32)

Atakakup, Joseph: B-39, Joseph Atakakup, baptized 26 September 1869, age 9 months, legitimate son of Antoine Atakakup and Judith Bellanger, Godfather: Jean Baptiste Lafont, Godmother: Marie Tastawits, V. Vegreville p.m.a.o.m.i. (page 108)

Atayokan, Therese: S-48, Therese Atayokan, buried 19 April 1868, died yesterday, age 22 years, daughter of Abraham Atayokan, Present: Eugene Wawieyenam and Louison Sisawapas, Maisonneuve A. p.o.m.i. (page 89-90)

Atekamck, Louise: B-42, Louis Atekamek, baptized 28 May 1854, age 2 years, daughter of Atekamek and Catherine, Godfather: Francois Decoing, M. R. Remas p.o.m.i. (page 8)

Atoyokan, Therese; See Jean Baptiste Kakikekamik and Therese Atoyokan

Attikamek, Antoine: B-109, Antoine Attikamek, baptized 18 January 1856, age about one year, son of Victor Attikamek and Catherine Nabes (Durant), Godfather: James McGuay, Maisonneuve A. priest o.m.i. (page 21)

Attikamek, Rosalie: B-250, Rosalie Attikamek, baptized 19 March 1862, age one month, daughter of Victor Attikamek and Catherine Durand, Godfather: Alexis Cardinal, Alb. Lacombe priest o.m.i. (page 47)

Attinakwawis, Marie-Lucie: B-5, Marie-Lucie, baptized 1 February 1877, age about 30 years, Godfather: Mr. l'abbe Jolys (signed J. M. Jolys), Godmother: Marie-Lucie Fortier, F. Le Serrec priest o.m.i. (page 166-167)

Attinakwawis, Marie-Lucie; See Baptiste Cris and Marie-Lucie Attinakwawis

Auge, Antoine: B-12, Antoine Auge, baptized 31 March 1872, age about 20 years, son of Alexis Auge and Abittawiyasik, Godfather: Adam Ladouceur, Godmother: Genevieve Ladouceur, M. R. Remas priest o.m.i. (page 128)

Auge, Augustin: B-29, Augustin Auge, baptized 21 September 1869, age 8 months, son of John Auge and Etawisikmeniw, Godfather: Francois Dubois, Godmother: Caroline Johnston, M. R. Remas priest o.m.i. (page 106)

Auge, Francois: B-28, Francois Auge, baptized 22 September 1869, age about 2 years and 10 months, daughter [sic] of John Auge and Etawisikmeniw, Godfather: Abraham Yasaskamikkatew, Godmother: Agathe Cardinal, M. R. Remas priest o.m.i. (page 105_106)

Auge, Marie-Eugenie;B-31, Marie Eugenie Auge, baptized 6 September 1875, born yesterday, legitimate daughter of Augustin Auge and Sylvie Bruno, Godmother: Marie_Georgina Hudon (signed), M. R. Remas priest o.m.i. (page 156)

Auge, Melie: B-13, Melie Auge, baptized 12 July 1870, 10 July 1870, of the legitimate marriage of Augustin Auge and Silvy Bruneau, Godmother: Melie Bruneau, M. R. Remas p.m.a.o.m.i. (page 112)

Lac la Biche Baptisms, Marriages and Burials 1853-1884

Auger, Adam (Oger): B-19, Adam Oger [Auger], baptized 15 June 1871, age 8 months, legitimate son of Toussaint Oger and Angelique Kiyakikwanepiw, Godmother: Marguerite Laroque, V. Vegreville p.m.a.o.m.i. (page 122)

Auger, Agathe; See Charly Johnston and Agathe Auger

Auger, Augustin: B-3, Augustin Auger, baptized 8 February 1878, born today, of the legitimate marriage of Pierre Auger and Julia Rivet, Godfather: Augustin Auger, Godmother: Silvy Bruneau, Collignon p.o.m.i. (page 176)

Auger, Baptiste: B-23, Baptiste Auger, baptized 16 August 1879, about age 6, of Wabaskaw, son of John Auger and Missis, no Godfather, E. Grouard priest o.m.i. (page 190)

Auger, Chromance: B-14, Chromance Auger, baptized __ May 1878, age 2 days, legitimate son of Augustin Auger and Rosalie Labonne [Sylvie Bruneau], Godfather: Baptiste Castor, Godmother: Nancy Quintal, J. M. Jolys priest (page 178)

Auger, David (Oger) and Philomene Cardinal: M-72, David Oger, minor son of Augustin Oger and the late [..] Labonne (Beaudoin), married 1 December 1868, Philomene Cardinal, minor daughter of Alexis Cardinal and Nancy Quintal, Present: Joseph Duquette and Nancy Quintal, V. Vegreville p.m.a.o.m.i. (page 96-97)

Auger, Elise (Oger) and Siyapokiskwepiw: M-71, Elisa Oger, minor daughter Augustin Oger and Rosalie Labonne (Beaudoin), married 26 October 1868, Siyapokisikwepiw, Present: Augustin Oger and Joseph Duquette, V. Vegreville p.m.a.o.m.i. (page 96)

Auger, Emelie (Oger): S-3, Emelie Oger, bu. 17 June 1871, died yesterday, age 11 months, daughter of Augustin Oger and Silvie Bruneau, Witnesses: Charles Houle and Joseph Ladouceur, V. Vegreville p.m.a.o.m.i. (page 122)

Auger, Emile Pierre: B-1, Emile Pierre Auger, baptized 10 January 1880, born today, of the legitimate marriage of Pierre Auger and Julie Rivet, Godfather: Charles House, Godmother: Julie Auger, Collignon o.m.i. (page 193)

Auger, Eulalie: B-13, Eulalie Auger, baptized 20 May 1883, born yesterday of the legitimate marriage of Augustin Auger and Sylvia Bruneau, Godfather: Alec Johnston, Godmother: Angele Hoole, Collignon o.m.i.p. (page 227)

Auger, Euphrosine: S-6, Euphrosine Oger [Auger], buried 31 August 1873, daughter of ___, V. Vegreville p.m.a.o.m.i. (page 138)

Auger, Felix: B-15, Felix Auger, baptized 3 June 1872, born today, legitimate son of Augustin Auger and Silvy Bruneau, Godfather: Francois Laroque, Godmother: Isabelle Bruneau, V. Vegreville p.m.a.o.m.i. (page 130)

Auger, Jean Marie: S-8, Jean-Marie Auger, buried 26 June 1857, died yesterday, age 19 years, son of Baptiste Auger and Susanne Gray, Witnesses: Joseph Ladouceur and Joseph Roy, Maisonneuve A. priest o.m.i. (page 23)

Lac la Biche Baptisms, Marriages and Burials 1853-1884

Auger, Julie: B-275, Julie Auger, baptized 18 March 1863, born 23 January 1863, of the legitimate marriage of Augustin Auger and Silvie Bruneau, Godfather: Joseph Ladouceur, Godmother: Julie Auger, Tissot Jn. priest o.m.i. (page 51)

Auger, Julie: S-1, Julie Auger, buried 1 February 1877, died yesterday age 55 years, wife of Joseph Ladouceur, Present: Joseph Ladouceur and Pierre Ladouceur, H. Leduc priest o.m.i. (page 167)

Auger, Julie; See Narcisse Ladouceur and Julie Auger

Auger, Julien-Gregoire: B-35, Julien-Gregoire Auger, baptized 26 November 1880, born today, of the legitimate marriage of Augustin Auger and Silie Bruneau, Godfather: Paul Pichon, Godmother: Marguerite Fosseneuve, Collignon o.m.i.p. (page 201)

Auger, Marguerite: B-344, Marguerite Auger, baptized 27 May 1865, born the same day, of the legitimate marriage of Augustin Auger and Sylvie Bruneau, Godfather: Jacques Dumont, Godmother: Marianne Bruneau, Masionneuve, A. priest o.m.i. (page 66)

Auger, Marie (Oger): B-448, Marie Oger, baptized 6 October 1868, age 2 months, legitimate daughter of Toussaint Oger and Angelique Kiyakikwanepiw, Godmother: Catherine Pepamisowepiw, V. Vegreville, p.m.a.o.m.i. (page 96)

Auger, Marie-Adele: B-13, Marie-Adele Auger, baptized 4 April 1875, age about 60 years, daughter of Auger, widow of Andre Gladu, Godfather: Brother Alexandre, Godmother: Sister Daunais, A. Bruneaut priest o.m.i. A. Lambert o.m.i. (page 151)

Auger, Marie-Christine: B-9, Marie-Christine Auger, baptized 26 March 1882, born yesterday, of the legitimate marriage of Pierre Auger and Julie Rivet, Godfather: Thomy Huppe, Godmother: Sister Youville (signed), Collignon o.m.i.p. (page 217)

Auger, Marie-Christine: S-6, Marie-Christine Auger, buried 22 June 1882, died yesterday, age about 4 months, daughter of Pierre Auger and Julia Rivet, Witnesses: Augustin Auger and Pierre, Collignon o.m.i.p. (page 219)

Auger, Marie-Emilie: B-11, Marie-Emilie Auger, baptized 11 May 1883, born day before yesterday, of the legitimate marriage of Pierre Auger and Julie Rivet, Godmother: Sister Donnet, Collignon o.m.i.p. (page 226)

Auger, Michel: B-137, Michel Auger, baptized 4 October 1857, son of Antoine Auger and Louise Boucher, Godfather: Michel Normand, Godmother: Catherine Boucher, Tissot Jn. priest o.m.i. (page 26)

Auger, Narcisse: B-24, Narcisse Auger, baptized 16 August 1879, about age 3, of Wabaskaw, son of John Auger and Missis, Christened at Lac Wabaskaw by Paulette Desjarlais, E. Grouard priest o.m.i. (page 190)

Auger, Paulette: S-29, Paulette Auger, buried 12 October 1865, died 11 October 1865, age about 18 years, Present: Paul Decoin and Augustin Auger, Maisonneuve A. priest o.m.i. (page 68)

Lac la Biche Baptisms, Marriages and Burials 1853-1884

Auger, Pierre and Julia Rivet: M-1, Pierre Auger, legitimate adult son of Augustin Auger and Rosalie Labonne, married 8 January 1877, Julia Rivet, legitimate minor daughter of Louis Rivet and Marguerite Hamel, Present: Pierre Ladouceur and Augustin Auger, H. Leduc priest o.m.i. (page 166)

Auger, Therese: B-434, Therese Auger, baptized 20 January 1868, born yesterday, legitimate d/o Augustin Auger and Sylvie Bruneau, Godfather: Adam Ladouceur, Godmother: Therese Ladouceur, V. Vegreville p.m.a.o.m.i. (page 88)

Aulianille, Eugenie: B-88, Eugenie Aulianille, baptized 30 March 1856, age 3 months, legitimate daughter of Augustin Aulianille and Clotilde Thekas, Godfather: Alexis Aubichon, Godmother: Catherine Ekenakuope, Tissot Jn. o.m.i. (page 16)

Autsethethed, Louise: B-353, Louise Autsethethed, baptized 20 September 1865, legitimate daughter of Gregoire Autsethethed and Francoise Tsutsez, Godfather: Antoine Derez, Godmother: Victoire, V. Vegreville priest o.m.i. (page 68)

Ayamihakan, Moise: B-186, Moise Ayamihakan, baptized 20 April 1859, age 3 months and 8 days, daughter of Louis Ayamihakan and Susanne Assiniboinisse, Godmother: Julie Auge, Tissot Jn. priest o.m.i. (page 34)

Ayikisan, Julie-Victoria: B-11, Julie-Victoria Ayikisan, baptized 14 March 1880, age about 5 months, daughter of Baptiste Ayikisan and Misinikapawiw, Godmother: Domitilde Jean-Marie, Collignon o.m.i. priest. (page 195)

Aymawiniw, Pierre: B-29, Pierre Aymawiniw, baptized 16 July 1876, age 7 years, son of Nanimis dit Chatelain and Wapasakaye, Godfather: brother Lecomte (signed H. Lecomte o.m.i.), Godmother: Catherine Simpson, E. Petitot priest o.m.i. (page 163)

Aytamatam, Adelaide: B-46, Adelaide Aytamatam, baptized 9 July 1854, born 8 July 1854, of Aytamatam and Wiyapittulhip, Godmother: Angelique, M. R. Remas p.o.m.i. (page 8)

Baptisis, Joseph: B-32, Joseph Baptisis, baptized 8 October 1876, age about 2 years, son of Baptiste and Atinakwawis, Godfather: Ducharme, Godmother: Marie, Collignon p.o.m.i. (page 164)

Baptisis, Moise: B-15, Moise Baptisis, baptized 8 April 1877, age about 20 days, legitimate son of Baptisis and Marie, Godmother: Agathe, Collignon p.o.m.i. (page 169)

Batiche, Angelique: B-232, Angelique Batoche, baptized 19 August 1861, age about 25 years, daughter of Louis Batoche, Godmother: Marie Batoche, Tissot Jn. priest o.m.i. (page 43)

Batoche, Agnes: B-106, Agnes Batoche, baptized 10 October 1856, age about 21 years, daughter of Louis Batoche and Marguerite Okimawaskamikinam, Godmother: Julie Auge, Tissot Jn, priest o.m.i. (page 20)

Batoche, Angelique; See Paul Pinakay and Angelique Batoche

Batoche, Angelique; See Joseph Pinakay and Angelique Batoche

Lac la Biche Baptisms, Marriages and Burials 1853-1884

Batoche, Francois: B-5, Francois Batoche, baptized 4 October 1853, age quelques months, son of Louis Batoche and Okimawaskamikinam, Godfather: Pepamasamowinin, Godmother: Marguerite Tshimakits, M. R. Remas p.o.m.i. (page 2-3)

Batoche, Louis and Marguerite Okimawaskanikinam: M-18, Louis Batoche, age about 60 years, married 16 October 1859, Marguerite Okimawaskanikinam, Present: Charles Houle and F. Salatse, Tissot Jn. priest o.m.i. (page 36)

Batoche, Louis: B-72, Louis Batoche, baptized 29 May 1855, age 50 years, Godfather: Pierre Boucher, M. R. Remas p.o.m.i. (page 13)

Batoche, Olive: B-231, Olive Batoche, baptized 18 August 1861, age about 12 days, daughter of Andre Batoche and Catherine Crise, Godmother: Marie Desjarlais, Maisonneuve A. priest o.m.i. (page 43)

Batoche, Rosalie: S-35, Rosalie Batoche, buried 5 January 1867, died yesterday, age 33 years, legitimate daughter of Louis Batoche and Marguerite Okimawaskamiskinam, Present: Joseph Ladouceur and Augustin Auger, V. Vegreville, priest mis. o.m.i. (page 78)

Batoche, Therese: B-302, Therese Batoche, baptized 6 April 1864, age 2 months, duaghter of Andre Batoche and Catherine Crise, Godmother: Isabelle Kakikekamik, Tissot Jn. priest o.m.i. (page 57)

Beaudry, Abraham: B-86, Abraham Beaudry, baptized 29 February 1856, born yesterday of the legitimate marriage of Joseph Beaudry and Suzanne Ladouceur, Godfather: Abraham Lariviere, Godmother: Nannecy Quintal, Tissot Jn. priest o.m.i. (page 16)

Beauregard, Marie: S-31, Marie Beauregard, buried 21 October 1865 at Fort Pitt, died yesterday, age 7 weeks, daughter of Charles Beauregard and Marie Bellerose, Witnesses: Johny Rowland and Henry Leblanc, V. Vegreville priest o.m.i. (page 71)

Beauregard, Ursule; See Moise Laroque and Ursule Beauregard

Bekeodidjaille, Pierre: B-75, Pierre Bekeodidjaille, baptized 3 August 1855, age about 30 years, Godfather: Clement Collins, Tissot Jn. priest o.m.i. (page 13-14)

Bekeodidjaille, Pierre: S-3, Pierre Bekeodidjaille, buried 4 August 1855, died in the evening, Present: Clement Collins and Baptiste Cardinal, Tissot Jn. priest o.m.i. (page 14)

Belanger, Marie; See Joseph Mallet and Marie Bellanger

Bellecourt, Jean-Baptiste and Isabelle Adam: M-1, Jean_Baptiste Belcourt, minor son of Jean_Baptiste Belcourt and Cecile Caliou, married 7 January 1870, Isabelle Adam, minor daughter of Georges Adam and Angelique Desjarlais, Present: Charles Johnston and Louis Daze, V. Vegreville p.m.a o.m.i. (page 109)

Bellecourt, Jean-Felix: B-49, Jean-Felix Bellecour, baptized 15 April 1881 [entry is between two 7 September 1881 entries], legitimate son of Baptiste Bellecour and Isabelle Desjarlais, Godmother: Flora Hope wife of Villeneuve, E. Grouard priest o.m.i. (page 213)

Bellecourt, John-Robert: B-_, John-Robert Bellecour, supplied the ceremonies on 25 February 1883 and baptized 21 January 1883, Collignon o.m.i.p. (page 225)

Bellecourt, John-Robert: B-1, John-Robert Bellecour, baptized 21 January 1883, age about 5 days, legitimate son of Jean-Baptiste Bellecour and Isabelle Desjarlais, [no godparents], E. Grouard o.m.i. priest. (page 223-224)

Bellecourt, Florine: S-5, Florine Bellecourt, buried 20 February 1879, died yesterday, age about 3 years, daughter of J. B. Bellecourt, Witnesses: Benjamin Belcourt and Narcisse Boucher, D. Collignon priest (page 185)

Bellecourt, Louisa: B-1, Louisa Bellecourt, baptised 5 January 1879, born yesterday of the legitimate marriage of Jean Baptiste Bellecourt and Isabelle Adam, Godfather: St.Pierre Quintal, Godmother: Marie his wife, Collignon priest (page 184)

Bellecourt, Magloire: B-6, Magloire Bellecourt, baptized 18 February 1877, age 3 days, legitimate son of Jean_Baptiste Bellecourt and Isabelle Adam, Godparents: Georges Adam and Angelique Desjarlais; D. Collignon priest (page 167)

Bellehumeur, Isabelle; See Norbert Sauve and Isabelle Bellehumeur

Bellerose, Leysa: B-315, Leysa Bellerose, baptized 20 September 1864, born 1 January 1864, daughter of Olivier Bellerose and Josephte Savard, Godfather: Joe Mallet, Godmother: Marie Bellanger, Maisonneuve A. priest o.m.i. (page 59)

Bews, Christine; See Paul Lapoudre and Christine Bews

Billaozaze, Charles: B-6, Charles Billaozaze, baptized 4 April 1873, age 16 months, legitimate son of Jean-Baptiste Billaozaze and Francoise Donathe, Godfather: Fabien Bisson, Godmother: Marie Gladu, V. Vegreville p.m.a.o.m.i. (page 136)

Billaozaze, Rosalie: B-25, Rosalie Billaozaze, baptized 12 September 1869, age 5 months, legitimate daughter of John Baptiste Billaozaze and Francoise A'asthe, Godmother: Marguerite [...], V. Vegreville p.m.a.o.m.i. (page 105)

Billiozaze, Jean Baptiste and Francoise Radousthe: M-45, Jean Baptiste Billiozaze married 10 April 1865 Francoise Radousthe, Present: Francois Ettioubet and Tsinaze, Tissot Jn. priest o.m.i. (page 65)

Bilnauzage, Justine: B-382, Justine Bilnauzage, baptized 15 September 1866, age 5 months, legitimate daughter of Jean Baptiste Bilnauzage and Francoise Padousthe, Godfather: Antoine Bisson, Godmother: Marianne Lanoure, V. Vegreville o.m.i. (page 75)

Bisson, Agnes, Fabien and Julie: B-18, 19 and 20, Agnes, Fabien and Julie Bission, baptized 19 January 1854, Agnes born last August, Fabien age 5 years, Julie age 4 years, the three children of the legitimate marriage of Alexis Bisson and Catherine, Godfather: Jean Baptiste Quintal, M. R. Remas p.o.m.i. (page 4)

Bisson, Agnes; See Alec Deltot and Agnes Bisson

Bisson, Alexandre: B-416, Alexandre Bisson, baptized 22 September 1867, age 5 months, legitimate son of Fabien Bisson and Marguerite Larossetete, Godfather: Jean_Baptiste Belloozage, Godmother: Angelique Ethalerda, V. Vegreville p.m.a.o.m.i. (page 84_85)

Bisson, Brigitte: B-25, Brigitte Theottine (Bisson), baptized 11 October 1882, age about 2 months, legitimate daughter of Fabien Theottine (Bisson) and Marguerite, Godmother: Angelique, E. Grouard priest o.m.i. (page 221)

Bisson, Christine: B-7, Christine Bisson, baptized 4 April 1873, age 16 months, legitimate daughter of Francois Bisson and Catherine Binorelnulle, Godfather: Fabien Bisson, Godmother: Marie Gladu, V. Vegreville p.m.a.o.m.i. (page 136)

Bisson, Clothilde; See Alek Deltat and Clothilde Bisson

Bisson, Fabien and Marguerite Lagrossette: M-51, Fabien Bisson, minor son of Alexis Bisson and Catherine Netasbae, married 16 September 1866, Marguerite Lagrossetete, minor daughter of Pierre Lagrossetete and Angelique Chaleria, Present: Alexis Bisson and Pierre Lagrossetete, V. Vegreville o.m.i. (page 75)

Bisson, Francois and Catherien Isakale: M-64, Francois Bisson, adult son of Alexis Bisson and Catherine Netasbaedme, married 8 June 1868, Catherine Isakale, widow of Jean Baptiste Tsadelas, Present: Jean Baptiste Billaozzaze and Marie Destoil, V. Vegreville p.m.a.o.m.i. (page 91-92)

Bisson, Francois: B-4, Francois Bison, baptized 12 February 1883, age 3 weeks, legitimate son of Paul Bison and Sophie Grosse-Tete, Godfather: Joseph Ezillale, E. Grouard priest o.m.i. (page 224)

Bisson, Josephine: B-22, Josephine Bisson, baptized 8 October 1871, age 17 months, daughter of Andre Bisson and Charlotte, Godmother: Marie Gladu, V. Vegreville p.m.a.o.m.i. (page 123)

Bisson, Julie; See Louis Nadlaitu and Julie Bisson

Bisson, Julien: B-31, Julien Bisson, baptized 12 October 1884, age 20 days, legitimate son of Fabien Bisson and Marguerite Grosse-Tete, Godmother: Isabelle Desjardins (signed), + Henri Ev. D'Anamour o.m.i. (page 242)

Bisson, Justine; See Francois Enalile and Justine Bison

Bisson, Louison: B-22, Louison Bisson, baptized 3 September 1869, age 8 months, legitimate son of Francois Bisson and Catherine, Godmother: Julie Gladu, V. Vegreville p.m.a.o.m.i. (page 104)

Bisson, Marguerite: B-27, Marguerite Bisson, baptized 15 September 1869, age about 10 months, daughter of Fabien Bisson and Marguerite Hornteray (Lagrisselote), Godmother: Caroline Johnston, M. R. Remas priest o.m.i. (page 105)

Lac la Biche Baptisms, Marriages and Burials 1853-1884

Bisson, Paul-Marcel (Tchilikwizami): B-19, Paul-Marcel (Tchilikwizami) Bisson, baptized 4 November 1873, age 4 months, legitimate son of Fabien Bisson dit Thi-Ottini and Marguerite Lagrosse-Tete, Godfather: Julien Beziaze, Godmother: Marie Judith, E. Petitot priest o.m.i. (page 139)

Bisson, Susanne: B-21, Susanne Bisson, baptized 8 October 1871, age 11 months, legitimate daughter of Fabien Bisson and Marguerite Lagrossetete, Godmother: Marie Gladu, V. Vegreville p.m.a.o.m.i. (page 123)

Boucher, Alexandre: B-17, Alexandre Boucher, baptized 19 July 1884, age 22 days, of the legitimate marriage of Narcisse Boucher and Judith McCarthy, Godfather: Julien Cardinal, Godmother: Liza Ladouceur, Collignon. (page 238)

Boucher, Alphonse: B-17, Alphonse Boucher, baptized 24 May 1875, of the legitimate marriage of Narcisse Boucher and Judith McCrathy, Godfather: Raphael Tremblay, Godmother: Julia Rivet, A. G. B. Brunet priest o.m.i. (page 152)

Boucher, Antoine: B-39, Antoine Boucher, baptized 4 September 1881, born yesterday, of the legitimate marriage of Narcisse Boucher and Judith McCarthy, Godfather: Antoine Laliberte, Godmother: Melanie Lavallee (signed), Collignon o.m.i.p. (page 210)

Boucher, Caroline: S-7, Caroline Boucher, buried 15 September 1881, age about 9 years, Witnesses: Louis Lavallee and Duncan Tremblay, Collignon o.m.i.p. (page 211)

Boucher, Emilien; B-22, Emilien Boucher, baptized 24 August 1878, born yesterday of the legitimate marriage of Narcisse Boucher and Judith McCarthy, Godfather: Pierre Ladouceur, Godmother: Marguerite; Collignon omi. (page 180)

Boucher, Narcisse and Caroline Ladouceur: M-3, Narcisse Boucher married 25 April 1882 Caroline Ladouceur, [no witnesses named], Collignon o.m.i.p. (page 217)

Boucher, Sophie: B-19, Sophie Boucher, baptized 15 July 1883, born this morning, legitimate daughter of Narcisse Boucher and Caroline Ladouceur, Godfather: Pierre Ladouceur, Godmother: Judith McCarty, Collignon o.m.i.p. (page 228)

Bourgard, Charles and Josephte Iroquois: M-1, Charles Bourgard, widower of Josephte Iroquois, married 6 September 1853, Angelique Merat, widow of Louis Olivier, Present: Louis Patnaude and Baptiste Pelletier, M. R. Remas p.o.m.i. (page 2)

Bourke, Arsene: B-337, Arsene Bourk, baptized 1 April 1865, born yesterday, of the legitimate marriage of George Bourk and Agathe Desjarlais, Godfather: Eugene Wawiyenam, Godmother: Esther Bruneau, Masionneuve, A. priest o.m.i. (page 65)

Bourke, Edouard: S-4, Edouard Bourk, buried 10 February 1879, age 11 years, son of Georges Bourk and Agathe Ladouceur, Witnesses: Paul Lavallee and Louison Fosseneuve, Collignon o.m.i. (page 185)

Bourke, Georges: S-5, Georges Bourke, buried 7 August 1881, died 5 August 1881, age 4 and one year, Witnesses: Alexandre Hamelin and Joseph Ladouceur, E. Grouard priest o.m.i. (page 208)

11

Bourke, Jean-Baptiste: B-1, Jean_Baptiste Bourke, baptized 14 January 1878, born of the legitimate marriage of George Bourke and Agathe Ladouceur, Godfather: Joseph Ladouceur, Godmother: Mary Jane Ladouceur, E. Grouard priest o.m.i. (page 175)

Bourk,e Joseph: B-391, Joseph Bourk, baptized 10 November 1866, born yesterday, of the legitimate marriage of George Bourk and Agathe Ladouceur, Godfather: Joseph Ladouceur, Godmother: Julie Auger, Masionneuve, A. priest o.m.i. (page 77)

Bourque, Alphonse-Marie-Ligori: B-26, Alphonse Marie Ligori Bourque, baptized 18 November 1872, born yesterday, legitimate son of Georges Bourque and Agathe Ladouceur, Godfather: Louison Fosseneuve, Godmother: Agnes Ladouceur, V. Vegreville priest omi. (page 132_133)

Bourque, Arsene and Marie Hoole: M-4, Arsene Bourque married 2 October 1883 Marie Hoole, Present: C. Racette (signed) and L. Boisrame (signed), + Henri Ev. D'Anemour o.m.i. (page 231-232)

Bourque, Bathelemie;B-19, Barthelemi Bourque, baptized 20 September 1874, born today, legitimate son of Georges Bourque and Agathe Ladouceur, Godfather: Augustin Auger, Godmother: Sylvie Bruneau, V. Vegreville priest omi. (page 145)

Bourque, Charles-Henry: B-4, Charles Henry Bourque, baptized 29 January 1882, born 2 days, of the legitimate marriage of the deceased Geores Bourque and Agathe Ladouceur, Godfather: Augustin Ladouceur, Godmother: Sister Youville (signed), Collignon o.m.i.p. (page 215)

Bourque, Edouard: B-442, Edouard Bourke, baptized 28 July 1868, born today, legitimate son of Geroges Bourque and Agathe Ladouceur, Godfather: Louis Daze, Godmother: Therese Ladouceur, V. Vegreville p.m.a.o.m.i. (page 93)

Bourque, George Silvestre: B-27, George Silvestre Bourque, baptized 15 August 1884, age 2 days, legitimate son of Arsene Bourque and Marie Hoole, Godfather: Silvestre Bourque, Godmother: Agathe Ladouceur, Collignon o.m.i.p. (page 240)

Bourque, Georges-Silvestre: B-2, Georges Silvestre Bourque, bt 29 January 1871, born yesterday, legitimate son of Georges Bourque and Agathe Ladouceur, Godfather: David Ladouceur, Godmother: Genevieve Ladouceur, M. R. Remas priest omi. (page 117)

Bourque, Marie-Agathe: B-8, Marie_Agathe Burque, baptized 14 March 1876, born in the evening, legitimate daughter of Georges Burque and Agathe Ladouceur, Godfather: Jemmy Tige, Godmother: Marie Fraser, Husson p.o.m.i. (page 159)

Bourque, Olivier Edouard: B-31, Olivier Edouard Bourque, baptized 12 October 1879, born yesterday, of the legitimate marriage of Georges Bourque and Agathe Ladouceur, Godfather: Olivier Courte-oreille, Godmother: Sophie Ladouceur, E. Grouard priest o.m.i. (page 191)

Lac la Biche Baptisms, Marriages and Burials 1853-1884

Bruneau, ___: B-16, __ Bruneau, baptized 14 September 1873, age 15 days, legitimate daughter of Paul Bruneau and Isabelle Kakikekamik, Godfather: Augustin Oger, Godmother: Sylvie Bruneau, V. Vegreville p.m.a.o.m.i. (page 138)

Bruneau, Agnes: B-18, Agnes Bruno, baptized 17 July 1875, age about 2 months, of the legitimate marriage of Paul Bruno and Isabelle Kakikekamik, Godfather: Francois Kakikekamik, Godmother: Julie Bruno, H. Leduc priest o.m.i. (page 153)

Bruneau, Baptiste and Marie Decoin: M-17, Baptiste Bruneau, minor son of Baptiste Bruneau and Marie Crise, married 24 May 1859, Marie Decoin, minor daughter of Francois Decoin and Josephte Desjarlais, Present: Francois Decoin and Isidore Decoin, Tissot Jn. priest o.m.i. (page 34)

Bruneau, Emelie; See Charles House and Emelie Bruneau

Bruneau, Esther and Marie Houle: S-38 and S-39, Esther Bruneau, legitimate daughter of Genevieve Ladouceur and Joachim Bruneau, and Marie Houle, age about 26 years, buried 17 March 1867, died 15 March 1867, Present: Augustin Auger and Francois Larocque, Maisonneuve A. priest o.m.i. (page 79)

Bruneau, Henry: B-366, Henry Bruneau, baptized 12 November 1865, born day before yesterday, legitimate son of Vital Bruneau dit Sikaskuto and Josephte Chatelain, Godmother: Rosille Beauregard, V. Vegreville priest o.m.i. (page 71)

Bruneau, Isabelle; See Patrick Pruden and Isabelle Bruneau

Bruneau, Joachim: S-3, Joachim Bruneau, buried 29 June 1878, drowned in Lac La Biche 22 June 1878, Witnesses: Augustin Auger and Paul Montagnais, Collignon o.m.i. (page 179)

Bruneau, Joseph and Isabelle Aniskwewin: M-6, Joseph Bruno married 16 October 1854 Isabelle Aniskwewin, Present: Joseph Ladouceur and St.Luc Cardinal, M. R. Remas p.o.m.i. (page 10)

Bruneau, Josephine: B-31, Josephine Bruneau, baptized 10 November 1869, born today, daughter of Paul Bruneau and Emilie Kakikekamik, Godfather: Louis Tissawapas, Godmother: Emilie Bruneau, M. R. Remas priest o.m.i. (page 106)

Bruneau, Lisette: S-17, Lisette Bruneau, buried 14 March 1863, died 7 March 1863, Present: Charles Houle and Joseph Ladouceur, Tissot Jn. priest o.m.i. (page 51-52)

Bruneau, Lisette: S-53, Lisette Bruneau, buried 25 October 1868, died day before yesterday, age 33 years, wife of Paulette Desjarlais, Present: Luc Cardinal and Paulette Desjarlais, V. Vegreville, p.m.a.o.m.i. (page 96)

Bruneau, Madeleine: B-38, Madeleine Bruneau, baptized 26 May 1854, born 26 May 1854, of Louis Bruneau and Angele Dumont, Godfather: Michel Bruneau, Godmother: Catherine Ladouceur, M. R. Remas p.o.m.i. (page 7)

Lac la Biche Baptisms, Marriages and Burials 1853-1884

Bruneau, Madeleine: B-438, Madeleine Bruneau, baptized 21 June 1868, born yesterday, legitimate daughter of Paul Bruneau and Isabelle Kakekamik, Godfather: Johny Sisawapas, Godmother: Rosalie Kekekamik, V. Vegreville p.m.a.o.m.i. (page 92-93)

Bruneau, Marguerite Eliza: B-59, Marguerite Eliza Bruno, baptized 1 November 1854, born 31 October 1854, of Joachim Bruno and Catherine Ladouceur, Godfather: Pierre Chrysologue Pambrun (signed), M. R. Remas p.o.m.i. (page 10-11)

Bruneau, Marie-Rose: B-24, Marie-Rose Bruno, baptized 4 October 1882, born yesterday, of the legitimate marriage of Paul Bruno (Montagnais) and Isabelle Kakikekamik, Godfather: Marcel Tremblay, Godmother: Kakikekamik, E. Grouard priest o.m.i. (page 221)

Bruneau, Michel and Marguerite Gladu dite Janvier: M-2, Michel Bruneau, son of __ Bruneau and Josephte, widower of his 1st marriage ___ Ladouceur, married 7 February 1871, Marguerite Gladu dite Janvier, daughter of Louis Gladu and Genevieve Grey, widow of J. Bte Pepamawew, Present: Monseigneur Faraud and Angele Desjarlais, V. Vegreville p.m.a.o.m.i. (page 118)

Bruneau, Paul and Isabelle Kakekamik: M-53, Paul Bruneau, minor son of Michel Bruneau and Catherine Ladouceur, married 21 May 1867, Isabelle Kakekamik, minor daughter of Jean Baptiste Kakekamik and Charlotte Kanitawinisk, Present: Jean Baptiste Kakekamik and Isidore Decoine, V. Vegreville p.m.a.o.m.i. (page 80)

Bruneau, Therese; See Moise Cardinal and Therese Bruneau

Buisson, Antoine and Marianne Montagnaise: M-26, Antoine Buisson married 25 October 1861 Marianne Montagnaise Present: Gregoire Nateetthel and Andre Yoseogalra, Tissot Jn. priest o.m.i. (page 44-45)

Burk, Georges and Agathe Ladouceur: M-37, Georges Burk married 18 April 1864 Agathe Ladoucer, Present: Joseph Ladouceur and Augustin Auger, Tissot priest o.m.i. (page 57)

Cardinal, Adam: B-91, Adam Cardinal, baptized 18 May 1856, age about 3 months, legitimate son of Aubichon Cardinal and Cecile Labonne (Beaudoin), Godfather: Isidore Decoin, Godmother: Eugenie Ladouceur, Tissot Jn. priest o.m.i. (page 17)

Cardinal, Adele: B-296, Adele Cardinal, baptized 8 March 1863, age over 14 months, daughter of Antoine Cardinal and Marie, Godmother: Adele Desjarlais, Maisonneuve A. priest o.m.i. (page 56)

Cardinal, Adele: S-7, Adele Cardinal, buried 17 August 1874, died 3 days, age 11 years and 8 months, daughter of Antoine Cardinal and Marie Nisto, present: Joseph Nisto and Eugene Wawiyenam, V. Vegreville p.m.a.o.m.i. (page 144)

Cardinal, Albert: B-187, Albert Cardinal, baptized 28 May 1859, age about 6 months, son of Pierre Cardinal and Apistsiskwesis, Godmother: Genevieve Cardinal, Tissot Jn. priest o.m.i. (page 34)

Lac la Biche Baptisms, Marriages and Burials 1853-1884

Cardinal, Albert: S-11, Albert Cardinal, buried 8 December 1859, died yesterday, age one year and one month, son of Pierre Cardinal and Apistsiskwesis, Present: Baptiste Lafreniere and Paul Decoin, Tissot Jn. priest o.m.i. (page 36)

Cardinal, Alexis: B-22, Alexis Cardinal, baptized 31 July 1875, age about 16 days, legitimate son of Francois Cardinal and Adele Desjarlais, Gdofather: Pierre Auger, Godmother: Caroline Johnston, Alexis Jn Bte. Brunet. priest (page 154)

Cardinal, Alexis: S-5, Alexis Cardinal, buried 15 October 1855, died yesterday, age about 35, Present: Clement Collins and Joseph Beaudry, Maisonneuve A. priest o.m.i. (page 14)

Cardinal, Alphonse: B-48, Alphonse (Cardinal), baptized 7 November 1881, age about two months, son of Capetius (Cardinal) and Batinera, Godfather: Georges Adam, Godmother: Francoise Decoine, E. Grouard priest o.m.i. (page 212)

Cardinal, Amede: B-25, Amede Cardinal, baptized 13 June 1881, age about one month, legitimate son of Johny Cardinal and Angele Desjarlais, Godmother: Isabelle Cardinal, the priest served as godfather, Collignon o.m.i. p. (page 207)

Cardinal, Angele: B-193, Angele Cardinal, baptized 7 August 1859, age 3 years, daughter of Laventure Cardinal and Josephte Gladu, Godfather: Jacques Cardinal, Godmother: Lisette Cardinal, Tissot Jn. priest o.m.i. (page 35)

Cardinal, Angele: B-423, Angele Cardinal, baptized 18 January 1868, age 10 days, legitimate daughter of Pierre Cardinal and Angelique Apistiskwisis, Godmother: Nancy Quintal, V. Vegreville p.m.a.o.m.i. (page 88)

Cardinal, Angele: B-22, Angele Cardinal, baptized 22 August 1872, born yesterday of the legitimate marriage of Dominique Cardinal and Marianne Desjarlais, Godfather: Jules Desjarlais, Godmother: Brigitte Cardinal, V. Vegreville priest o.m.i. (page 131)

Cardinal, Angelique: B-13, Angelique Cardinal, baptized 22 June 1873, age about 9 months, legitimate daughter of Louison Cardinal Moustatip and Judith Desjarlais, Godfather: Antoine Wapamun, Godmother: Isabelle Kakikekamik, M. R. Remas priest o.m.i. (page 137-138)

Cardinal, Anne: B-1 and 2, Anne and Julienne Cardinal, baptized 1 January 1877, born yesterday of the legitimate marriage of Johny Cardinal and Angele Desjarlais, Godfather: Julien Cardinal, H. Leduc priest o.m.i. (page 166)

Cardinal, Anonyme: S-37, Anonyme Cardinal, buried 4 March 1867, died 4 days, age 4 days, infant of Lavanture Cardinal and Josephte Gladu, Present: Charly Johnston and Louis Decoin, Maisonneuve A. priest o.m.i. (page 79)

Cardinal, Antoine: B-25, Antoine Cardinal, baptized 1 August 1875, born October 1874, son of Baptiste Cardinal and Josephte Leponce., Godmother: Pelagie Cardinal, M. R. Remas priest o.m.i. (page 155)

Cardinal, Arsene: B-267, Arsene Cardinal, baptized 12 October 1862, age 2 months, son of Gabriel Cardinal and Marie Bruneau, Godmother: Isabelle Kakikekamik, Tissot Jn. priest o.m.i. (page 50)

Cardinal, Aubichon John and Cecile Labonne: M-3, Aubichon John Cardinal married 2 May 1854 Cecile Labonne, Present: Basile Labonne (Beaudoin) and Joseph Ladouceur, Alex Ev. de St.Boniface o.m.i. (page 6)

Cardinal, Augustin: B-76, Augustin Cardinal, baptized 28 August 1855, born day before yesterday, of the legitimate marriage of St.Luc Cardinal and Marguerite Desjarlais, Godmother: Louisa Desjarlais, Tissot Jn. priest o.m.i. (page 14)

Cardinal, Baptiste: B-20, Baptiste Cardinal, baptized 29 July 1878, age 16 days, legitimate son of Xavier Louison Cardinal and Mary Jane, Godfather: Baptiste Kakekekamik, Godmother: Marie-Anne Cardinal, E. Grouard priest o.m.i. (page 180)

Cardinal, Baptiste: B-230, Baptiste Cardinal, baptized 7 July 1861, age about 9 months, son of Baptiste Cardinal and Pimutew, Godmother: Agathe Laoduceur, Maisonneuve A. priest o.m.i. (page 43)

Cardinal, Baptiste: B-325, Baptiste Cardinal, baptized 25 October 1864, born 8 October 1864, son of Joseph Cardinal and Marianne Berland, Godfather: Baptiste Kakikekamik, Godmother: Marie Desjarlais, Maisonneuve A. priest o.m.i. (page 61)

Cardinal, Elise: B-400, Elise Cardinal, baptized 7 April 1867, age two months, legitimate daughter of Antoine Cardinal and Cecile Boucher, Godfather: Jean Baptiste Kakekamik, Godmother: Marguerite Laroque, V. Vegreville, priest mis. o.m.i. (page 79-80)

Cardinal, Basile and Isabelle Kekenittawikin: M-47, Basile Cardinal married 9 November 1865 Isabelle Kekenittawikin, Present: Marguerite widow of Jacques Cardinal and Josephte Desjarlais, Maisonneuve A. priest o.m.i. (page 69)

Cardinal, Benit: B-12, Benit Cardinal, baptized 8 June 1879, born yesterday, legitimate son of Johny Cardinal and Angele Desjarlais, Godmother: Isabelle, Collignon priest o.m.i. (page 187)

Cardinal, Benjamin: B-22, Benjamin Cardinal, baptized 3 September 1870, born today, son of Francois Cardinal and Adele Desjarlais, Godfather: Baptiste Sauve, Godmother: Agathe Cardinal, M. R. Remas priest o.m.i. (page 114)

Cardinal, Benjamin: B-96, Benjamin Cardinal, baptized 21 August 1856, age over seven months, legitimate son of Antoine Cardinal and Cecile Boucher, Godmother: Julie Auge, Tissot Jn priest o.m.i. (page 18)

Cardinal, Bethsy; See Paulet Desjarlais and Bethsy Cardinal

Cardinal, Brigitte: B-277, Brigitte Cardinal, baptized 7 April 1863, born yesterday, of the legitimate marriage of Laventure Cardinal and Josephte Gladu, Godfather: Jacques Cardinal, Godmother: Pelagie Samaskekapo, Tissot Jn. priest o.m.i. (page 52)

Lac la Biche Baptisms, Marriages and Burials 1853-1884

Cardinal, Casimir: B-356, Casimir Cardinal, baptized 6 November 1865, age 8 days, legitimate son of John Cardinal and Cecile Labonne, Godmother: Josephte Chalfoux, Maisonneuve A. priest o.m.i. (page 68-69)

Cardinal, Catherine; See Jacques Miyosaskamikutew dit Opiwitew

Cardinal, Cecile: B-264, Cecile Cardinal, baptized 14 September 1862, age about 13 months, daughter of Jerome Cardinal and Josephte Desjarlais, Godfather: Johny Cardinal, Godmother: Catherine Ladouceur, Tissot Jn. priest o.m.i. (page 50)

Cardinal, Cecile: B-273, Cecile Cardinal, baptized 14 December 1862, age about 15 days, daughter of Baptiste Cardinal and Opimutew, Godfather: Jacques Cardinal, Godmother: Josephte Crise, Tissot Jn. priest o.m.i. (page 51)

Cardinal, Cecile: B-450, Cecile Cardinal, baptized 25 October 1868, age 16 days, legitimate daughter of Gabriel Cardinal and Marie Bruneau, Godmother: Julie Dagneau, V. Vegreville, p.m.a.o.m.i. (page 96)

Cardinal, Cecile; See Joseph Desjarlais and Cecile Cardinal

Cardinal, Charles: B-17, Charles Cardinal, baptized 8 July 1883, age 22 days, legitimate son of Dominique Cardinal and Marianne Desjarlais, Godfather: Michel Grosse-Tete, Godmother: Julie Desjarlais, Collignon o.m.i.p. (page 227)

Cardinal, Charles: B-319, Charles Cardinal, baptized 15 October 1864, age 18 days, legitimate son of Charles Cardinal and Angelique Gladu [?], Godmother: Marguerite Tsimakis, Tissot Jn. priest o.m.i. (page 60)

Cardinal, Christine: B-14, Christine Cardinal, baptized 11 July 1870, age over one month, daughter of Jacques Cardinal and Pelagie Samaskekabew, Godfather: Louis Gladu, Godmother: Genevieve Gray, Alb. Lacombe priest o.m.i. (page 112)

Cardinal, Clement: B-188, Clement Cardinal, baptized 29 May 1859, age 2 months, of the legitimate marriage of John Cardinal and Cecile Labonne, Godmother: Nancy Quintal, Tissot Jn. priest o.m.i. (page 34)

Cardinal, Dameon: B-30, Dameon Cardinal, baptized 4 October 1879, born yesterday, of the legitimate marriage of Julien Cardinal and Eliza Ladouceur, Godfather: Absalom Ladouceur, Godmother: Florestine Ladouceur (signed), Collignon o.m.i. (page 191)

Cardinal, David: B-430, David Cardinal, baptized 5 April 1868, age 55 days, of the legitimate marriage of Luc Cardinal and Marguerite Desjarlais, Godfather: John Cardinal, Godmother: Angele Larocque, Alb. Lacombe priest o.m.i. (page 89)

Cardinal, Edouard: B-28, Edouard Cardinal, baptized 17 December 1872, born yesterday, legitimate son of Francois Cardinal and Adele Desjarlais, Godfather: James Tige, Godmother: Angelique Sauve, V. Vegreville p.m.a.o.m.i. (page 133)

Lac la Biche Baptisms, Marriages and Burials 1853-1884

Cardinal, Eleonore: B-208, Eleonore Cardinal, baptized 29 June 1860, born the 26 of the month, daughter of Luc Cardinal and Marguerite Desjarlais, Godfather: Francois Decoin, Godmother: Josephte Desjarlais, Tissot Jn. priest o.m.i. (page 38)

Cardinal, Elie dit Mustatip Napesis: B-11, Elie Cardinal Mustatip Napesis, baptized 23 April 1882, age about two months, legitimate son of Joseph Cardinal Mustatip and Mathilde Tremblay, Godfather: Duncan Tremblay, Godmother: Olive Tremblay, Collignon o.m.i.p. (page 217)

Cardinal, Elisa: B-258, Elisa Cardinal, baptized 25 May 1862, age 6 months, legitimate daughter of Charles Cardinal and Angelique Berland, Godfather: Isidore Decoin, Godmother: Genevieve Ladouceur, Tissot Jn. priest o.m.i. (page 48)

Cardinal, Elisa; See Eugene Wawiyenam and Elisa Cardinal

Cardinal, Elisabeth: B-20, Elisabeth Cardinal, baptized 14 August 1870, age about one month, daughter of Moise Cardinal and Therese Bruneau, Godfather: Jules Cardinal, Godmother: Elisabeth Kekinittawikiw, M. R. Remas priest o.m.i. (page 114)

Cardinal, Eustache: B-9, Eustache Cardinal, baptized 22 April 1879, born 10 April 1879, legitimate son of St.Paul Cardinal and Marguerite Tremblay, Godfather: Louis Hamelin (signed), Godmother: Olive Tremblay (signed), E. Grouard priest o.m.i. (page 187)

Cardinal, Eve-Marie: B-6, Eve Marie Cardinal, baptized 4 October 1853, age about 2 months, daughter of St. Pierre Cardinal and Apitsiskwes, Godfather: Joseph Gray, M. R. Remas pr. o.m.i. (page 3)

Cardinal, Francois and Rosalie Kisikawikutsin: M-8, Francois Cardinal, adult son of Cardinal and Nikikiskwew, married 22 November 1871, Rosalie Kisikawikutsin, minor daughter of Kisikawikutsin and a Sauteuse, Present: Baptiste Kakikekamik and Melie Pittukekapaw, M. R. Remas priest o.m.i. (page 125)

Cardinal, Francois and Adele Desjarlais: M-21, Francois Cardinal married 13 November 1860 Adele Desjarlais in the presence of witnesses: Tissot Jn. priest o.m.i. (page 40)

Cardinal, Francois: B-24, Francois Cardinal, baptized 22 November 1871, age about 40 years, son of a Cardinal and Nikikiskwew, Godfather: Baptiste Kakikekamik, Godmother: Melie Pittukekapaw, M. R. Remas priest o.m.i. (page 125)

Cardinal, Francois: B-301, Francois Cardinal, baptized 28 March 1864, son of Baptiste Cardinal and Oipimutew, Godmother: Catherine Decoin, Tissot Jn. priest o.m.i. (page 57)

Cardinal, Francois: B-27, Francois Cardinal, baptized 28 September 1879, age 18 days, legitimate son of Dominique Cardinal and Marianne, Godfather: Petit Louis Martin, Godmother: Cecile Cardinal, Collignon, o.m.i. (page 191)

Cardinal, Frederic (Cayatins): B-28 Frederic Cardinal (Cayatins), baptized 2 July 1881, age 8 days, legitimate son of Olivier Cardinal and Adelaide, Godfather: Thomas, Godmother: Catherine Cardinal, Collignon o.m.i. p. (page 207)

Lac la Biche Baptisms, Marriages and Burials 1853-1884

Cardinal, Gabriel and Marie Piwapiskapaw: M-4, Gabriel Cardinal married 22 May 1854 Marie Piwapiskapaw, Witnesses: Michel Bruno and Michel Gray, M. R. Remas p.o.m.i. (page 7)

Cardinal, Gabriel: S-1, Gabriel Cardinal, buried 28 September 1870, age 12 or 13 years, Witnesses: Paul Bruneau and Julien Cardinal, M. R. Remas priest o.m.i. (page 114)

Cardinal, Genevieve: B-126, Genevieve Cardinal, baptized 17 May 1857, age one year, daughter of Edouard Cardinal and Charlotte Atimuskweyaw, Godfather: Edouard Genevieve, Godmother: Marianne Beaudry, Tissot Jn. priest o.m.i. (page 24)

Cardinal, Genevieve: B-395, Genevieve Cardinal, baptized 30 December 1866, age 23 days, legitimate daughter of Jacques Cardinal and Pelagie Samaskekapaw, Godmother: Genevieve Cardinal, V. Vegreville, priest mis. o.m.i. (page 78)

Cardinal, Genevieve; See Jean-Marie Desjarlais and Genevieve Cardinal,

Cardinal, Guillaume: B-248, Guillaume Cardinal, baptized 19 January 1862, born 17 January 1862, son of Luc Cardinal and Marguerite Desjarlais, Godfather: Michel Nipising, Godmother: Josephte Desjarlais, Maisonneuve, A. priest o.m.i. (page 47)

Cardinal, Guillaume: S-30, Guillaume Cardinal, buried 22 December 1865, died 21 December 1865, age 3 years and one month, Present: John Cardinal and Basile Cardinal, Maisonneuve A. priest o.m.i. (page 69)

Cardinal, Helene (Kamiyoatamut): B-257, Helene Kamiyoatamut (Cardinal), baptized 11 May 1862, age 5 months, daughter of Albert Kamiyoatamut and Nannecy Labonne (Beaudoin), Godfather: Charly Johnson, Godmother: Cecile Labonne, Tissot Jn. priest o.m.i. (page 48)

Cardinal, Helene: S-3, Helene Cardinal, buried 4 January 1873, age about one month, Witness: Joseph Cardinal, Collignon o.m.i. (page 134)

Cardinal, Ignace and Charlotte Takutsin: M-3, Ignace Cardinal, minor son of Charles Cardinal and Angelique, married 24 April 1878, Charlotte Takutsin, minor daughter of Takutsin and Susanne Cardinal, Witness: Cardinal Julien, Collignon o.m.i. (page 177)

Cardinal, Ignace: B-180, Ignace Cardinal, baptized 1 February 1859, age one month, son of Charles Cardinal and Angelique Berland, Godfather: Joseph Cardinal, A. Lacombe o.m.i. (page 33)

Cardinal, Isabelle: B-19, Isabelle Cardinal, baptized 25 July 1869, age 5 or 6 days, legitimate daughter of Baptiste Cardinal and Josephine Canard, Godfather: Louis Cardinal, Godmother: Isabelle Adam, M. R. Remas, priest o.m.i. (page 102)

Cardinal, Isabelle: B-155, Isabelle Cardinal, baptized 20 June 1858, age 15 days, of the legitimate marriage of Luc Cardinal and Marguerite Desjarlais, Godmother: Isabelle Quintal, Tissot Jn. priest o.m.i. (page 29)

Lac la Biche Baptisms, Marriages and Burials 1853-1884

Cardinal, Isidore: B-15, Isidore Cardinal, baptized 16 August 1874, b. 17 Jul, legitimate son of Dominique Cardinal and Marianne Dejarlais, Godfather: Isidore Pambrun, Godmother: Marie Mognon, Alb. Pascal priest o.m.i. (page 144)

Cardinal, Jacob: S-4, Jacob Cardinal, buried 10 April 1872, died yesterday, age about 45 years, son of Jacques Cardinal and Sikak. (page 129)

Cardinal, Jacques and Pelagie Samaskekabo: M-33, Jacques Cardinal married 19 June 1862 Pelagie Samaskekabo, Present: Francois Decoin and Joseph Ladouceur, Tissot Jn. priest o.m.i. (page 49)

Cardinal, James: B-4, James Cardinal, baptized 30 January 1871, born 24 January 1871, legitimate child of Baptiste Cardinal and Francoise Hope, Godmother: Flora Hope, M. R. Remas priest o.m.i. (page 118)

Cardinal, Jamy: B-11, Jamy Cardinal, baptized 12 April 1875, born today, of the legitimate marriage of Francois Cardinal dit Kiskekamik and Caroline Johnstone, Godfather: Jamy Tyique (Tige), Godmother: Agathe Cardinal, J. V. Fourmond priest o.m.i. (page 151)

Cardinal, Jamy dit Kakekamik: S-5, Jamy Cardinal dit Kakekamik, buried 7 June 1875, age two months, Witnesses: Francois Charley and Baptist Desjardins, A. J. B. Brunet, priest (page 153)

Cardinal, Jean: B-317, Jean Cardinal, baptized 2 October 1864, age 11 days, son of Gabriel Cardinal and Marie Bruneau, Godmother: Magdeleine Wishipasiku, Maisonneuve A. priest o.m.i. (page 60)

Cardinal, Jean: B-8, Jean Cardinal, baptized 5 April 1874, legitimate son of Basile Cardinal and Isabelle, Godfather: Jeannet Pambrun, Godmother: Marguerite Desjarlais, wife of Castor, E. Petitot priest o.m.i. (page 142)

Cardinal, Jean Baptiste: B-290, Jean-Baptiste Cardinal, baptized 22 October 1863, born yesterday, of the legitimate marriage of Jacques Cardinal and Pelagie Samaskekabo, Godfather: Paul, Godmother: Agathe, Tissot Jn. priest o.m.i. (page 54-55)

Cardinal, Jean- Marie: B-2, Jean_Marie Cardinal, baptized 13 January 1869, age 6 days, legitimate son of Dominique Cardinal and Marianne Desjarlais, Godfather: Julien Cardinal, V. Vegrevillle, p.m.a.o.m.i. (page 97)

Cardinal, Jean-Baptiste and Francoise Hope: M-4, Jean-Baptiste Cardinal, adult son of the late Laurent Cardinal and Marie Mognon, married 21 April 1869, Francoise Hope, minor daughter of the late James Hope and Judith Desjarlais, Present: Joseph Duquette and Judith Desjarlais, V. Vegreville p.m.a.o.m.i. (page 100)

Cardinal, Jean-Baptiste and Josephine Martin dit Cisip: M-62, Jean-Baptiste Cardinal, minor son of the late Louison Cardinal and Susanne Courte-oreille, married 8 January 1868, Josephine Martin, minor daughter of Martin (dit Cisip) and the late Marie, Present: Martin and Louison Cardinal, V. Vegreville p.m.a.o.m.i. (page 87-88)

Cardinal, Jean-Baptiste: B-16, Jean Baptiste Cardinal, baptized 11 July 1869, age over one month, legitimate son of Joseph Cardinal and Marie Nonamepekinam, Godfather: Georges Adam, Godmother Francoise Decoine, V. Vegreville p.m.a.o.m.i. (page 102)

Cardinal, Jean-Baptiste Cayatius: S-6, Jean-Baptiste Cayatius (Cardinal), buried 7 December 1884, died day before yesterday, age about 55 years, Witnesses: Petit Louis Lavallee and Duncan Tremblay, Collignon o.m.i.p. (page 242)

Cardinal, Jerome and Josephte Desjarlais: M-35, Jerome Cardinal married 15 August 1863 Josephte Desjarlais, Present: Joseph Ladouceur and Jean_Baptiste Amiskuiyinisis, Tissot Jn. priest o.m.i. (page 54)

Cardinal, John: B-18, John Cardinal, baptized 24 June 1877, age about 5 months, of the legitmate marriage of Joseph Cardinal and Marie Desjarlais, Godparents: Louison [Cardinal ?] and Judith Desjarlais, the infant was previously christened by Jerome Cardinal, F. Le Serrec, priest o.m.i. (page 170)

Cardinal, Johny and Angele Desjarlais: M-50, Johny Cardinal, adult son of Pierre Cardinal and Marguerite Tsimakits, married 28 August 1866, Angele Desjarlais, minor daughter of Francois Desjarlais and Euphrosine Auger, Present: Francois Desjarlais and Marguerite Tsimakits, V. Vegreville o.m.i. (page 74-75)

Cardinal, Joseph and Niyanampekinam: M-31, Joseph Cardinal married June 1861 Niyanampekinam, crise not baptized, Present: Maisonneuve, Tissot Jn. priest o.m.i. (page 46)

Cardinal, Joseph and Marie Desjarlais: M-1, Joseph Cardinal, minor son of Louison Cardinal and Susanne Sauteuse married 3 January 1876, Marie Desjarlais, minor daughter of Paulette Desjarlais and Lisette Bruno, Witnesses: Louis Cardinal and Augustin Cardinal, M. R. Remas priest o.m.i. (page 157-158)

Cardinal, Joseph and Angelique Kakikekamik: M-9, Joseph Cardinal, widower of Marie Nanamepehinam, married 13 September 1875, Angelique Kakikekamik, adult daughter of Baptiste Kakikekamik and Madeleine Wiskinasikuw, Witnesses: Baptiste Kakikekamik, father of the bride, and Cardoline Johnston, M. R. Remas priest o.m.i. (page 155)

Cardinal, Joseph and Modeste Niyanampekinam: M-45, Joseph Cardinal married 10 November 1864 Modeste Niyanampekinam, Present: P. Bourk and Marguerite Larocque, Tissot Jn. priest o.m.i. (page 62)

Cardinal, Joseph: B-143, Joseph Cardinal, baptized 1 November 1857, age about 6 months, son of Baptiste Cardinal and Opimatew, Godfather: Louis Leveille, Tissot Jn. priest o.m.i. (page 27)

Cardinal, Joseph: B-179, Joseph Cardinal, baptized 1 February 1859, age 3 months, son of Joseph Cardinal and Josephte Apispitumis, Godfather: Alexis Cardinal, A. Lacombe o.m.i. (page 33)

Cardinal, Joseph: B-3, Joseph Cardinal, baptized 8 March 1884, age 26 days, legitimate son of Paul Cardinal and Marguerite Tremblay, Godfather: Julien Cardinal, Godmother: Liza Ladouceur, Collignon o.m.i.p. (page 235)

Cardinal, Joseph: B-357, Joseph Cardinal, baptized 8 November 1865, age 3 days, son of St.Luc Cardinal and Marguerite Desjarlais, Godmother: Euphrosine Auger, Maisonneuve A. priest o.m.i. (page 69)

Cardinal, Joseph: B-154, Joseph Cardinal, baptized 3 June 1858, age 4 months, son of Louis Cardinal and Susanne Courteoreille, Godmother, Josephte Desjarlais, Tissot, Jn. priest o.m.i. (page 29)

Cardinal, Joseph: B-159, Joseph Cardinal, baptized 17 October 1858, age 3 months, of the legitimate marriage of Gabriel Cardinal and Marie Bruneau, Godmother: Lisette Bruneau, Tissot Jn. priest (page 29)

Cardinal, Joseph: B-20, Joseph Cardinal, baptized 9 July 1877, born during the night of the legitimate marriage of Julien Cardinal and Elisa Ladouceur, Godparents Pierre Ladouceur and his wife, F. Le Serrec priest o.m.i. (page 170)

Cardinal, Joseph: B-251, Joseph Cardinal, baptized 20 March 1862, age over one year, son of Antoine Cardinal and Marie, Godfather: Louis Cardinal, Godmother: Susanne Courteoreille, Alb. Lacombe priest o.m.i. (page 47)

Cardinal, Joseph Mustatip and Domitille Desjarlais: M-5, Joseph Mustatip Cardinal, adult son of Antoine Cardinal and Marie, married 19 September 1881, Domitille Desjarlais, minor daughter of Jean-Marie Desjarlais and Rosalie Batoche, Witnesses: Cleophas Racette (signed C. Racette) and Eugene Wawiyenam (signed with x), Collignon o.m.i.p. (page 211)

Cardinal, Joseph: S-3, Joseph Cardinal, buried 2 November 1854, age over 98 years, interred last September, M. R. Remas p.o.m.i. (page 11)

Cardinal, Josephte, B-303, Josephte Cardinal, baptized 17 April 1864, age over one month, illegitimate daughter of Dominique Cardinal and Brigitte Desjarlais, Godmother: Isabelle Marie, Tissot Jn. priest o.m.i. (page 57)

Cardinal, Josephte; See Louis Matsunta and Josephte Cardinal

Cardinal, Josette: S-11, Josette Cardinal, buried 8 May 1875, died 4 days, age 90 years, wife of Desjarlais, Witnesses: Charles Johnston (signed) and Gaillard, J. V. Fourmond priest o.m.i. (page 152)

Cardinal, Jules: B-13, Jules Cardinal, baptized 30 May 1869, born today, legitimate son of Jerome Cardinal and Josephte Desjarlais, Godfather: Jules Desjarlais, Godmother:; Susanne Desjarlais, V. Vegreville p.m.a.o.m.i. (page 101)

Cardinal, Julie: B-415, Julie Cardinal, baptized 14 August 1867, age 20 months, natural daughter of Antoine Cardinal and Marie Kakeokanepiw, Godmother: Marguerite Cardinal, V. Vegreville p.m.a.o.m.i. (page 84)

Cardinal, Julie: B-46, Julie Cardinal, baptized 22 October 1881, age about one month, legitimate daughter of Paul Cardinal and Marguerite Tremblay, , Godmother: Eulalie Hamelin, E. Grouard priest o.m.i. (page 212)

Cardinal, Julie;S-46, Julie Cardinal, buried 12 December 1867, died yesterday, age 2 years, daughter of Antoine Cardinal and Marie Kakeskanapiw, V. Vegreville p.m.a.o.m.i. (page 87)

Cardinal, Julien and Elisa Ladouceur: M-4, Julien Cardinal , adult son of Laurent Cardinal and Marie Mongnon, m. 29 Sep1874, Elisa Ladouceur, minor daughter of Agapit Ladouceur and Marguerite Fraser, Present: Pierre Ladouceur and Racette, V. Vegreville p.m.a.o.m.i. (page 146)

Cardinal, Julien-Laurent: B-54 (2nd), Julien Laurent Cardinal, baptized 1 October 1854, age 2 days, son of Laurent Cardinal and Marie Monyon, Godmother: Betshy Ladebauche, M. R. Remas p.o.m.i. (page 9)

Cardinal, Julienne: B-1 and 2, Anne and Julienne Cardinal, baptized 1 January 1877, born yesterday of the legitimate marriage of Johny Cardinal and Angele Desjarlais, Godfather: Julien Cardinal, H. Leduc priest o.m.i. (page 166)

Cardinal, Katy: B-14, Katy Cardinal, baptized 23 May 1882, age about 15 days, legitimate daughter of Julien Cardinal and Liza Ladouceur, Godfather: brother Boisrame, Godmother: Caroline Ladouceur, Collignon o.m.i.p. (page 218)

Cardinal, LaLouise; See Francois Enullile and LaLouise Cardinal

Cardinal, Laurent: S-4, Laurent Cardinal, buried 16 August 1855, died in the evening, age about 36 years, Present: Baptiste Cardinal and Pierre Labonne, Tissot Jn. priest o.m.i. (page 14)

Cardinal, Laventure and Josephte Gladu: M-23, Laventure Cardinal married 24 December 1860 Josephte Gladu, Present: Francois Cardinal and Aubichon Cardinal, Tissot Jn. priest o.m.i. (page 40)

Cardinal, Lisette and Naniwotakusiw: M-30, Lisette Cardinal married 3 June 1861 Naniwotakusiw, Tissot Jn. priest o.m.i. (page 46)

Cardinal, Lisette: B-171, Lisette Cardinal, baptized 2 December 1858, age 7 months, daughter of Antoine Cardinal and Cecile Boucher, Godmother: Julie Auger, Tissot Jn. priest o.m.i. (page 31)

Cardinal, Lisette: B-202, Lisette Cardinal, baptized 10 January 1860, age about 2 years, daughter of Jacques Cardinal and Samaskekebo, Godfather: J. B. Maskutepwan, Godmother: Euphrosine Cardinal, Alb. Lacombe priest o.m.i. (page 37)

Cardinal, Lisette: B-110, Lisette Cardinal, baptized 18 January 1857, age one year and three months, daughter of Kakinus Cardinal (Charles) and Isabelle Berland, Godmother: Angelique Berland, Maisonneuve A. priest o.m.i. [The mother named is the godmother and the godmother is the mother of Lisette.] (page 21_22)

Cardinal, Lisette: B-306, Lisette Cardinal, baptized 7 June 1864, age about 10 months, daughter of Joseph Cardinal and Marianne Berland, Godmother: Genevieve Ladouceur, Tissot, Jn., priest, o.m.i. (page 58)

Cardinal, Lisette; See Joseph Nanehotakusiw and Lisette Cardinal

Cardinal, Louis and Judith Desjarlais: M-10, Louis Cardinal married 10 November 1869 Judith Desjarlais, Present: Jacob Cardinal grandfather of the groom and Angelique Sauve, M. R. Remas priest o.m.i. (page 106)

Cardinal, Louis: B-7, Louis Cardinal, baptized 8 March 1875, born today, of the legitimate marriage of Charles Cardinal and Emilie Bruno, Godfather: Baptiste Castor, Godmother: Isabelle Bruno, A. J. B. Brunet priest o.m.i. (page 149)

Cardinal, Louis Xavier: B-58, Louis-Xavier Cardinal, baptized 27 October 1854, age about one month, son of Louison Cardinal and Suzane Courteoreille, Godfather: Louis St.Arnaud, M. R. Remas p.o.m.i. (page 10)

Cardinal, Louise: B-292, Louise Cardinal, baptized 13 December 1863, age 25 days, daughter of Jerome Cardinal and Josephte Desjarlais, Godfather: John Desjarlais, Godmother: Marianne Desjarlais, Tissot Jn. priest o.m.i. (page 55)

Cardinal, Luc: S-2, Luc Cardinal, buried 6 May 1871, died a few days, age about 35 years, Witnesses: Johny Cardinal and Julien Cardinal, M. R. Remas priest (page 121)

Cardinal, Lucinien: B-245, Lucinien Cardinal, baptized 10 December 1861, born yesterday, of the legitimate marriage of Cecile Labonne and Andre (John) Cardinal, Godmother: Josephte Desjarlais, Tissot Jn. priest o.m.i. (page 45-46)

Cardinal, Lucinien: S-14, Lucinien Cardinal, buried 7 March 1862, died 4 March 1862, Present: Francois Cardinal and Pierre Cardinal, Tissot Jn. priest o.m.i. (page 47)

Cardinal, Magdeleine: B-25, Magdeleine Cardinal, baptized 19 June 1875, age 3 months, of the legitimate marriage of Joseph Cardinal and Euphrosine Lemyre, Godmother: Henriette Mercredi (McCarthy), J. M. A. Blanchet priest o.m.i. (page 154)

Cardinal, Magdeleine: B-30, Magdeleine Cardinal, baptized 24 December 1872, age nine days, legitimate daughter of Baptiste Cardinal and Josephine Metashew, Godfather: Joseph Cardinal, Godmother: Marie Charle, Collignon p.o.m.i. (page 133-134)

Cardinal, Magdeleine; S01, Magdeleine Cardinal, buried 14 January 1873, died 12 January 1873, age 25 days, Witnesses: Joseph Cardinal and Xavier Cardinal, Collignon o.m.i. (page 134)

Cardinal, Marcelline: B-295, Marcelline Cardinal, baptized 24 December 1863, age 25 days, legitimate daughter of Luc Cardinal and Marguerite Desjarlais, Godmother: Therese Cardinal, Tissot Jn. priest o.m.i. (page 55)

Cardinal, Marguerite: B-1, Marguerite Cardinal, baptized 1 January 1875, age about 3 days, of Johny Cardinal and Angele Piyesis, Godfather: Pierre Pjerante, Godmother: Marguerite Dejarlais, J. V. Fourmond priest o.m.i. (page 147)

Cardinal, Marguerite: B-399, Marguerite Cardinal, baptized 2 March 1867, age 10 days, legitimate daughter of Dominique Cardinal and Marianne Desjarlais, Godfather: Julien Cardinal, V. Vegreville priest mis. o.m.i. (page 79)

Cardinal, Marguerite Kamiyotamut: B-67, Marguerite Kamiyotamut (Cardinal), baptized 20 April 1855, age about 2 months, daughter of Albert Kamiyotamut (Cardinal) and Nancy (Anne Beaudoin), Godfather: Paulette Desjarlais, Godmother: Marie Labonne (Beaudoin), M. R. Remas p.o.m.i. (page 12)

Cardinal, Marguerite; See Alexis Courte-Oreille and Marguerite Cardinal

Cardinal, Maria: B-17, Maria Cardinal, baptized 13 September 1874, age 21 months, daughter of Antoine Cardinal and Marie Okistot, Godfather: Isidore Decoine, Godmother: Catherine, V. Vegreville, p.m.a.o.m.i. (page 145)

Lac la Biche Baptisms, Marriages and Burials 1853-1884

Cardinal, Marianne: B-342, Marianne Cardinal, baptized 8 May 1865, age 10 days, child of Jeroeme Cardinal and Josephte Desjarlais, Godmother: Angelique Desjarlais, Masionneuve, A. priest o.m.i. (page 66)

Cardinal, Marianne; See Absalon Ladouceur and Marianne Cardinal

Cardinal, Marie Aloise: B-57, Marie_Aloise Cardinal, baptized 27 October 1854, age about one month, daughter of Antoine Cardinal and Cecile Boucher, Godfather: Louis St.Arnaud, M. R. Remas p.o.m.i. (page 10)

Cardinal, Marie: B-226, Marie Cardinal, baptized 2 June 1861, age about 3 months, daughter of Louis Cardinal and Susanne Courte-oreille, Godmother: Silvie Bruneau, Maissoneuve priest o.m.i. (page 42)

Cardinal, Marie: B-3, Marie Cardinal, baptized 29 January 1871, age about 2 months, legitimate daughter of Dominique Cardinal and Marianne Desjarlais, Godfather: Jules Desjarlais, Godmother: __ Desjarlais, M. R. Remas priest o.m.i. (page 117)

Cardinal, Marie: B-44, Marie Cardinal, baptized 28 May 1854, age 4 years, daughter of Charlot Cardinal and Angelique Berland, Godfather: Decoing, M. R. Remas p.o.m.i. (page 8)

Cardinal, Marie: B-20, Marie Cardinal, baptized 1 October 1872, legitimate daughter of Johnny Cardinal and Angele Cardinal [Desjarlais], Godfather: Guillaume Desjarlais, Godmother: Isabelle Capotvert, Collignon o.m.i. (page 131)

Cardinal, Marie: B-374, Marie Cardinal, baptized 25 March 1866, born 1 March 1866, of the legitimate marriage of Joseph Cardinal and Modeste Niyanamekinum, Godmother: Cecile Beaudoin (dit Labonne), Maisonneuve A. p. o.m.i. (page 73)

Cardinal, Marie;B-381, Marie Cardinal, baptized 24 August 1866, age 13 days, legitimate daughter of Francois Cardinal and Angele Desjarlais, Godmother: Marie Cardinal, V. Vegreville priest mis. o.m.i. (page 74)

Cardinal, Marie Mustatip: B-19, Marie_Mustatip (Cardinal), baptized 24 June 1877, age 5 months, of the legitmate marriage of Xavier Mustatip and Marie Jim, Godfather: Joseph Desjarlais, Godmother: Marie Desjarlais, F. Le Serrec priest o.m.i. (page 170)

Cardinal, Marie; See Etienne Quintal and Marie Cardinal

Cardinal, Marie-Caroline Napesis: B-20, Marie-Caroline Napesis Cardinal, baptized 17 July 1884, age 7 days, legitimate daughter of Joseph Napesis Cardinal and Mathilde Tremblay, Godfather: Louis Lavallee, Godmother: Catherine L'Esperance, Lecorre priest o.m.i. (page 239)

Cardinal, Marie-Josephte: B-43, Marie_Josephte Cardinal, baptized 24 December 1877, born about 5 weeks, legitimate daughter of Jerome Cardinal and Josephte, Godmother: Marianne Cardinal, Collignon o.m.i. (page 174)

Cardinal, Marie-Magdeleine (LaBatoche): B-28, Marie-Magdeleine Cardinal (LaBatoche), baptized 21 September 1884, age about 6 months, legitimate daughter of Joseph Cardinal La Batoche dit Wikwekem and

Lac la Biche Baptisms, Marriages and Burials 1853-1884

Marguerite Desjarlais, Godfather: Absalon Ladouceur, Godmother: Agathe Ladouceur, Collignon o.m.i.p. (page 241)

Cardinal, Marie-Rose: B-1, Marie_Rose Cardinal, baptized 22 January 1871, age 2 months, legitimate daughter of Gabriel Cardinal and Marie Pwapiskekapaw, Godfather: Julien Cardinal, Godmother: Elise McGillis, V. Vegreville p.m.a.o.m.i. (page 117)

Cardinal, Marie-Rose Kapetuess: B-19 Marie-Rose Kapetuess (Cardinal), baptized 6 June 1880, age about 11 months, daughter of Kapetuess and Patenow (of Lac Castor), Godmother: Christine Kakikamik, E. Grouard priest o.m.i. (page 197)

Cardinal, Mary-Jane: B-409, Mary-Jane Cardinal, baptized 11 July 1867, agte 25 days, legitimate daughter of Jerome Cardinal and Josephte Desjarlais, Godmother: Bethsy Cardinal, V. Vegreville, p.m.a.o.m.i. (page 83)

Cardinal, Mathilde: B-297, Mathilde Cardinal, baptized 8 March 1864, age over one month, legitimate daughter of Louison Cardinal and Susanne Courte_oreille, Godmother: Therese Ladouceur, Maisonneuve A. pr. o.m.i. (page 56)

Cardinal, Melanie: B-109, Melanie Cardinal, baptized 27 November 1856, born 21 November 1856, of the legitimate marriage of Luc Cardinal and Marguerite Desjarlais, Godmother: Josephte Cardinal, Tissot Jn. priest o.m.i. (page 20-21)

Cardinal, Moise and Therese Bruneau: M-11, Moise Cardinal married 28 November 1869 Therese Bruneau, Present: Louis Cardinal, brother of the groom, and Josephte Sicard, M. R. Remas priest o.m.i. (page 107)

Cardinal, Moise: B-262, Moise Cardinal, baptized 10 August 1862, son of Joseph Cardinal and ___, Godmother: Lisette Bruneau, Tissot Jn. priest o.m.i. (page 49)

Cardinal, Moise: S-1, Moise Cardinal, buried 6 March 1880, of Lac du Male, age 17 years, Witnesses: Baptiste Kakikamik and Louison Kakekamik, E. Grouard priest o.m.i. (page 194-195)

Cardinal, Monique: B-7, Monique Cardinal, baptized 25 March 1872, born 15 March 1872, legitimate daughter of Jerome Cardinal and Josephte Desjarlais, Godfather: Isidore Pambrun, Godmother: Marie Cardinal, M. R. Remas priest o.m.i. (page 127)

Cardinal, Monique: S-5, Monique Cardinal, buried 14 April 1874, age two years, Witnesses: Dominique Cardinal and Natsakam, E. Petitot priest o.m.i. (page 142-143)

Cardinal, Narcisse: B-19, Narcisse Cardinal, baptized 24 July 1875, born about 8 weeks, legitimate son of Jerome Cardinal and Josephte Desjarlais, Godfather: Charles Quintal, Godmother: Josephte Desjarlais, M. R. Remas pret o.m.i. (page 153)

Cardinal, Narcisse: B-32, Narcisse Cardinal, baptized 23 November 1869, b. day before yesterday, legitmate son of Luc Cardinal and Marguerite Desjarlais, Godfather: Joseph Ladouceur, Godmother: [J...] Ladouceur, V. Vegreville p.m.a.o.m.i. (page 106_107)

Lac la Biche Baptisms, Marriages and Burials 1853-1884

Cardinal, Narcisse: B-40 Narcisse Quintal [Cardinal], baptized 18 December 1877, born today of the legitimate marriage of Basile Quintal [Cardinal] and Isabelle Osakumanapiw, Godmother: Eleonore Quintal [Cardinal], Collignon o.m.i. (page 174)

Cardinal, Narcisse: S-1, Narcisse Cardinal, buried 6 January 1879, age about one year, son of Basile Cardinal and Isabelle in the presence of Basile Cardinal and Johny Cardinal, E. Grouard priest o.m.i. (page 184)

Cardinal, Olivier and Adelaide Seyapukyikwepiw: M-2, Oliver Cardinal, minor son of Jean_Baptiste Cardinal Cayatius and Josephte Jolifaux, married 8 January 1878, Adelaide, minor daughter of Seyapukyikwepiw dit Pitsikuwinis and the deceased Atsakwapiw, Present: Wapamun and Pitsikuwinis, Collignon o.m.i. (page 175)

Cardinal, Olivier: B-194, Olivier Cardinal, baptized 7 August 1859, age 2 months, son of Laventure Cardinal and Josephte Gladu, Godfather: Francois Cardinal, Godmother: Josephte Cardinal, Tissot Jn. priest o.m.i. (page 35)

Cardinal, Olivier Labatoche: B-62, Olivier Labatoche (Cardinal), baptized 17 December 1854, age a few days, son of Labatoche (Cardinal) and Opimontew, Godfather: Olivier Ladouceur, Godmother: Jessie Ladouceur, R. M. Remas p.o.m.i. (page 11)

Cardinal, Olivier: S-1, Olivier Cardinal, buried 19 January 1871, Witnesses: Georges Adam and Antoine Cardinal, M. R. Remas o.m.i. (page 117)

Cardinal, Patrik: B-220, Patrik Cardinal, baptized 21 March 1861, born the same day, son of Jacques Cardinal dit Kokohokan and Samaskiykapiw, Godfather: Jean Cardinal, Godmother: Cecile Labonne, Maisonneuve A. priest o.m.i. (page 41)

Cardinal, Paul and Marguerite Tremblay: M-4, Paul CardinalL, adult son of the deceased Leon Cardinal, and the surviving Marie Moyon, married 12 September 1876, Marguerite, minor daughter of Raphael Tremblay and Catherine McDougall, Present: Raphael Tremblay and Duncan Tremblay, Henri Ev. L' amour, o.m.i. (page 164)

Cardinal, Paul: B-35, Paul Cardinal, baptized 26 November 1876, age about one month, legitimate son of Dominique Cardinal and Marianne, Godfather: Paul Cardinal, Godmother: Marguerite Tremblay, Collignon o.m.i. (page 164_165)

Cardinal, Pelagie: B-426, Pelagie Cardinal, baptized 7 April 1868, age one month and 3 weeks, natural daughter of Antoine Cardinal and Marie Kakeskamepiw, Godmother: Elise Cardinal, V. Vegreville p.m.a.o.m.i. (page 88-89)

Cardinal, Philippe Charlot: B-39, Philippe Charlot (Cardinal), baptized 26 May 1854, age about 10 months, son of Charlot and Angelique (Berland), Godfather: Bazile Cardinal, M. R. Remas p.o.m.i. (page 7)

Cardinal, Philomene (Quintal); See Jules Desjarlais and Philomene Quintal (Cardinal)

Cardinal, Philomene; See David (Oger) Auger and Philomene Cardinal

Cardinal, Pierre and Angelique Apitsiskwesis: M-22, Pierre Cardinal married 30 November 1860 Angelique Apitsiskwesis, Present: Jacques Cardinal and Baptiste Pepamowew, Tissot Jn. priest o.m.i. (page 40)

Cardinal, Pierre: B-19, Pierre Cardinal, baptized 1 October 1872, legitimate son of Johnny Cardinal and Angele Desjarlais, Godfather: Guillaume Desjarlais, Godmother: Christine Desjarlais, Collignon o.m.i. (page 131)

Cardinal, Pierre: S-2, Pierre Cardinal, buried 28 February 1875, Present, his brothers Gerante, Pierre and Alexandre, Alex. J. B. Brunet priest o.m.i. (page 149)

Cardinal, Raphael: B-37, Raphael Cardinal, baptized 15 December 1883, age about 25 days, legitimate son of Johny Cardinal and Angele Desjarlais, Godfather: Joseph Bourque, Godmother: Agathe Ladouceur, Collignon o.m.i.p. (page 232)

Cardinal, Raphael: B-39, Raphael Cardinal, baptized 13 December 1877, legitimate son of Paul Cardinal and Marguerite Tremblay, Godfather: Raphael Tremblay, Godmother: Catherine McDougall, wife of Raphael Tremblay, E. Grouard priest o.m.i. (page 174)

Cardinal, Raphael: S-4, Raphael Cardinal, buried 9 July 1878, died yesterday, age about 8 months, Witnesses: Pierre Ladouceur and Raphael Tremblay, Collignon o.m.i. (page 179)

Cardinal, Rosalie: B-7, Rosalie Cardinal, baptized 4 October 1853, age 3 days, daughter of Jacques Cardinal and Tiamaskekapaw [?], Godfather: Joseph Gray, M. R. Remas p.o.m.i. (page 3)

Cardinal, Rosalie dit Mustatip: S-3, Rosalie Cardinal-Mustatip, buried 20 April 1882, age about 5 years, daughter of Joseph Cardinal Mustatip and Angelique Kakikekamik, Witnesses: Francois Kakikekamik and Jean-Baptiste Laroque, E. Grouard priest o.m.i. (page 217)

Cardinal, Scholastique: B-286, Scholastique Cardinal, baptized 27 June 1863, born yesterday, daughter of Antoine Cardinal and Cecile Boucher, Godmother: Adele Desjarlais, Tissot Jn. priest o.m.i. (page 53)

Cardinal, Silvestre La Batoche: B-24, Silvestre La Batoche (Cardinal), baptized 29 July 1883, age 2 months, legitimate son of Joseph La Batoche (Cardinal) and Eliza Desjarlais, Godfather: Thomas, Godmother: Melanie Desjarlais, Collignon o.m.i.p. (page 229)

Cardinal, St.Luc and Marguerite Desjarlais: M-5, St.Luc Cardinal married 15 October 1854, Marguerite Desjarlais, Witnesses: Decoin Sr. and Paul Decoin, M. R. Remas p.o.m.i. (page 10)

Cardinal, Suzanne Thibly: B-37, Suzanne Thibly (Cardinal), baptized 26 May 1854, age one year, daughter of Pierre Thibly and Catherine Pakaque, Godfather: Adam Ladouceur, M. R. Remas p.o.m.i. (page 7)

Cardinal, Virginie (Mustatip): B-23, Virginie Cardinal (Mustatip), baptized 29 September 1882, age 7 days, legitimate daughter of Joseph (Antoine) Cardinal (Mustatip) and Domitille Desjarlais (Jean-Marie), Godmother: Catherine Lavalleee (signed), E. Grouard priest o.m.i. (page 221)

Lac la Biche Baptisms, Marriages and Burials 1853-1884

Cardinal, William: B-18, William Cardinal, baptized 3 April 1881, age 12 days, legitimate son of Dominique Cardinal and Maria Desjarlais, Godfather: Charles Quintal, Godmother: Angelique Desjarlais wife of Adam, E. Grouard priest o.m.i. (page 205)

Cardinal, William: B-229, William Cardinal, baptized 7 July 1861, age over one year, son of Baptiste Cardinal and Kimawapikes, Godfather: Isidore Decoin, Maisonneuve A. priest o.m.i. (page 43)

Cardinal, William: S-23, William Cardinal, buried 24 February 1865, died 6 days, Present: Baptiste Lafrayniere and Paulette Auger, Maisonneuve A. Priest o.m.i. (page 64)

Cardinal, Xavier and Marie Jim: M-1, Xavier Cardinal, son of Louison Cardinal dit Mustatip and Susan Metheomet (Courte_Oreille)., married 28 February 1875, Marie Jim, daughter of Baptiste Jim and Betsi, Present: Guilluame Vilbrun, cousin of the groom, and Julien Cardinal, J. V. Fourmond priest o.m.i. (page 148)

Castor, Eulalie-Agathe: B-35, Eulalie-Agathe Castor, baptized 4 December 1883, age about 2 months, legitimate daughter of Francois Castor and Marguerite Desjarlais, Godmother: Marie Hoole, Collignon o.m.i.p. (page 232)

Castor, Francis: B-4, Francis Castor, baptized 22 March 1874, age 8 days, legitimate son of Francois Castor and Marguerite Desjarlais, Godfather: Joseph Desjarlais, Godmother: Agathe Ladouceur, V. Vegreville p.m.a.o.m.i. (page 142)

Castor, Jean Baptiste: S-7, Jean Baptiste Castor, buried 22 September 1875, died 10 days, age 10 years, son of Baptiste Castor and Nancy Quintal, Present: Le Serrec (signed) and L. Dupire (signed), Husson Ate. p.o.m.i. (page 156)

Castor, Lalouise: B-24, Lalouise Castor, baptized 12 June 1881, age about 2 months, legitimate daughter of Francois Castor and Marguerite Desjarlais, Godfather: Petit Loius Hamelin, Godmother: Veronique Desjarlais, Collignon o.m.i. p. (page 206-207)

Castor, Nicolas: B-20, Nicolas Castor, baptized 25 July 1875, born the middle of the month, legitimate son of Francois Castor and Marguerite Desjarlais, Godmother: Nancy Quintal, M. R. Remas pret o.m.i. (page 153)

Castor, Rose de Lima; B-20, Rose de Lima Castor, baptized 7 July 1879, age 20 days, legitimate daughter of Francois Castor and Marguerite Desjarlais, Godfather: Francois Desconane, Godmother: Adelaide Decouane, E. Groaurd priest o.m.i. (page 189)

Cayatius, Francis: B-9, Francis Cayatius, baptized 27 April 1884, born yesterday, of the legitimate marriage of Olivier Cayatius and Adelaide Pitikuninis, Godfather: Francis Isidore Decoine, Godmother: Florestine Ladouceur, Collignon o.m.i.p. (page 236)

Celkailerou, Elisabeth: B-31, Elisabeth Celkailerou, baptized 9 July 1881, age about 3 months, legitimate daughter of Charles Celkailerou and Marguerite Intaraze, Godmother: Angele wife of Pascal, E. Grouard priest o.m.i. (page 208)

Celkailerou, Madeleine; See Alexandre Ekittesh and Madeleine Celkailerou

Celkelin, Charles and Marguerite Edoyaze: M-66, Charles Celkelin, adult son of Francois Izonanyz and Therese Shaynned, married 11 June 1868, Marguerite Edoyaze, adult daughter of Isakeli and Marie Beruyini, Present: Antoine Bisson and Jean Baptiste Billyozzaze, V. Vegreville p.m.a.o.m.i. (page 92)

Charland, Emerence: B-289, Emerence Charland, baptized 8 September 1863, age 2 months, daughter of Charland and Julie Dagneau, Godfather: Ambroise Philippe Durocher, Godmother: Scholastique Vivier, Tissot Jn. priest o.m.i. (page 54)

Charland, Felix: B-405, Felix Charland, baptized 16 June 1867, born yesterday, legitimate son of Louis Charland and Julie Dagneau, Godmother: Rosille Beauregard, Godfather: Francois Larocque, V. Vegreville, p.m.a.o.m.i. (page 82)

Charland, Felix: S-42, Felix Charland, buried 24 June 1867, died yesterday, age 8 days, son of Louis Charland and Julie Dagneau, Present: Louis Charland and Pierre Ladouceur, V. Vegreville, p.m.a.o.m.i. (page 82)

Charland, Madeleine: B-441, Madeleine Charland, baptized 19 July 1868, born yesterday, legitimate daughter of Louis Charland and Julie Dagneau, Godfather: Louis Daze, Godmother: Therese Ladouceur, V. Vegreville p.m.a.o.m.i. (page 93)

Charles, Jean-Marie: B-10, Jean-Marie (Charles), baptized 21 March 1877, age 5 years, son of Charles __, F. Le Serrec priest o.m.i. (page 168)

Charles, Louis: B-11, Louis (Charles), baptized 21 March 1877, age 10 months, son of Charles __, F. Le Serrec priest o.m.i. (page 168)

Charles, Pascal and Angele Montagnais: M-3, Pascal, adult legitimate son of Charles and Marguerite, married 10 June 1877, Angele, minor daughter of ___, Present: Antoine and Pierre, E. Grouard priest o.m.i. (page 169-170)

Cicip, Marie wife of: S-41, Marie, wife of Cicip, buried 14 June 1867, died yesterday, age about 55 years, Present: Theodore Decoine and Louison Cardinal, V. Vegreville, p.m.a.o.m.i. (page 82)

Colin, Anselme: B-14, Anselme Colin, baptized 20 May 1872, born 18 May 1872, legitimate son of Clement Colin and Elisabeth Quintal, Godfather: Isidore Pambrun, Godmother: Betsy Quintal, M. R. Remas priest omi. (page 129)

Colin, Marie: B-16, Marie Kolen, baptized 2 May 1875 born 3 days, of the legitimate marriage of Clement Kolen and Isabelle Quintal, Godfather: Guillaume Vilbrun, Godmother: Florence Hope, J. V. Fourmond priest o.m.i. (page 152)

Collin, Anselme: S-7, Anselme Collin, buried 30 December 1878, age 7 years, Witnesses: R. P. Collignon, Thomy Huppe, E. Grouard priest omi. (page 184)

Collin, Clement: S-3, Clement Collin, buried 23 May 1881, died 21 May 1881, age about 70 years, Witnesses: Charley Johnston and Duncan Tremblay, E. Grouard priest o.m.i. (page 206)

Lac la Biche Baptisms, Marriages and Burials 1853-1884

Collin, Hubert: B-73, Hubert Colin, baptized 17 March 1879, born 16 March 1879, son of Clement Collin and Elisabeth Quintal, Godfather: Charlie Quintal, Godmother: Mathild Collin, E. Grouard priest o.m.i.

Collin, Marcel: B-398, Marcel Collin, baptized 30 January 1867, born yesterday, legitimate son of Clement Collin and Isabelle Quintal, Godmother: Nancy Quintal, V. Vegreville, priest mis. o.m.i. (page 78)

Collins, Clement and Isabelle Quintal: M-11, Clement Collins, adult son of the late Joseph Collins and Javotte Gaudin, married 28 January 1856, Isabelle Quintal, minor daughter of the late Quintal and Charlotte Desjarlais, Present: Maisonneuve (signed Maisonneuve A. priest o.m.i.) and Alexandre Beaudry, Tissot Jn. priest o.m.i. (page 16)

Collins, Mathilde: B-215, Mathilde Collins, baptized 30 November 1860, born yesterday, of the legitimate marriage of Clement Collins and Isabelle Quintal, Godfather: Alexis, Godmother: Esther Bruneau, Tissot Jn. priest o.m.i. (page 40)

Courte-Oreille, Carron Boussaul: B-10, Carron Boussaul Courte-Oreille, baptized 15 April 1883, age 10 days, legitimate son of Olivier Courte-Oreille and Jany Ladouceur, Godfather: David Ladouceur, Godmother: Sophie Ladouceur, Collignon o.m.i.p. (page 226)

Courteoreille, Alexis and Marguerite Cardinal: M-39, Alexis Courte-Oreille married 28 August 1864, Marguerite Cardinal, Present: Jacques Cardinal and Eugene Kaniyenam, Tissot Jn. priest o.m.i. (page 59)

Courteoreille, Oliver and Jane Ladouceur: M-4, Olivier Courte-oreille, widower of [Sarah Pruden], legitimate son of Louison Courteoreille and the deceased [Francoise], married 2 June 1878, Jane Ladouceur, adult daughter of Joseph Ladouceur and the deceased Julie Auger, Present: Joseph Ladoucer (x) and Thomy Huppe (x), E. Grouard priest o.m.i. (page 178)

Cris, Agnes: B-33, Agnes Cris, baptized 7 August 1881, age about 2 months, legitimate daughter of Xavier Cris and Jeanne, Godfather: Moyse Cris, Godmother: his wife, Collignon o.m.i.p. (page 208-209)

Cris, Andre: B-26, Norbert (Cris), baptized 8 July 1877, age about 2 years, legitimate son of Peter and Nancy (Cris), E. Grouard priest o.m.i. (page 171)

Cris, Baptiste and Marie-Lucie Atinakwawis: M-2, Baptiste Cris, married 2 February 1877, Marie-Lucie Atinakwawis, Present: R. P. Leduc (signed H. Leduc priest o.m.i.), Mr. l'Abbe Jolys (signed J. M. Jolys priest), F. Le Serrec priest (page 166-167)

Cris, Marguerite: B-27, Marguerite (Cris), baptized 21 June 1881, age about 3 months, daughter of Pierre (Cris) and Marie (Montagnaise), no godparents, E. Grouard priest o.m.i. (page 207)

Cris, Marie-Josephine: B-40, Marie-Josephine Cris, baptized 25 December 1883, age about 2 months, legitimate daughter of Xavier Cris and Jeanne-Marie, Godfather: Alec Johnston, Godmother: Josephine Lavallee (signed), Collignon o.m.i.p. (page 233)

Cris, Norbert: B-25, Norbert (Cris), baptized 8 July 1877, age about 6 months, legitimate son of Peter and Nancy (Cris), E. Grouard priest o.m.i. (page 171)

Crise, Cecile: B-25, Cecile Crise baptized 10 July 1878, age about 2 months, daughter of Paul (Cris from Fort McMurray) and Justine, no godfather, E. Grouard priest o.m.i. (page 181)

Crise, Lalouise: B-43, Lalouise Crise, baptized 10 October 1869, age 18 months, daughter of Jean-Baptiste (Crise) and Napunokwes, Godmother: Julie McGillis, V. Vegreville p.m.a.o.m.i. (page 108)

Crise, LaLouise: B-26, LaLouise Crise baptized 10 July 1878, age about 2 years, daughter of Paul (Cris) and Josette, no godfather, E. Grouard priest o.m.i. (page 181)

Crise, Marie: B-223, Marie Crise, conditional baptism 18 March 1861 abjuration of Marie Nanakawas, age 24 years, Godmother: Magdeleine Deschamps, Tissot Jn. priest o.m.i. (page 41-42)

Cshimanaskuts, Michel: B-31, Michel Cshimanaskuts, bt 29 April 1854, age about 4 months, son of Cshimanaskuts and Atshakwapiw, Godmother: Eugenie Ladouceur, M. R. Remas p.o.m.i. (page 6)

Dagneau, Daniel: B-80, Daniel Dagneau, baptized 25 August 1855, age 3 months and a few days, legitimate son of Pierre Dagneau and Julie Larence, Maisonneuve A. priest o.m.i. (page 15)

Dagneau, Elise: B-133, Elise Dagneau, baptized 23 September 1857, age over two months, daughter of Isaac Dagneau and Julie Larence, Godfather: John Rollin (Rowland), Godmother: Marguerite Desjarlais, Tissot Jn. priest o.m.i. (page 25_26)

Dagneau, Felix: B-349, Felix Dagneau, baptized 3 August 1865 at Fort Pitt, age 17 months, legitimate son of Isaac Dagneau and Julie Larence, Godmother: Marie Bellerose, V. Vegreville priest o.m.i. (page 67)

Daigneault, David Marie: B-1, David Marie Daigneault, baptized 19 August 1853 at Fort de la Corne, born 17 September 1853, of the legitimate marriage of Isaac Daigneault and Julie Larance, Godfather: Augustin Lajeunesse, M. R. Remas p.o.m.i. (page 2)

Dares, Angelique: B-288, Angelique Dares, baptized 5 September 1863, age over 6 months, daughter of Antoine Dares and Marie Tsakrale, Godmother: Isabelle Sauteuse, Tissot Jn. priest o.m.i. (page 54)

David, Philomene: B-246, Philomene David, baptized 16 January 1861, age about 3 months, daughter of David Cris and Metomatsakwewis, Godfather: Louison Sawapas, Maisonneuve, A. priest o.m.i. (page 46)

Daze, Louis and Sophie Ladouceur: M-61, Louis Daze, widower of Caroline Genthon, married 8 January 1868, Sophie Ladouceur, minor daughter of Joseph Ladouceur and Julie Auger, Present: Joseph Ladouceur and Adam Ladouceur, V. Vegreville p.m.a.o.m.i. (page 87)

Decoigne, Narcisse: S-6, Narcisse Decoigne, buried 10 October 1872, age about one month, Witnesses: Charles Houle, Collignon o.m.i. (page 131)

Decoigne, Josette Dekwan: B-18, Josette Dekwan (Decoigne), baptized 4 August 1884, born 3 August 1884, of the legitimate marriage of Francois Dekwan and Pelagie Cardinal, Godfather: Moise Dekwan, Godmother: Josette Holl, A. Desmarais priest o.m.i. (page 238)

Decoigne, Marie: B-18, Marie Decoigne, baptized 29 September 1872, age about 24 days, legitimate daughter of Pierre Decoigne and Rosalie Sisawokaskwet, Godfather: Narcisse Ladouceur, Godmother: Marie Laroque, Collignon o.m.i. (page 130-131)

Decoigne, Marie-Adelaide: B-2, Marie-Adelaide Decoigne, baptized 1 February 1879, age 8 days, legitimate daughter of Isidore Decoigne and Catherine Bews, Godfather: Alec Johnston, Godmother: Adelaide Decoigne, Collignon o.m.i. (page 185)

Decoigne, Pelagie; See Andre Fortier and Pelagie Decoigne

Decoin, Adelaide: B-225, Adelaide Decoin, baptized 12 May 1861, born 2 May 1861, of the legitimate marriage of Francois Decoin and Josephte Desjarlais, Godfather: Charles Quintal, Godmother: Ester Bruneau, Tissot Jn. priest o.m.i. (page 42)

Decoin, Catherine; See Louison Fosseneuve and Catherine Decoin

Decoin, Francois and Pelagie Moustatip: M-1, Francois Decoin married 8 January 1880 Pelagie Moustatip, Present: Petit Louis Lavallee and Thomas Faller, Collignon o.m.i. (page 193)

Decoin, Francois: B-345, Francois Decoin, baptized 15 June 1865, age 6 months, legitimate son of Isidore Decoin and Catherine Tawits, Godfather: Francois Cardinal, Godmother: Catherine Decoin, J. M. Th. Caer priest o.m.i. (page 66-67)

Decoin, Henry and Christianne Viviers: M-9, Henry Decoin, minor son of Pierre Decoin dit Lapoudre and Therese Cardinal, married 5 December 1871, Christianne Viviers, widow of Theodore Decoin, daughter of the late Viviers and Louise Lavallee, Witnesses: Paul [sic] Decoin, father of Henry and Caroline Johnston, M. R. Remas priest o.m.i. (page 125_126)

Decoin, Jenny: B-51, Jenny Decoin, baptized 11 November 1881, age about 10 days, legitimate daughter of Francois Decoin and Pelagie Mustatip Laventure, Godfather: Alex Johnston, Godmother: Catherine Mustatip Laventure, Collignon o.m.i.p. (page 213)

Decoin, Julie; See Leon Desjarlais and Julie Decoin

Decoin, Louis: B-14, Louis Decoin, baptized 24 September 1871, age one year, legitimate son of Pierre Decoin and Rosalie Sisowekaskwet, Godmother: Catherine Cardinal, M. R. Remas priest o.m.i. (page 121-122)

Decoin, Magdeleine: B-3, Magdeleine Decoin, baptized 9 March 1870, born 9 March 1870, daughter of Isidore Decoin and Catherine, widow Bews, Godfather: Moise Decoin, Godmother: Josephte Desjarlais, M. R. Remas priest o.m.i. (page 110)

Decoin, Marie; See Baptiste Bruneau and Marie Decoin

Lac la Biche Baptisms, Marriages and Burials 1853-1884

Decoin, Moise: B-274, Moise Decoin, baptized 28 February 1863, born today, of the legitimate marriage of Francois Decoin and Josephte Desjarlais, Godfather: Joseph Ladouceur, Godmother: Catherine Ladouceur, Tissot Jn. priest o.m.i. (page 51)

Decoin, Olivier: B-21, Olivier Decoin, baptized 6 December 1874, age 20 days, legitimate son of Henry Decoin and Christine Viviers, Godfather: Isidore Decoin, Godmother: Catherine Eauits, M. R. Remas priest o.m.i. (page 147)

Decoin, Paul and Marguerite Fosseneuve: M-46, Paul Decoine married 26 April 1865 Marguerite Fosseneuve, Present: Joachim Bruneau and Joseph Ladouceur, Tissot Jn. priest o.m.i. (page 65-66)

Decoin, Pelagie: B-157, Pelagie Decoin, baptized 19 September 1858, born 13 September 1858, of the legitimate marriatge of Francois Decoin and Josephte Desjarlais, Godmother: Nancy Quintal, Godmother: Olivier Laderoute, Tissot Jn. priest o.m.i. (page 29)

Decoin, Theodore: S-2, Theodore Decoine, buried 1 October 1870, age about 25 years, Witnesses: Isidore Decoin and Charles Houle, M. R. Remas priest o.m.i. (page 114-115)

Decoine, Adelaide:; See Edward Villeneuve and Adelaide Decoine

Decoine, Albert and Catherine Maskawanis: M-3, Albert Decoine married 2 April 1875 Catherine Maskawanis, Present: Alexis Cardinal and Ema Siwastimaw, M. R. Remas priest o.m.i. (page 150)

Decoine, Alexandre: B-24, Alexandre Decoine, baptized 2 October 1872, born yesterday, legitimate son of Harry Decoine and Christine Viviers, Godfather: Narcisse Boucher, Godmother: Marguerite Tremblay, V. Vegreville p.m.a.o.m.i. (page 132)

Decoine, Augustin: B-30, Augustin Decoin, baptized 4 September 1876, born 1 September 1876, legitimate son of Isidore Decoin and Catherine Bews, Godfather: Francois Decoin, Godmother: Julie Decoin, L. Dupire priest (page 163)

Decoine, Francis Isidore and Isabelle Osisis: M-6, Francis Isidore Decoine married 2 September 1884 Isabelle Osisis, Present: Francois Laroque (x) and Francois Decoine (x), + Henri Ev. D'Anamour o.m.i. (page 240)

Decoine, Francois: B-90, Francois Decoin, baptized 11 May 1856, age 4 days, of the legitimate marriage of Francois Decoin and Josephte Desjarlais, Godfather: Francois Desjarlais, Godmother: Euphrosine Auge, Tissot Jn. priest o.m.i. (page 17)

Decoine, Joseph: B-4, Joseph Decoine, baptized 8 February 1876, age about 2 months, born of the legitimate marriage of Alex Decoine and Catherine Mastahuganis, Godfather: Johnny Pambrun, Husson pt. o.m.i. (page 158)

Decoine, Louis: S-4, Louis Decoine, buried 7 October 1871, age one year, son of Pierre Decoine and Rosalie Sisawakaskwep, Witnesses: Norbert Decoine and Augustin Decoine, V. Vegreville p.m.a.o.m.i. (page 122-123)

Lac la Biche Baptisms, Marriages and Burials 1853-1884

Decoine, Louise: B-10, Louise Decoing [Decoine], baptized 9 October 1853, age 3 months and 7 days, legitimate daughter of Francois Decoing and Josephte Kwetsheit (Desjarlais), Godmother: Louis Desjarlais, M. R. Remas p.o.m.i. (page 3)

Decoine, Louise; See Thomas Hupe and Louise Decoine

Decoine, Madeleine; See Julien Lapoudre and Madeleine Decoine

Decoine, Marie: B-406, Marie Decoine, baptized 26 June 1867, born today, legitimate daughter of Isidore Decoine and Catherine, Godfather: Theodore Decoine, Godmother: Francoise Decoine, V. Vegreville, p.m.a.o.m.i. (page 82)

Decoine, Narcisse: B-23, Narcisse Decoigne, baptized 22 August 1872, born yesterday, legitimate son of Isidore Decoine and Catherine Tawits, Godfather: Narcisse Boucher, Godmother: Julie Decoine, V. Vegreville p.m.a.o.m.i. (page 131)

Decoine, Paul: B-24, Paul Decoine, baptized 8 September 1869, born today, son of Theodore Decoine and Christianna Viviers, Godfather: Paul Decoine, Godmother: Marguerite Buisson, M. R. Remas priest o.m.i. (page 105)

Decoine, Pierre (Sacob) and Agnes Batoche: M-13, Pierre Sacob married 10 October 1856 Agnes Batoche, Present: Baptiste Kakikekamik and Louis Batoche, Tissot Jn, priest o.m.i. (page 20)

Decoine, Sophie: B-2, Sophie Decoine, bt 21 January 1874, age 13 days, legitimate daughter of Isidore Decoine and Catherine Tawits, Godfather: Theophile Ladouceur, Godmother: Judith MacCarthy, V. Vegreville priest o.m.i. (page 140_141)

Decoine, Theodore and Christianne Viviers: M-70, Theodore Decoine, adult son of the late Francois Decoine and Josephte Desjarlais, married 29 September 1868, Christianne Viviers, minor daughter of the late Viviers and Louise Vallee, Present: Joseph Duquette and Louise Vallee, V. Vegreville, p.m.a.o.m.i. (page 95-96)
Decoine, Francoise; See Charles Houle and Francoise Decoine

Deisthi, Nanette: B-26, Nanette Deisthi, baptized 12 September 1869, age 3 months, daughter of Ma.... Deisthi, Godmother: Melanie, V. Vegreville p.m.a.o.m.i. (page 105)

Dekayro, Jean Baptiste: B-256, Jean-Baptiste Dekayro, baptized 25 April 1862, age 4 months, son of Charles Dekayro and Marguerite Intoyaze, Godmother: Marguerite Gladu, Tissot Jn. priest o.m.i. (page 48)

Delgayero, Cecile: B-387, Cecile Delgayero, baptized 30 September 1866, born 24 September 1866, legitimate daughter of Charles Delgayero and Marguerite Nitohage, Godmother: Bethsy Cardinal, Maisonneuve A. priest o.m.i. (page 76)

Delgayero, Therese: B-299, Therese Delgayero, baptized 27 March 1864, age over 2 months, daughter of Charles Delgayero and Marguerite Sutokazirugee [?], Godmother: Marie Montagnaise, Tissot Jn. priest o.m.i. (page 56)

Lac la Biche Baptisms, Marriages and Burials 1853-1884

Delkayero, Francois: B-183, Francois Delkayero, baptized 27 March 1859, age about one year, son of Charles Delkayero and Marguerite Intohaze, Godfather: Francois Deschamp, Godmother: Marguerite Hainault, Tissot Jn priest o.m.i. (page 33)

Deltat, Abraham: B-28, Abraham Deltatt, baptized 5 October 1875, born 25 December 1874, natural child of Alexandre Deltatt and Marie Destsie, Godfather: Antoine Dzensedildille, Husson p.o.m.i. (page 156)

Deltat, Alek and Clothilde Bisson: M-6, Alek Deltat, married 1 June 1875, Clothilde Bisson dit Sikwes, Witnesses: Raphael Trembly and Narcisse Boucher, M. R. Remas priest om.i. (page 152-153)

Deltat, Emilie: B-8, Emilie Deltat, baptized 4 April 1873, age one year, legitimate daughter of Alec Deltat and Agnes Bisson, Godfather: Fabien Bisson, Godmother: Marie Gladu, V. Vegreville p.m.a.o.m.i. (page 136)

Deltat, Jean-Marie: B-21, Jean-Marie Deltat, baptized 15 June 1876, age about 4 months, legitimate son of Alexandre Deltat and Clothild Cherak'ais (Bisson), Godfather: Andre, Collignon p.o.m.i. (page 161)

Deltat, Suzanne: B-8, Suzanne Deltat, baptized 16 April 1870, age 5 months, legitimate son of Alec Deltat and Agnes Bisson, Godfather: Fabien Bisson, Godmother: Marie Gladu, M. R. Remas priest o.m.i. (page 110-111)

Deltot Alec and Agnes Bisson: M-8, Alec Deltot, adult son of Alexandre Deltot and Tsekedyede, married 8 September 1869, Agnes Bisson, minor daughter of Alexis Bisson and Catherine, Present: Charles Tethlens [?] and Pascal [...], V. Vegreville p.m.a.o.m.i. (page 104)

Deneltti, Gregoire: B-11, Gregoire Deneltti, baptized 8 May 1870, age 6 months, of the legitimate marriage of Louis Deneltti and Marie Tsinaiyazigan, Godmother: Constance Deneltti, M. R. Remas priest o.m.i. (page 111)

Depez, Louise: B-95, Louise Depez, baptized 27 July 1856, age 15 days, legitimate daughter of Antoine Depez and Marie Paydese, Godmother: Marie Deneyonille, Tissot Jn. priest o.m.i. (page 18)

Depez, Marie: B-158, Marie Depez, baptized 7 October 1858, age 2 months, of the legitimate marriage of Antoine Depez and Marie Paydeze, Godfather: Andre Woule, Godmother: Eupogini [?], Tissot Jn. priest o.m.i. (page 29)

Deprez, Antoine and Marie Paydeze: M-8, Antoine Deprez married 16 July 1855 Marie Paydeze, Present: Alexandre Janvier and Louison Janvier, Tissot Jn. priest o.m.i. (page 13)

Derez, Angelique; See Noe Otsebes and Angelique Derez

Derez, Magdeleine: B-340, Magdeleine Derez, baptized 15 April 1865, age over two months, daughter of Antoine Derez and Marie Rayerze, Godmother: Francoise Tsekintseze, Tissot Jn. priest o.m.i. (page 65)

Deschamp, Elise; See Narcisse Mognon and Elise Deschamp

Deschamps, Marguerite: B-336, Marguerite Deschamps, baptized 21 January 1865, age 7 months, daughter of Baptiste deschamps and Isabelle Honore, Godfather: Antoine Houle, Godmother: Josephte Deschamps, Tissot Jn. priest o.m.i. (page 64)

Lac la Biche Baptisms, Marriages and Burials 1853-1884

Deschamps, Marie: B-161, Marie Deschamps, baptized 3 September 1858, born 16 July 1858, of the legitimate marriage of Francois Deschamps and Marguerite Haineault, Godfather: John Nolin, Godmother: Sophie Chatlain, Maisonneuve A. priest o.m.i. (page 30)

Desjardins, Adeline: B-30, Adeline Desjardins, baptized 8 October 1884, born yesterday, of the legitimate marriage of Baptiste Desjardins and Madeleine Lafleur, Godmother: Eulalie Hamelin (signed), Godmother: Louis Hamelin (signed), Collignon o.m.i.p. (page 241)

Desjardins, Arsene: B-18, Arsene Desjardins, buried 2 July 1882, born yesterday, of the legitimate marriage of Baptiste Desjardins and Madeleine Lafleur, Godfather: Milsens, (signed), Godmother: Agathe Ladouceur, Collignon o.m.i.p. (page 219)

Desjardins, Baptiste: B-2, Baptiste Desjardins, baptized 15 January 1878, born today of the legitimate marriage of Baptiste Desjardins and Isabelle Lafleur, Godfather: Alexandre Salomon Hamelin, Godmother: Marie McGillis, Colligonon o.m.i. (page 175)

Desjardins, Felix: B-7, Felix Desjardins, baptized 18 February 1880, born today, of the legitimate marriage of Baptiste Desjardins and Isabelle Lafleur, the godfather was the attending priest, Godmother: Sister Donet, Collignon o.m.i. (page 194)

Desjardins, Julie: B-2, Julie Desjardins, baptized 29 January 1876, born in the night of the legitimate marriage of Baptiste Desjardins and Isabelle Lafleur, Godfather: Antoine Laroque, Godmother: his wife, Husson p.o.m.i. (page 158)

Desjarlais, Abaslom: B-15, Absalom Desjarlais, baptized 14 June 1879, age 2 months and 10 days, legitimate son of Paulette Desjarlais and Betsy, Godfather: fr. Cleophas Racette, Godmother: Sister Carroll (signed), E. Grouard priest o.m.i. (page 188)

Desjarlais, Adelaide: B-12, Adelaide Desjarlais, baptized 9 June 1873, age about 26 days, illegitimate daughter of Christine Desjarlais, Godmother: Caroline Ladouceur, Collignon o.m.i. (page 137)

Desjarlais, Adele; See Francois Cardinal and Adele Desjarlais

Desjarlais, Alfred: B-30, Alfred Desjarlais, baptized 19 September 1883, age 7 days, legitimate son of Paulette Desjarlais and Betsy, Godmother: Mary Jane Cardinal (signed), Collignon o.m.i.p. (page 231)

Desjarlais, Alisa: B-206, Alisa Desjarlais, baptized 28 May 1860, age 17 days, daughter of Francois Desjarlais and Euphrosine Auger, Godfather: Paul Desjarlais, Godmother: Eugenie Ladouceur, Tissot Jn priest o.m.i. (page 38)

Desjarlais, Alphonse: B-50, Alphonse Desjarlais, baptized 7 November 1881, age 17 days, legitimate son of Joseph Desjarlais dit Akayasiw and Betsy Tsimanaskat, Godfather: Georges Adam, Godmother: Isabelle Desjarlais, Collignon o.m.i. priest. (page 213)

Lac la Biche Baptisms, Marriages and Burials 1853-1884

Desjarlais, Amable: B-156, Amable Desjarlais, baptized 8 August 1858, age about 2 months, son of Paul Desjarlais and Iskwesis, Godmother: Eugenie Ladouceur, Tissot Jn. priest o.m.i. (page 29)

Desjarlais, Angele; See Johny Cardinal and Angele Desjarlais

Desjarlais, Antoine and Marguerite Kikikuwatam: M-4, Antoine Desjarlais, minor son of Marcel Desjarlais and Nakwestakay, married 22 October 1877, Marguerite Kikikuwatam, minor daughter of Kikikuwatam, Present: brother Lorfevre and Catherine L'Esperance, Collignon o.m.i. (page 173)

Desjarlais, Archange: B-384, Archange Desjarlais, baptized 23 September 1866, age 9 days, legitimate daughter of Paulet Desjarlais and Lisette Bruneau, Godfather: Jean-Baptiste Amistawiyinisis, Godmother: Francoise Decoine, V. Vegreville o.m.i. (page 76)

Desjarlais, Baptiste: B-6, Baptiste Desjarlais, baptized 25 February 1883, age 19 days, legitimate son of Antoine Desjarlais and Marguerite Kaayatapiyis, Godfather: Narcisse Boucher, Godmother: Marianne, Collignon o.m.i.p. (page 225)

Desjarlais, Betsy: B-16, Betsy Desjarlais, baptized 11 April 1880, age 9 days, legitimate daughter of Antoine Desjarlais and Marguerite Kaayatapiyis, Godfather: George Adam, Godmother: Angelique Desjarlais, Collignon o.m.i. priest. (page 196)

Desjarlais, Christine: B-89, Christine Desjarlais, baptized 13 April 1856, age about 3 months, legitimate daughter of Francois Desjarlais and Euphrosine Auge, Godfather: Charles Quintal, Godmother: Isabelle Quintal, Tissot Jn. priest o.m.i. (page 17)

Desjarlais, Delphine: B-16, Delphine Desjarlais, baptized 28 September 1871, born yesterday, legitimate child of Francois Desjarlais and Fresine Auge, Godmother: Louise Decoin, M. R. Remas priest o.m.i. (page 122)

Desjarlais, Delphine: S-4, Delphine Desjarlais, buried 15 October 1871, daughter of Francois Desjarlais and Frezine Auge, Witnesses: Norbert Sauve and Guillaume Desjarlais, M. R. Remas priest o.m.i. (page 124)

Desjarlais, Domitilde: B-355, Domitilde Desjarlais, baptized 24 October 1865, born yesterday, of the legitimate marriage of Jean Marie Desjarlais and Rosalie Batauche, Godmother: Catherine Decoin, Maisonneuve A. priest o.m.i. (page 68)

Desjarlais, Domitille; See Joseph Mustatip Cardinal and Domitille Desjarlais

Desjarlais, Edouard: B-1, Edouard Desjarlais, baptized 4 January 1872, born today, legitimate son of Guillaume Desjarlais and Marguerite Sauve, Godfather: Norbert Sauve, Godmother: Marie Sauve, M. R. Remas priest o.m.i. (page 126)

Desjarlais, Edouard: S-5, Edouard Desjarlais, buried 13 April 1872, died 12 April 1872, age about 4 months, Witnesses: St.Luc Cardinal and Leon Desjarlais, Colliginon o.m.i. (page 129)

Lac la Biche Baptisms, Marriages and Burials 1853-1884

Desjarlais, Elaiza: B-26, Elaiza Desjarlais, baptized 21 December 1871, age 18 months, legitimate daughter of Paul Desjarlais and Bethsy Cardinal, Godfather: Jules Desjarlais, Godmother: Angelique Desjarlais, M. R. Remas priest o.m.i. (page 126)

Desjarlais, Eliza; See Joseph LaBatoche and Eliza Desjarlais

Desjarlais, Francois: B-173, Francois Desjarlais, baptized 8 December 1858, born 28 November 1858, of the legitimate marriage of Jean Marie Desjarlais and Rosalie Batauche, Godfather: Francois Desjarlais, Godmother: Agnes Batauche, Maisonneuve A. Priest o.m.i. (page 32)

Desjarlais, Francois: B-27, Francois Desjarlais, baptized 30 August 1880, age about 3 months, legitimate son of Leon Desjarlais and Julie Decoin, Godfather: Andre Fortier (signed), Godmother: Francoise Decoin, Collignon o.m.i. (page 198)

Desjarlais, Gabriel: B-190, Gabriel Desjarlais, baptized 13 June 1859, born yesterday, illegitimate son of Josephte Desjarlais, Godmother: Josephte Desjarlais, Tissot Jn. priest o.m.i. (page 35)

Desjarlais, Guillaume and Marguerite Sauve: M-6, Guillaume Desjarlais, minor son of Francois Desjarlais and Fresine Auge, married 27 July 1870, Marguerite Sauve, minor daughter of Norbert Sauve and Josephte St.Pierre, Present: Francois Desjarlais and Norbert Sauve, M. R. Remas priest o.m.i. (page 113)

Desjarlais, Guillaume: B-29, Guillaume Desjarlais, baptized 1 September 1877, age 12 days, legitimate son of Jules Desjarlais and Philomene Cardinal, Godfather: Eugene Waweyinam, Godmother: Caroline Johnson, E. Grouard priest o.m.i. (page 172)

Desjarlais, Henriette Paulette: B-26, Henriette Paulette Desjarlais, baptized 22 August 1880, age about 3 weeks, legitimate daughter of Joseph Desjarlais Paulette and Cecile Cardinal, Godmother: Eleonore Cardinal, E. Grouard priest o.m.i. (page 198)

Desjarlais, Henriette: S-2, Henriette Desjarlais, buried 4 September 1883, age about 3 years and 3 days, Witnesses: Francois Decoine and Leon Dejarlais, Collignon o.m.i.p. (page 230)

Desjarlais, Hyacinthe: B-34, Hyacinthe Desjarlais, baptized 14 August 1881, age 15 days, legitimate son of Guillaume Desjarlais and Marguerite, Godfather: Louison Fosseneuve, Godmother: Marie-Jeanne Desjarlais, Collignon o.m.i.p. (page 209)

Desjarlais, Isabelle: B-142, Isabelle Desjarlais, baptized 24 October 1857, age 3 months, daughter of Jean-Marie Desjarlais and Lisette Batoche, Godfather: Joseph Ladouceur, Godmother: Isabelle Quintal, Tissot Jn. priest o.m.i. (page 27)

Desjarlais, Jean:: B-191, Jean Desjarlais, baptized 24 July 1859, age 9 days, of the legitimate marriage fo Paulette Desjarlais and Lisette Bruneau, Godfather: Aubichon Cardinal, Godmother: Cecile Labonne, Tissot Jn. priest o.m.i. (page 35)

Lac la Biche Baptisms, Marriages and Burials 1853-1884

Desjarlais, Jean-Baptiste: B-31, Jean-Baptiste Desjarlais, baptized 19 September 1880, age about 15 days, legitimate son of Joseph Desjarlais dit Apiskwesimun and Marie Desjarlais, Godfather: Jean-Baptiste Cis, Godmother: Josephte, Collignon o.m.i.p. (page 199)

Desjarlais, Jean-Marie and Genevieve Cardinal: M-55, Jean_Marie Desjarlais, widower Lisette Batoche, married 28 May 1867, Genevieve Cardinal, minor daughter of Jacob Cardinal and Marguerite Desjarlais, Present: Paulette Desjarlais and Julie Auger, V. Vegreville, p.m.a.o.m.i. (page 81)

Desjarlais, Joseph and Betsy Tsimanaskat: M-3, Joseph Desjarlais married 26 April 1880 Betsy Tsimanaskat, Present: T. Gonat (signed) and J. Larfeuvre (signed), Collignon o.m.i. priest. (page 196)

Desjarlais, Joseph and Cecile Cardinal: M-1, Joseph Desjarlais, married 11 August 1879, Cecile Cardinal, Present: Paulette Desjarlais (x) and Joseph Apichimon (x), Collignon o.m.i. (page 189)

Desjarlais, Joseph: B-11, Joseph Desjarlais, baptized 30 May 1884, age 26 days, illegitimate son of Jules Desjarlais and Monique Petit Castor, Godfather: Absalom Ladouceur, Godmother: Cecile Hoole, Collignon o.m.i.p. (page 237)

Desjarlais, Joseph: B-148, Joseph Desjarlais, baptized 4 February 1858, born 3 January 1858, of the legitimate marriage of Francois Desjarlais and Euphrosine Auger, Godfather: Adam Ladouceur, Godmother: Therese Ladouceur, Tissot Jn. priest o.m.i. (page 28)

Desjarlais, Marguerite; See Francis Nitanikamuw and Marguerite Desjarlais

Desjarlais, Joseph: B-3, Joseph Desjarlais, baptized 12 January [February] 1883, age about one month, legitimate son of Joseph Paulette Desjarlais and Cecile Cardinal, Godmother: Marie-Jeanne [signed Mary-Jane Cardinal), Collignon o.m.i.p. (page 224)

Desjarlais, Joseph: B-5, Joseph Desjarlais, baptized 7 March 1875, born 4 days, of the legitimate marriage of Jules Desjarlais and Philomene Cardinal, Godfather: St.Pierre Quintal, Godmother: Marie Gladu, J. V. Fourmond priest o.m.i. (page 149)

Desjarlais, Joseph: B-15, Joseph Desjarlais, baptized 24 July 1870, born 10 July 1870, son of Paul Desjarlais and Veronique Otakinatikwe, Godfather: Pierre Lambert, Godmother: Elizabeth Adam, M. R. Remas priest omi. (page 113_114)

Desjarlais, Joseph: S-20, Joseph Desjarlais, buried 18 August 1863, died yesterday, son of Paulette Desjarlais, Present: Joseph Ladouceur and Francois Decoin, Tissot Jr., priest o.m.i. (page 54)

Desjarlais, Joseph: S-2, Joseph Desjarlais, buried 30 November 1854, husband of Josephte Cardinal, Present: Joseph Ladouceur and Louis Decoine, M. R. Remas p.o.m.i. (page 11)S-2, Joseph Desjarlais, buried 30 November 1854, husband of Josephte Cardinal, Present: Joseph Ladouceur and Louis Decoine, M. R. Remas p.o.m.i. (page 11)

Lac la Biche Baptisms, Marriages and Burials 1853-1884

Desjarlais, Josephte: B-35, Josephte Desjarlais, baptized 12 December 1878, age about 2 months, legititmate daughter of Antoine Desjarlais and Marguerite Kaayatapiyis, Godfather: Jules Desjarlais, Godmother: Nakwestakay, Collignon o.m.i. (page 183-184)

Desjarlais, Josephte: S-3, Josephte Desjarlais, buried 3 February 1879, age about 4 months, daughter of Antoine Desjarlais and Marguerite Kaayatapiyis, Witnesses: Antoine Desjarlais and Alec Johnston, E. Grouard priest o.m.i. (page 185)

Desjarlais, Josephte; See Jerome Cardinal and Josephte Desjarlais

Desjarlais, Judith; See Louis Cardinal and Judith Desjarlais

Desjarlais, Jules and Philomene Quintal (Cardinal): M-5, Jules Desjarlais, minor son of Marcel Desjarlais and Brigitte Cardinal, married 10 September 1871, Philomene Quintal, adult daughter of Alexis Cardinal and Nancy Quintal, and widow of David Auge, Witnesses: Georges Adam and Baptiste Bellecourt, M. R. Remas p.m.a.o.m.i. (page 123-124)

Desjarlais, Julie: B-285, Julie Desjarlais, baptized 10 June 1863, born 17 February 1863, of the legitimate marriage of Paulette Desjarlais and Lisette Bruneau, Godmother: Josephte Desjarlais, Tissot Jn. priest o.m.i. (page 53)

Desjarlais, Julie; See Michel Grosse-Tete and Julie Desjarlais

Desjarlais, Leon and Julie Decoin: M-8, Leon Desjarlais, adult son of Paulette Desjarlais and Lisette Bruno, married 25 August 1875, Julie Decoin, adult daughter of Francois Decoin and Josephte Desjarlais, Witnesses: Paulette Desjarlais and Augustin Cardinal, M. R. Remas priest o.m.i. (page 154-155)

Desjarlais, Leon: B-55, Leon Desjarlais, baptized 3 October 1854, born 2 October 1854, son of Paulette Desjarlais and Lisette Bruno, Godfather: Joseph Ladouceur, Godmother: Louise Desjarlais, M. R. Remas p.o.m.i. (page 10)

Desjarlais, Leon: B-68, Leon Dejarlais, baptized 22 April 1855, age about 3 months, son of Jean-Marie Dejarlais and Rosalie Nakwe, Godfather: St.Luc Cardinal, Godmother: Margueritte Dejarlais, M. R. Remas p.o.m.i. (page 12)

Desjarlais, Louise: B-24, Louise Desjarlais, baptized 22 August 1875, born 20 March 1875, legitimate daughter of Paulette Desjarlais and Bethsy Cardinal, Godmother: Julie Decoin, M. R. Remas priest o.m.i. (page 154)

Desjarlais, Louise Paulette: S-4, Louise Desjarlais Paulette, buried 29 June 1880 at the mission, died the end of May last, Witnesses: Leon Desjarlais and Tousaint Gladu, E. Grouard priest o.m.i. (page 197)

Desjarlais, Louise: S-7, Louise Desjarlais, buried 1 December 1856, died 29 November 1856, age about 16 years, Present: Joseph Ladouceur and Abraham Lariviere, Tissot Jn. priest o.m.i. (page 21)

Desjarlais, Madeleine: B-36, Madeleine Desjarlais, baptized 28 December 1884, age 8 days, natural daughter of Mathilde Desjarlais, Godmother: Eulalie Hamelin (signed), Collignon o.m.i.p. (page 244)

Desjarlais, Madeleine: S-7, Madeleine Desjarlais, buried 30 December 1884, died yesterday, age 9 days, Witnesses: F. Boisrame and Baptiste Laroque, Collignon o.m.i.p. (page 245)

Desjarlais, Magdeleine: B-233, Magdeleine Desjarlais, baptized 20 August 1861, age 2 months, daughter of Jean-Marie Desjarlais and Rosalie Batoche, Godmother: Catherine Ladouceur, Tissot Jn. priest o.m.i. (page 43)

Desjarlais, Marguerite: B-8, Margueritte Desjarlais, baptized 9 October 1853, age 3 months, daughter of the legitimate marriage of Francois Desjarlais and Josephte Cardinal, Godmother: Marguerite Desjarlais, M. R. Remas p.o.m.i. (page 3)

Desjarlais, Marguerite: S-32, Marguerite Desjarlais, buried 15 January 1866, died yesterday, age about 60 years, daughter of Desjarlais and a Sauteuse, Witnesses: Pierre Cardinal and Cardinal, V. Vegreville priest o.m.i. (page 72)

Desjarlais, Marguerite; St.Luc Cardinal and Marguerite Desjarlais

Desjarlais, Marie: B-144, Marie Desjarlais, baptized 15 November 1857, age 9 days, daughter of Paulette Dejarlais and Lizaette Bruno, Godfather: John Nollin, Godmother: Henriette, Tissot Jn. priest o.m.i. (page 27)

Desjarlais, Marie Iskwesis; See Baptiste Fosseneuve and Marie Iskwesis (Desjarlais)

Desjarlais, Marie; See Joseph Cardinal and Marie Desjarlais

Desjarlais, Marie-Agnes: B-41, Marie-Agnes Desjarlais, baptized 12 September 1881, age 3 months, legitimate daughter of Paulette Desjarlais and Betsy, Godmother: Eulalie Hamelin (signed), E. Petitot p.o.m.i. (page 210)

Desjarlais, Marie-LaLouise: B-28, Marie-LaLouise Desjarlais, baptized 15 September 1884, age 9 days, legitimate daughter of Joseph Desjarlais dit Anaskasun and Marie Paulette, Godmother: Louisa Hamelin (signed), Collignon o.m.i.p. (page 241)

Desjarlais, Marie-Rose: B-15, Marie-Rose Desjarlais, baptized 19 May 1878, age about one year, legitimate daughter of Paulette Desjarlais and Betsi, Godfather: George Bourk, Godmother: Marguerite Louison, Collignon o.m.i. (page 178)

Desjarlais, Marie-Rose: S-5, Marie-Rose Desjarlais, buried 8 December 1878, age one year and 8 months, Witnesses: Pierre Ladouceur and Paulette Desjarlais, E. Grouard priest o.m.i. (page 183)

Desjarlais, Marie-Vitaline: B-19, Marie-Vitaline Desjarlais, baptized 3 July 1882, age about 3 months, legitimate daughter of Julien Desjarlais and Philomene Cardinal, Godfather: C. Racette (signed), Godmother: Marianne Cardinal, Collignon o.m.i.p. (page 219)

Desjarlais, Mary Jane;B-401, Mary Jane Desjarlais, baptized 19 April 1867, born 23 February, legtimate daughter of Francois Desjarlais and Euphrosine Auger, Godfather: George Bourque, Godmother: Agathe Ladouceur, V. Vegreville p.m.a.o.m.i. (page 80)

Lac la Biche Baptisms, Marriages and Burials 1853-1884

Desjarlais, Maxime: B-14, Maxime Desjarlais, baptized 5 July 1873, age 2 days, legitimate son of Guillaume Desjarlais and Marguerite Sauve, Godfather: St.Luc Cardinal, Godmother: Angelique Desjarlais, Collignon o.m.i. (page 138)

Desjarlais, Michel: B-12, Michel Desjarlais, baptized 14 May 1869, age 8 days, legitimate s/o Francois Desjarlais and Euphrosine Oger, Godfather: Augustin Ladouceur, Godmother: Agnes Ladouceur, V. Vegreville p.m.a.o.m.i. (page 100_101)

Desjarlais, Michel dit Apichimen: B-10, Michel Desjarlais dit Apichimen, baptized 9 April 1882, age about one month, legitimate son of Joseph Desjarlais dit Apichimen and Marie Desjarlais Paulette, Godfather: Michel Grosse-Tete, Godmother: Julie Desjarlais, Collignon o.m.i.p. (page 217)

Desjarlais, Moyse: B-417, Moyse Desjarlais, baptized 26 September 1867, age 16 days, legitmate son of Paul Desjarlais and Otakinatukewisk, Godfather: Jean_Baptiste Kakekamik, Godmother: Suzanne Osawamikek, V. Vegreville p.m.a.o.m.i. (page 85)

Desjarlais, Parisit (Nikwestakay): S-1, Parisit Desjarlais dit Nikwestakay, buried 6 March 1884, died 3 March 1884, age about 80 years, Witnesses: Alex Hamelin (signed) and George Martin (signed), Collignon o.m.i.p. (page 235)

Desjarlais, Paul: B-33, Paul Desjarlais, baptized 3 November 1876, age 3 days, legitimate son of Guillaume Desjarlais and Julie Decoigne, Godfather: Francois Decoigne, Godmother: Pelagie Decoigne, C. Mignon o.m.i. (page 164)

Desjarlais, Paul: S-7, Paul Desjarlais, buried 20 March 1879, age 2 years, died yesterday, son of Leon Desjarlais and Julie Decouanne, Witnesses: Andre Fortier and Narcisse Boucher, Collingnon priest (page 186)

Desjarlais, Paulet and Bethsy Cardinal: M-3, Paulet Desjarlais, widower of Lisette Bruneau, married 13 April 1869, Bethsy Cardinal, adult daughter of the late Louison Cardinal and Susane Courte-Oreille, Present: Joseph Duquette and Susanne Courte-Oreille, V. Vegreville p.m.a.o.m.i. (page 100)

Desjarlais, Paulette and Lisette Bruno: M-3, Paulette Desjarlais married 7 May 1854 Lisette Bruno, Present: Joseph Ladouceur and Aubichon (John) Cardinal, Alex Ev. de St.Boniface o.m.i. (page 6-7)

Desjarlais, Petit Louis (Akayasiw): B-1, Petit Louis Desjarlais (Akayasiw), baptized 27 February 1884, age one month, legitimate son of Joseph Desjarlais dit Akayasiw and Betsy, Godmother: Angelique Desjarlais, Collignon o.m.i.p. (page 234-235)

Desjarlais, Pierre: B-21, Pierre Desjarlais, baptized 21 August 1872, age 8 days, legitimate son of Jules Desjarlais and Philomene Cardinal, Godmother: Brigitte Cardinal, V. Vegreville p.m.a.o.m.i. (page 131)

Desjarlais, Pierre Paulette and Catherine Matsimuttaw: M-2, Pierre Paulette Desjarlais married 5 February 1884 Catherine Matsimuttaw, Present: Charles Johnstone (signed) and George Martin (signed), Collignon o.m.i.p. (page 234)

Lac la Biche Baptisms, Marriages and Burials 1853-1884

Desjarlais, Rupert: B-192, Rupert Desjarlais, baptized 24 July 1859, age 3 days, illegitimate son of a Crise and Michel Desjarlais, Godmother: Euphrosine Auger, Tissot Jn. priest o.m.i. (page 35)

Desjarlais, Sara: B-23, Sara Desjarlais, baptized 24 August 1878, age 13 days, born of the legitimate marriage of Francois Desjarlais and Marie Yatisekinam, Godfather: Louis Lavallee, Godmother: Eliza Desjarlais, E. Grouard priest o.m.i. (page 180)

Desjarlais, Sylivie: S-6, Sylvie Desjarlais, buried 28 October 1856, age about 3 months, daughter of Paulette Desjarlais and Lisette Bruno, Present: Joseph Pepamwew and Abraham Lariviere, Tissot Jn. priest o.m.i. (page 20)

Desjarlais, Veronique: B-293, Veronique Desjarlais, baptized 13 December 1863, born 5 December 1863, daughter of Francois Desjarlais and Euphrosine Auger, Godfather: Augustin Auger, Godmother: Julie Auger, Tissot Jn. priest o.m.i. (page 55)

Desjarlais, Vitaline: B-15, Vitaline Desjarlais, baptized 1 June 1882, born yesterday, of the legitimate marriage of Leon Desjarlais and Julie Decouane, Godfather: Joseph Desjarlais Paulette, Godmother: Pelagie Foriter, E. Grouard priest o.m.i. (page 218-219)

Desmarais, Marguerite; See Adam Ladouceur and Marguerite Desmarais

Desrocher, Magdeleine; See Joseph Paquette and Magdeleine Desrocher

Desrochers, Edouard: B-127, Edouard Desrochers, baptized 17 May 1857, age 5 days, son of Philippe Desrochers and Catherine Parrant, Godfather: Edouard Genereux, Godmother: Marianne Beaudry, Tissot Jn. priest o.m.i. (page 24)

Desrochers, Sara: B-304, Sara Desrochers, baptized 1 May 1864, age over three months, daughter of Philippe Desrochers and Catherien Parent, Godfather: Joachim Bruneau, Godmother: Josephte Cardinal, Tissot priest o.m.i. (page 57)

Dliyeros; See Jeremie Eklethene and Dliyeros

Dubois, Francois: S-2, Francois Dubois, buried 26 February 1872, age 15 years, of the Assiniboine nation, Witnesses: Julien Cardinal and Jacques Piwitew, M. R. Remas priest o.m.i. (page 127)

Duchame, Antoine and Sophie Ladouceur: M-6, Antoine Ducharme, minor son of Baptiste Ducharme and Catherine Marie, married 19 November 1878, Sophie Ladouceur, widow of the deceased Louis Daze, adult daughter of Joseph Ladouceur and the deceased Julie Auger, Witnesses: Antoine Ducharme (x) and Joseph Ladouceur (x) , Collignon o.m.i. (page 182)

Ducharme, Adelaide: B-99, Adelaide Ducharme, baptized 6 September 1856, born 30 July 1856, legitimate daughter of Charles Ducharme and Nancy Sauteuse, Godmother: Sophie Chalifoux,Maisonneuve A. priest o.m.i. (page 19)

Ducharme, Angelique; See Joseph Timanaskak and Angelique Ducharme

Lac la Biche Baptisms, Marriages and Burials 1853-1884

Ducharme, Angelique; See J. B. Kakikekamik and Angelique Ducharme

Ducharme, Antoine: S-2, Antoine Ducharme of Lac Manitoba, bu. 17 January 1879, died 15 January 1879, age about 19 years, Witnesses: Louis Fosseneuve and Adam Ladouceur, E. Grouard priest o.m.i. (page 184_185)

Ducharme, Marguerite: B-34, Marguerite Ducharme, baptized 25 November 1883, born today of the legitimate marriage of Antoine Ducharme and Caroline Fidler, Godfather: Julien Cardinal, Godmother: Marguerite Fosseneuve, Collignon o.m.i.p. (page 232)

Ducharme, Rosalie: B-21, Rosalie Ducharme, baptized 1 September 1870, born 20 August 1870, daughter of Pierre Ducharme and Marie Desjarlais, Godmother: Marie Desjarlais, M. R. Remas priest o.m.i. (page 114)

Dufresne, Isabelle; See Isidore Pambrun and Isabelle Dufresne

Dufretois, Olive: B-8, Olive Dufretois, baptized 21 March 1877, born 30 January 1877, of Alfred Dufretois and Emelie Vivier, F. Le Serrec priest o.m.i. (page 168)

Duquet, Joseph: B-129, Joseph Duquet, baptized 17 May 1857, born 17 April 1857, son of Joseph Duquet and Marianne Constant, Godfather: Joseph Parisien, Godmother: Julie Larence, Tissot Jn. priest o.m.i. (page 24)

Duquet, Marisis; See Gregoire Malaterre and Marisis Duquet

Duquette, Andre: B-414, Andre Duquette, baptized 28 June 1867, born 10 May 1866, illegitimate son of William Duquette and Lalouise Tsimmak, Godfather: Cyrille Lafond, Maisonneuve A. priest o.m.i. (page 84)

Duquette, Genevieve; See Abraham and Genevieve Duquette

Dzinlchule, Judith; See Pierre Lagrossetete and Judith Dzinlchule

Easawiskamikutew, Jean Baptiste: B-383, Jean-Baptiste Easawiskamikutew, baptized 22 September 1866, age 4 days, son of Abraham Easawiskamikutew and Nepawis, Godmother: Catherine Cardinal, V. Vegreville o.m.i. (page 76)

Eatawatam, Jamy-Jacques: B-31, Jamy-Jacques Eatawatam, baptized 9 December 1870, age 8 days, of the legitimate marriage of Moise Eatawatam and Catherine Kakkwetsutamowisk, Godmother: Sophie St.Sauveur, + Henri, Eveq d'Anomore [?] o.m.i. (page 116)

Edoyaze, Marguerite; See Charles Celkelin and Marguerite Edoyaze

Eelkelero, Thomas and Eugenie Nadarenlyeille: M-3, Thomas Eelkelero, son of Charles Eelkelero and Marguerite Edoeyose, married 20 September 1874, Eugenie Nadarenlyeille, daughter of Augustin Nadarenlyeille and Emelie Tsekais, Present: Pierre Lagrossetete and Antoine Bisson, V. Vegreville priest omi. (page 145-146)

Lac la Biche Baptisms, Marriages and Burials 1853-1884

Eelkilero, Eugenie: B-9, Eugenie Eelkilero, baptized 4 April 1873, age one year, legitimate daughter of Charles Eelkilero and Marguerite Ittoyaze, Godfather: Fabien Bisson, Godmother: Marie Gladu, V. Vegreville p.m.a.o.m.i. (page 136)

Ek'Aliru, Edouard: B-13, Edouard Ek'Aliru, baptized 31 March 1877, age 3 months, legitimate son of Thomas Ek'aliru and Eugenie Piche, Godfather: Pascal Ek'ali, Godmother: Philomene Gendron, E. Grouard priest o.m.i. (page 168)

Ek'elene, Moise: B-41, Moise Ek'elene, baptized 19 December 1877, age one month, legitimate son of Jeremie Ek'elene and Gheros, Godfather: Pascal, Godmother: Angele his wife, E. Grouard priest o.m.i. (page 174)

Ek'elthene, Andre and Marie Piche: M-2, Andre Ek'elthene, minor son of the deceased Ek'elthene and the surviving Francoise, married 16 June 1876, Marie Piche, minor daughter of the deceased August Piche and the surviving Clothilde Bisson, Present: Joseph Ek'elthene and Alexandre Delttatt, Henri Ev. d'Anemour o.m.i. (page 161-162)

Ek'line, Rosalie: B-8, Rosalie Ek'line, baptized 13 April 1884, age 3 months, daughter of Andre Ek'line and Marie Admalginille, Godmother: Lisette Bison, Collignon o.m.i.p. (page 236)

Ekedhene, Narcisse: B-84, Narcisse Ekedhene, baptized 16 January 1856, age about 3 years, son of Ekedhene and Francoise Dliyellwas, Godfather: Joseph Dzisealkal, Tissot Jn. priest o.m.i. (page 16)

Ekelene, William: B-15, William Ekelene, baptized 24 September 1871, age about one year, legitimate son of Joseph Ekelene and Francoise Dliyeost, Godfather: Alexandre Delttall, M. R. Remas priest o.m.i. (page 122)

Ekeline, Julien: B-377, Julien Ekeline, baptized 1 April 1866, age 4 months, legitimate daughter of Jeremie Ekeline and Francois Duyekhoz, Godmother: Charlotte, V. Vegreville priest mis. o.m.i. (page 73)

Ekittesh, Alexandre and Madeleine Celkailerou: M-3, Alexandre Ekittesh, adult son of the deceased Francois Ekittesh and his widow Charlotte, married 9 July 1881, Madeleine Celkailerou, minor daughter of Charles Celkailerou and the deceased Marie Dacstoi, Present: Antoine Pichon and Charles Celkailerou, E. Grouard priest o.m.i. (page 208)

Eklethene, Jeremie and Dliyeros: M-27, Jeremie Eklethene married 26 October 1861 Dliyeros, Prsent: Antoine Buisson and Gregoire Natsetthel, Tissot Jn. priest o.m.i. (page 45)

Eklethene, Jeremie: B-241, Jeremie Eklethene, baptized 26 October 1861, age about 4 years, Godfather: Gregoire Nalsetthel, Tissot Jn. priest o.m.i. (page 45)

Elkedhene, Baptiste: B-263, Baptiste Elkedhene, baptized 5 September 1862, age 4 years, son of Elkedhene and Dliyeros, Godmother: Marianne Montagne, Tissot Jn. priest o.m.i. (page 49)

Enalile, Francois and Justine Bison: M-2, Francois Enalile married 26 March 1883 Justine Bison, Present: Jean-Baptiste Bison (signed), Fabien Bison (signed), + Henri Eveque d'Amemour o.m.i. (page 226)

Lac la Biche Baptisms, Marriages and Burials 1853-1884

Ennatshi, Joseph: B-443, Joseph Ennatshi, baptized 19 September 1868, age 5 months, legitimate son of Antoine Ennatshi and Louise Gladu, Godmother: Louise Vallee, V. Vegreville, p.m.a.o.m.i. (page 94)

Enouilleille, Adele: B-18, Adele Enouilleille, baptized 16 September 1874, age 6 months, legitimate daughter of Francois Enouilleille and Marie, Godmother: M. Emelie Esekais, V. Vegreville, p.m.a.o.m.i. (page 145)

Enouilleille, Angelique: B-23, Angelique Enouilleille, baptized 10 September 1870, age 8 months, daughter of Nicolas Enouilleille and Emilie Sokais, Godmother: Charlotte Ekeyite, V. Vegreville priest o.m.i. (page 114)

Enouilleille, Jean: B-437, Jean Enouilleille, baptized 6 June 1868, age 13 months, legitimate son of Nicolas Enouilleille and Emelie Sekais,Godfather: Francois Bisson, Godmother: Catherine Isakale, V. Vegreville p.m.a.o.m.i. (page 91)

Enouleille, Caroline: B-3, Caroline Enouleille, baptized 3 April 1873, age 6 months, illegitimate daughter of Nicolas Enouleille and Emelie Tsekais, Godfather: Fabien Bisson, Godmother: Francoise Tielros, V. Vegreville p.m.a.o.m.i. (page 135)

Enouleille, Francois and Marie Iliyekitson: M-1, Francois Enouleille, minor son of Nicolas Enouleille and Therese Ekides, married 5 April 1873, Marie Iliyekitson, minor daughter of Andre Iliyekitson and Marie Daistsic, Present: Pierre Lagrosse-Tete and Nicolas Enouleille, V. Vegreville p.m.a.o.m.i. (page 136)

Enouleille, Pascal: B-376, Pascal Enouleille, baptized 1 April 1866, age over one year, son of Nicolas Enouleille and Emilie Sekais, Godmother: Marie Daestsi, V. Vegreville priest mis. o.m.i. (page 73)

Enullile, Francois and LaLouise Cardinal: M-4, Francois Enullile married 30 June 1884 LaLouise Jerome Cardinal, Present: Julien Cardinal (x) and Louis Boisrame (x), + Henri Ev. D'anemour o.m.i. (page 237)

Etapitonew, Sara Raphaele: B-14, Sara-Raphaele Etapitonew, baptized 24 October 1853, born last March, of Etapitonew and Sawewisk, Godmother: Frosine Auge, M. R. Remas p.o.m.i. (page 4)

Etawihapaw dit Kiyakikikwepiw, Angelique: B-420, Angelique Etawihapaw dit Kiyakikikwepiw, baptized 12 November 1867, age about 26 years, daughter of Etawihapaw and Oteyaniskamikepiw, Godmother: Julie Auger, V. Vegreville p.m.a.o.m.i. (page 86)

Etawihapaw dit Kiyakikikwepiw, Angelique; See Toussaint Gladu and Angelique Etawihapaw dit Kiyakikikwepiw

Etehelle, Constance; See Isidore Gladu and Constance Etehelle

Eyeze Kathe, Madeleine: B-9, Madeleine Eyeze Kaythe, baptized 24 March 1883, age 15 days, legitimate daughter of Alexandre Eyeze Kaythe and Madeleine Bisson, Godfather: Andre, Collignon o.m.i.p. (page 225-226)

Eyiskala, Jean: B-20, Jean Eyiskala, baptized 4 November 1873, age 4 months, illegitimate son of Andre Eyiskala and Judith Tsiankuaze, Godfather: Julien Bedziaze, Godmother: Marie Aytoze, E. Petitot priest o.m.i. (page 139)

Eyitawyanawap, Susanne: B-147, Susanne Eyitawyanawap, baptized 30 January 1858, age about one year, daughter of Eyitawyanawap and Marie Sakatsiwis, Godmother: Julie Lavallee, Tissot Jn. priest o.m.i. (page 28)

Eyotowataw, Anne: B-26, Anne Eyotowataw, baptized 24 April 1854, age 5 years, daughter of Eyotowataw and Niyopitshitshep, Godfather: Joseph Gray, M. R. Remas p.o.m.i. (page 4-5)

Eyotowotaw, Paul: B-25, Paul Eyotowotaw, baptized 24 April 1854, age 3 years, son of Eyotowataw and Neyopitshitshafe, Godfather: Joseph Gray, M. R. Remas p.o.m.i. (page 5)

Fidler, Maxime and Henriette Molligan: M-1, Maxime Fidler married 15 January 1884 Henriette Molligan, Present: Antoine Ducharme (x) and Peter Pruden (signed), Collignon o.m.i.p. (page 234)

Forcier, Marie-Luce: S-2, Marie-Luce Forcier, buried 9 June 1878, died 8 June 1878, at the Sister of Charity Convent, Present: R. P. Collignon (signed) and fr. Patrick Bowes (signed), E. Grouard priest o.m.i. (page 178)

Fortier, Andre and Pelagie Decoigne: M-1, Andre Fortier, adult son of the deceased Pierre Fortier and the deceased Marie Desgauldrand, married 8 January 1878, Pelagie Decoigne, minor daughter of the deceased Francois Decoigne and Josephte Desjarlais, Present: Petit Louis Lavallee and Pierre Ladoucer, Collignon o.m.i. (page 175)

Fortier, Marie-Euphrosine: B-27, Marie-Euphrosine Fortier, baptized 25 August 1883, born today of the legitimate marriage of Andre Fortier and Pelagie Decoine, Godfather: Alexandre Hamelin (signed Alex Hamelin), Godmother: Sister Youville (signed), Collignon o.m.i.p. (page 229-230)

Fortier, Marie-Hermile: B-36, Marie Hermile Fortier, baptized 14 August 1881, born yesterday, of the legitimate marriage of Andre Fortier and Pelagie Decoigne, the priest served as the godfather, Godmother: Pelagie Laventure (signed), Collignon o.m.i.p. (page 209)

Fortier, Vitaline: B-33, Vitaline Fortier, baptized 17 November 1879, born the same day, of the legitimate marriage of Andre Fortier and Pelagie Decouanne, Godfather: Francois Decouanne, Godmother: Adelaide Decouanne, E. Grouard priest o.m.i. (page 192)

Fosseneuve, Alfred: B-2, Alfred Fosseneuve, baptized 11 January [February] 1883, age 8 days, legitimate son of Louison Fosseneuve and Therese Ladouceur, Godfather: Narcisse Ladouceur, Godmother: Julie Auger, Collignon o.m.i.p. (page 224)

Fosseneuve, Baptiste and Marie Iskwesis (Desjarlais): M-32, Baptiste Fosseneuve (dit Bisillier) married 21 March 1862 Marie Iskwesis (Desjarlais), Present: Louis Chatelain and Charles Beauregard, Tissot Jn. priest o.m.i. (page 48)

Fosseneuve, David: B-39, David Fosseneuve, baptized 12 December 1876, age 5 days, legitimate son of Louison Fosseneuve and Therese Ladouceur, Godfather: Augustin Ladouceur, Godmother: Agnes Ladouceur, Collignon o.m.i. (page 165)

Fosseneuve, Elphrosine: B-1, Elphrosine Fosseneuve, baptized 5 January 1882, born 25 December 1881, legitimate daughter of Louis Fosseneuve and Therese Ladouceur, Godmother: Marguerite Fosseneuve, Husson priest o.m.i. (page 214)

Fosseneuve, Emile: B-34, Emile Fosseneuve, baptized 7 December 1878, age 2 days, of the legitimate marriage of Louison Fosseneuve and Therese Ladouceur, Godmother: Sophie Ladouceur, Collegnon o.m.i. (page 183)

Fosseneuve, Jean: B-15, Jean Fosseneuve, baptized 29 April 1875, age 4 days, of the legitimate marriage of Louison Fosseneuve and Therese Ladouceur, Godfather: Joseph Ladouceur, Godmother: Julie Auger the grandparents, J. V Fourmon priest o.m.i. (page 152)

Fosseneuve, Julie-Victoire: B-18, Julie_Victoire Fosseneuve, baptized 21 September 1873, born today, legitimate daughter of Louis Fosseneuve and Therese Ladouceur, Godfather: Georges Bourque, Godmother: Agathe Ladouceur, V. Vegreville p.m.a.o.m.i. (page 138)

Fosseneuve, Louison and Therese Ladouceur: M-4, Louison Fosseneuve, adult son of Baptiste Fosseneuve and Marguerite Beaulieu, married 12 November 1872, Therese Ladouceur, adult daughter of Joseph Ladouceur and Julie Auger, Present: Joseph Ladouceur and Francois Laroque, V. Vegreville p.m.a.o.m.i. (page 132)

Fosseneuve, Louison and Catherine Decoin: M-57, Louison Fosseneuve, adult son of Jean_Baptiste Fosseneuve and Julie Morin, married Catherine Decoin, adult daughter of Francois Decoin and Josephte Desjarlais, Present: Ignace MacKay and Paul Decoin, V. Vegreville p.m.a.o.m.i. (page 83)

Fosseneuve, Marguerite; See Paul Decoin and Marguerite Fosseneuve

Fosseneuve, Marie: B-330, Marie Fausseneuve, baptized 8 January 1865, age 18 days, daughter of Baptiste Fausseneuve and Marie Iskwesis (Desjarlais), Godfather: Joseph Mallet, Godmother: Marie Bellanger, Tissot Jn. priest o.m.i. (page 63)

Fraser, Mary; See James Tige and Mary Fraser

Gadoua, Betsy: S-10, Betsy Gadoua, wife of Benjamin Belcourt, buried 12 October 1879, died 10 October 1879, age about 25 years, Witnesses: Louis Martin and Jean-Baptiste Desjarlais, E. Grouard priest o.m.i. (page 191-192)

Gane, Jean and Charlotte Nanetehan: M-5, Jean Gane, son of the deceased Gane and the living Julie Gladu, married 10 May 1870, Charlotte Nanetehan, minor daughter of the deceased Jean-Marie Nanetehan and the living Charlotte Enaestchoeiyazi [?], Present: Joseph Ducet and Julien Cardinal, V. Vegreville p.m.a.o.m.i. (page 112)

Gendron, Philomene: S-1, Philomene Gendron, buried 4 April 1878, died 3 April 1878 at the Sisters of Charity Convent, age about 18 years, Present: Pierre Ladouceur and Louis Martin Lavallee, E. Grouard priest o.m.i. (page 177)

Michel, Adam: B-10, Adam Michel, baptized 20 April 1878, age about 8 months, legitimate son of Louis Michel and Julie, Godfather: Jean-Baptiste Belozaze, E. Grouard priest o.m.i. (page 177)

Lac la Biche Baptisms, Marriages and Burials 1853-1884

Genereux, Archange: B-13, Archange Genereux, baptized 16 April 1872, age 6 months, daughter of Edouard Genereux and Marie Chatelain, Godfather: Monseigneur Grandin eveque de St.Albert (signed), Godmother: Sister of Charity Ursule Charlesbois (signed), M. R. Remas priest o.m.i. (page 129)

Georges, Joseph: B-17, Joseph Georges, baptized 17 September 1873, age 6 months, legitimate son of Georgers and Nagats, Godmother: Marguerite Tremblay, V. Vegreville p.m.a.o.m.i. (page 138)

Gibbot, Louis: B-213, Louis Gibbot, baptized 21 October 1860, age about one year, son of Joseph Gibbot and Angelique Gladu, Godmother: Josephte Cardinal, Tissot Jn priest o.m.i. (page 39)

Gibott, Silvestre: B-270, Silvestre Gibott, baptized 1 November 1862, age one year, son of Joseph Gibott and Angelique Wapestakay, Godmother: Adele Desjarlais, Tissot Jn. priest o.m.i. (page 50)

Gibotte, Cecile: B-149, Cecile Gibotte, baptized 2 March 1858, age 8 months, daughter of Sakiskanip and Siwyastimew, Tissot Jn. priest o.m.i. (page 28)

Gladu, Alexandre: B-447, Alexandre Gladu, baptized 28 September 1868, age 8 days, legitimate son of Antoine Gladu and Madeleine Kale, Godmother: Julie Gladu, V. Vegreville, p.m.a.o.m.i. (page 95)

Gladu, Alexandre dit Janvier: B-10, Alexandre Gladu dit Janvier, baptized 13 July 1871, age 5 months, son of Pierre Gladu dit Janvier and Melanie Naali, Godmother: Victoire Naali, + Henri Ev. D'Anomour o.m.i. (page 121)

Gladu, Angelique dit Janvier: B-324, Angelique Gladu dit Janvier, baptized 23 October 1864, age 2 years, daughter of Louison Gladu dit Janvier and Lisette Tsakuthe, Godfather: Baptiste Kakikekamik, Maisonneuve A. priest o.m.i. (page 61)

Gladu, Betsy: B-3, Betsy Gladu, baptized 21 January 1880, age about 11 months, daughter of Louison Gladu and Paskwawiskwew, Godmother: Mikwaskwesis, Collignon o.m.i. (page 193)

Gladu, Catherine: B-25, Catherine Gladu, baptized 23 July 1876, age about 3 years, legitimate daughter of Louis Gladu and Susanne Paskwaw-iskwew, Godmother: Catherine MacDougall, M. R. Remas priest o.m.i. (page 162)

Gladu, Constance-Angelique: B-7, Constance-Angelique Gladu, baptized 20 February 1876, age about 40 years, Godfather: Joseph Milsens, Godmother: Sister Donet, F. Le Serroc priest (page 159)

Gladu, Felicite; See Louison Gladu and Felicite Gladu

Gladu, Felix: B-12, Felix Gladu, baptized 13 July 1871, age 8 months, legitimate son of Louison Gladu and Felicite Gladu, Godmother: Therese Gladu, + Henri Ev. D'Anomour o.m.i. (page 121)

Gladu, Isidore and Constance Etehelle: M-4, Isidore Gladu, minor son of Mathias Gladu and the deceased Tlaeherida, married 10 May 1870, Constance Etehelle, minor daughter of the deceased Etehelli and Louise Kirelda, Present: V. Vegreville (signed) and R. Remas (signed), Henri Ev. D'Ammour o.m.i. (page 111-112)

Gladu, Jany: B-10, Jany Gladu, baptized 13 April 1873, age 14 days, legitimate daughter of Toussaint Gladu and Angelique Etawikapaw, Godfather: Adam Ladouceur, Godmother: Genevieve Ladouceur, Collignon o.m.i. (page 137)

Gladu, Jean-Marie (dit Janvier) and Lettor Antoine (Narebrin): M-65, Jean-Marie Gladu (dit Janvier), minor son of the late Jean-Marie Gladu (dit Janvier) and Charlotte Emma Crise, married 11 June 1868, Lettor Antoine (Narebrin), minor daughter of Antoine and Tsinnaze, Present: Antoine Bisson and Jean-Baptiste Billyozzaze, V. Vegreville p.m.a.o.m.i. (page 92)

Gladu, Joseph (Napesis): B-390, Joseph Napesis (Gladu), baptized 8 October 1866, age 19 days, son of Louis Napesis (Gladu) and Suzanne Batsis, Godfather: Julien Cardinal, Godmother: Isabelle Kakekemik, V. Vegreville o.m.i. (page 77)

Gladu, Joseph (Tsossede): B-5, Joseph Tsossede (Gladu), baptized 16 April 1870, age over one month, legitimate son of Jean-Marie Tsossede (Gladu) and Lettor (Antoine) Narelrin, Godfather: Fabien Bisson, Godmother: Marie Gladu, M. R. Remas priest o.m.i. (page 110)

Gladu, Joseph: S-44, Joseph Gladu, buried 3 November 1867, died 4 days, age over 13 months, son of Louison Gladu and Susanne Batsis (Paskwawiskwew), Witnesses: Francois Laroque and Joseph Duquette, V. Vegreville p.m.a.o.m.i. (page 85-86)

Gladu, Josephte: B-217, Josephte Gladu, baptized 24 December 1860, age about 30 years, daughter of Francois Gladu and Josephte, Tissot Jn. priest o.m.i. (page 40)

Gladu, Josephte: B-10, Josephte Gladu, baptized 9 April 1876, age about 11 months, legitimate daughter of Toussaint Gladu and Angele Tyetawikapaw, Godmother: Isabelle Gladu, M. R. Remas priest o.m.i. (page 159)

Gladu, Josephte; See Laventure Cardinal and Josephte Gladu

Gladu, Julia: B-2, Julia Gladu, baptized 6 February 1881, age about 5 weeks, legitimate daughter of Thomas Gladu and Marie Morin, Godfather: Nazaire Martel, Godmother: Paggie, Collignon o.m.i.p. (page 202)

Gladu, Louise: B-1, Louise Gladu, baptized 6 January 1869, age a few days, illegitimate daughter of Marguerite Gladu, Godmother: ... Charland, M. R. Remas priest o.m.i. (page 97)

Gladu, Louison and Felicite Gladu: M-69, Louison Gladu, widower of Lisette Tsakunthe, married 21 September 1868, Felicite Gladu, minor daughter of Louison Gladu and Suzanne Desjarlais, Present: Joseph Duquette and Therese Ladouceur, V. Vegreville, p.m.a.o.m.i. (page 95)

Gladu, Magdeleine: B-14, Magdeleine Gladu, baptized 15 April 1876, age about 23 years, Godfather: Joseph Ladouceur, Godmother: Julie Auge, Husson p.o.m.i. (page 160)

Gladu, Marcellin: B-24, Marcellin Gladu, baptized 23 July 1876, age about 11 months, daughter of Pierre Gladu and Lisette Ayhik, Godmother: Marguerite Tremblay, M. R. Remas priest o.m.i. (page 162)

Lac la Biche Baptisms, Marriages and Burials 1853-1884

Gladu, Pierre and Melanie: M-7, Pierre Gladu, adult son of Janvier Gladu and the late Gaillede, married Melanie, minor daughter of the late Antoine and Therese Tsinnaze, Present: Paul Decoine and Charles Telkelero, V. Vegreville p.m.a.o.m.i. (page 104)B-10,

Gladu, Marguerite: B-2, Marguerite Gladu, baptized 6 January 1882, age 5 months, legitimate daughter of Toussaint Gladu and Angelique, Godfather: Paul Lapoudre, Godmother: Marguerite Decoigne, Husson priest o.m.i. (page 214-215)

Gladu, Marguerite: B-25, Marguerite Gladu, baptized 28 September 1873, age one year, legitimate daughter of Antoine Gladu and Magdeleine Kaile, Godmother: Therese Gladu, V. Vegreville p.m.a.o.m.i. (page 140)

Gladu, Marguerite dite Janvier; See Michel Bruneau and Marguerite Gladu dite Janvier

Gladu, Marianne: B-9, Marianne Gladu, baptized 19 February 1881, age about 4 months, daughter of Louison Gladu and Paskwawiskwew, the priest served as godfather, Collignon o.m.i. p. (page 204)

Gladu, Marie: B-26, Marie Gladu, baptized 23 July 1876, age about 4 months, legitimate daughter of Louis Gladu and Susanne Paskwaw_iskwew, Godmother: Pegalie Decoine, M. R. Remas priest o.m.i. (page 162_163)

Gladu, Nancy: B-346, Nancy Gladu, baptized 30 July 1865, age one year, daughter of Augustin Gladu and Marguerite Mekwaskiwisk, Godmother: Isabelle Kakikekamik, Masionneuve, A. priest o.m.i. (page 67)

Gladu, Pierre Naubes: B-29, Pierre Naubes-Gladu, baptized 29 April 1854, age about 6 months, son of Naubes Gladu and Marguerite, Godfather: Joseph Ladouceur, M. R. Remas p.o.m.i. (page 5-6)

Gladu, Rosalie: B-26, Rosalie Gladu, baptized 28 September 1873, age 9 months, legitimate daughter of Pierre Gladu and Melanie Tsekwiyose, Godmother: Josephine Gladu, V. Vegreville p.m.a.o.m.i. (page 140)

Gladu, Toussaint and Angelique Etawikapaw; On 6 March 1868 discovered a 2nd degree relationship in the 12 November 1867 marriage of Toussaint Gladu and Angelique Etawikapaw, V. Vegreville p.m.a.o.m.i. (page 88)

Gladu, Toussaint and Angelique Etawihapaw dit Kiyakikikwepiw: M-60, Toussaint Gladu, adult son of the late Gladu and Auger, married 12 November 1867, Angelique Etawihapaw dit Kiyakikikwepiw, adult daughter of the late Etawihapaw and the late Oteyaniskamikepiw, Present: Julie Auger and Euphrosine Auger, V. Vegreville p.m.a.o.m.i. (page 86)

Gladu, Toussaint: B-419, Toussaint Gladu, baptized 12 November 1867, age about 24 years, son of Gladu and Auger, Godmother: Euphrosine Auger, V. Vegreville p.m.a.o.m.i. (page 86)

Gladu, William: B-328, William Gladu, baptized 18 December 1864, born today, son of Louison Gladu and Nepewis, Godfather: Cyrille Lafont, Godmother: Agathe Auge, Tissot Jn. priest o.m.i. (page 63)

Goin Adelaide: B-125, Adelaide Goin, baptized 4 May 1857, age 4 months, daughter of Antoine Goin and Francoise Bouche, Godfather: Pierre St.Sauvier, Godmother: Louise Bouche, Tissot Jn. priest o.m.i. (page 24)

Lac la Biche Baptisms, Marriages and Burials 1853-1884

Gouin, Jean Baptiste (Gwan); CB-103, Jean Baptiste Gwan (Gouin), baptized 6 September 1856, christened 11 September 1855, Godfather: Pierre Boucher, Godmother: Lalouise Boucher, Maisonneuve A. priest o.m.i. (page 19)

Gouin Jean-Baptiste: B-82, Jean_Baptiste Gwan (Gouin), baptized 11 September 1855 at Fort Pitt, age 9 months, legitimate son of Antoine Gwan (Gouin) and Francoise Boucher, Maisonneuve priest o.m.i. (page 15)

Grosse-Tete, Jean Baptiste: B-339, Jean-Baptiste Grosse-Tete, baptized 12 April 1865, age 2 months, son of Pierre Grosse-Tete and Angelique Tshanada, Godfather: Natsehel Gregoire, Tissot Jn. priest o.m.i. (page 65)

Grosse-Tete, Michel and Julie Desjarlais: M-4, Michel Grosse-Tete Montagnais, widower of his first wife Alice Leponce, married 27 August 1881, Julie Desjarlais, adult daughter of Paulette Desjarlais and the late Lisette, Present: Louis Lavallee and Joseph Dislets (signed Disilets), E. Grouard p.o.m.i. (page 210)

Grosse-Tete, Sophie: B-253, Sophie Grosse-Tete, baptized 5 April 1862, age 3 months, daughter of Pierre Grosse-Tete and Angelique Trarerdo, Godmother: Marie Tsoulkiyase, Tissot Jn. priest o.m.i. (page 48)

Gwanis, Melanie: B-370, Melanie Gwanis, baptized 28 January 1866, age about 9 months, daughter of William Gwanis and Marguerite (Jos. Flatt) Jamak, Godfather: Georges Bourk, Godmother: Sophie Ladouceur, Maisonneuve A. priest o.m.i. (page 72)

Hamelin, Eleonore: B-18, Eleonore Hamelin, baptized 20 June 1879, born today of the legitimate marriage of Alexandre Hamelin and Angelique Houle, Godfather: Louis Hamelin (signed), Godmother: Marie MacGillis, Collignon o.m.i. (page 188)

Hamelin, Elise: B-332, Elise Hamelin, baptized 9 January 1865, age 2 months, daughter of Alexandre Hamelin and Angelique Houle, Godfather: John Rolland, Godmother: Sophie Chatelain, Tissot Jn. priest o.m.i. (page 63)

Hamelin, Louis: B-42, Louis Hamelin, baptized 10 October 1869, age 2 months and 2 days, legitimate son of Alexandre Hamelin and Angelique Houle, Godfather: Louis Hamelin, Godmother: Elise St.Denis, V. Vegreville p.m.a.o.m.i. (page 108)

Hamelin, Marie: B-310, Marie Hamelin, baptized 31 July 1864, born 26 July 1864, of the legitimate marriage of Louis Hamelin and Marguerite Laroque, Godfather: Louis Laroque, Godmother: Marie Savoyard, Maisonneuve A. priest o.m.i. (page 58)

Hamelin, Noel: B-212, Noel Hamelin, baptized 3 October 1860, age 9 months and 9 days, son of Baptiste Hamelin and Susanne Neotsitsiwisk, Godfather: Baptiste Amiokuiyinisis, Godmother: Nancy Quintal, Tissot Jn priest o.m.i. (page 39)

Hodgson, Pierre (Hodson): B-411, Pierre Hodson, baptized 17 June 1867, age 3 days, legitimate son of Georges Hodson and Marie Rollan, Godmother: Helene Beauregarde, Maisonneuve A. priest o.m.i. (page 83-84)

Hoole, Clemence: B-14, Clemence Hoole, baptized 16 March 1880, born today, of the legitimate marriage of Charles Hoole and Francoise Decoane, Godfather: Alexandre Hamelin, Godmother: Louisa Hamelin, E. Grouard priest o.m.i. (page 195)

Hoole, Marie-Catherine: B-21, Marie-Catherine Hoole, baptized 12 June 1880, age about one month, legitimate daughter of William Hoole and Cecile, Godfather: Thomy Huppe, Godmother: Olive Tremblay, Collignon o.m.i. priest. (page 197)

Hope, Caroline: B-429, Caroline Hope, baptized 14 April 1868, age 2 years, legitimate daughter of James Hope and Judith Desjarlais, Godfather: Jerome Cardinal, Godmother: Elisa Cardinal, V. Vegreville p.m.a.o.m.i. (page 89)

Hope, Caroline: S-50, Caroline Hope, buried 26 April 1868, died yesterday, age 2 years, died of James Hope and Judith Desjarlais, Witnesses: Clement Collins and Charles Houle, Maisonneuve A. p.o.m.i. (page 90)

Hope, Eliza: B-9, Eliza Hope, baptized 9 October 1853, bron 22 July, of the legitimate marriage of James Hope and Judith Desjarlais, Godmother: Lisette Joachim, M. R. Remas p.o.m.i. (page 3)

Hope, Flora; See Guillaume Villebrun and Flora Hope

Hope, Francois: B-63, Francois Hope, baptized 18 February 1855, born yesterday, of Jamy Hope and Judith Desjarlais, Godfather: Charles Houlle, Godmother: Esther Bruno, M. R. Remas p.o.m.i. (page 12)

Hope, Francoise; See Jean-Baptiste Cardinal and Francoise Hope

Hope, Frederic: S-52, Frederic Hope, buried 28 July 1868, died yesterday, age over 9 years, son of James Hope and Judith Desjarlais, Present: Theodore Decoin and Jules Desjarlais, V. Vegreville p.m.a.o.m.i. (page 93)

Hope, Frederick: B-427, Frederick Hope, baptized 14 April 1868, age 9 years, legitimate son of James Hope and Judith Desjarlais, Godfather: Jerome Cardinal, Godmother: Euphrosine Auger, V. Vegreville p.m.a.o.m.i. (page 89)

Hope, Johny: B-446, Johny Hope, baptized 27 September 1868, age 2 years, natural son of Flora Hope, Godmother: Isabelle Quintal, V. Vegreville, p.m.a.o.m.i. (page 95)

Hope, William: B-428, William Hope, baptized 14 April 1868, age 5 years, legitimate son of James Hope and Judith Desjarlais, Godfather: Jerome Cardinal, Godmother: Euphrosine Auger, V. Vegreville p.m.a.o.m.i. (page 89)

Hope, William: S-49, William Hope, buried 26 April 1868, died day before yesterday, age 5 years, son of James Hope and Judith Desjarlais, Witnesses: Joseph Duquette and Francois Larocque, Maisonneuve A. p.o.m.i. (page 90)

Houle, Andre-Arthur: B-5, Andre-Arthur Hoole, baptized 9 March 1878, born the same day of the legitimate marriage of Charles Hoole and Francoise Decouanne, Godfather: Andre Fortier (signed), Godmother: Adelaide Decouanne, E. Grouard priest o.m.i. (page 176)

Lac la Biche Baptisms, Marriages and Burials 1853-1884

Houle, Caroline: B-199, Caroline Houle, baptized 4 December 1859, born yesterday, of the legitimate marriage of Charles Houle and Esther Bruneau, Godfather: Francois Deschamps, Godmother: Marguerite Haineault, Tissot Jn. priest o.m.i. (page 36)

Houle, Charles and Francoise Decoine: M-56, Charles Houle, widower of Esther Bruneau, married 4 June 1867, Francoise Decoine, minor daughter of the late Francois Decoine and Josephte Desjarlais, Present: Louis Daze and Paul Bruneau, V. Vegreville, p.m.a.o.m.i. (page 81)

Houle, Charles and Esther Bruno: M-7, Charles Houlle, son of Charles Houlle and ___ Berland, married 26 December 1854, Esther Bruno, daughter of Joachim Bruno and Catherine Ladouceur, Present: Clement Collins and Gilbert St.Luc (Cardinal), M. R. Remas p.o.m.i. (page 11)

Houle, Clemence: S-1, Clemence Hoole, buried 26 January 1883, age about 3 years, son of Charles Hoole and Francoise Decoine, Witnesses: Julien Cardinal and Paul Cardinal, E. Grouard priest o.m.i. (page 223)

Houle, Edmond: B-34, Edmond Houle, baptized 17 December 1875, born today, legitimate son of Charles Houle and Francoise Decoin, Godfather: Jamy Tige, Godmother: Pelagie Decoin, Husson p.o.m.i. (page 157)

Houle, Edmond: S-9, Edmond Hoole, buried 8 December 1881, age about 6 years, son of Charles Hoole and Francoise Decoine, Witnesses: Thomy Huppe and Duncan Tremblay, Collignon o.m.i.p. (page 213)

Houle, Francoise: B-35, Francoise Hoole, baptized 22 December 1884, age 7 days, legitimate daughter of Charles Hoole and Francoise Decoine, Godmother: Eulalie Hamelin (signed), Collignon o.m.i.p. (page 244)

Houle, Henri: B-261, Henri Houle, baptized 7 July 1862, born today, of the legitimate marriage of Charles Houle and Esther Bruneau, Godfather: Augustin Auger, Godmother: Agathe Ladouceur, Tissot Jn. priest o.m.i. (page 49)

Houle, Henri: S-9, Henri Houle, buried 28 October 1882, age 20 years, legitimate son of Charles Houle and Esther Bruneau, Witnesses: J. Milsons and William Houle, E. Grouard priest o.m.i. (page 222)

Houle, Josephte: B-3, Josephte Houle, baptized 18 January 1869, born today, legitimate daughter of Charles Houle and Francoise Decoine, Godfather: Theodore Decoine, Godmother: Julie Decoine, V. Vegrevillle, p.m.a.o.m.i. (page 97)

Houle, LaLouise: B-22, LaLouise Hoole, baptized 12 September 1882, born yesterday, of the legitimate marriage of Charles Hoole and Francoise Decoigne, Godfather: Petit Louis Lavallee, Godmother: Pelagie Decoine, Collignon o.m.i.p. (page 220)

Houle, Marie: B-329, Marie Houl, baptized 22 January 1865, born the same day, of the legitimate marriage of Charles Houl and Esther Bruneau, Godfather: Francois Larocque, Godmother: Angelique Sahis, Maisonneuve A. Priest o.m.i. (page 63)

Houle, Marie; Ond. 2, Marie Houle, christened 15 March 1867, born today, legitimate daughter of Charles Houle and Esther Bruneau, V. Vegreville priest mis. o.m.i. (page 79)

Lac la Biche Baptisms, Marriages and Burials 1853-1884

Houle, Marie; See Arsene Bourque and Marie Hoole

Houle, Marie-Pauline: B-28, Marie-Pauline Hoole, baptized 13 October 1882, born 9 days, of the legitimate marriage of William Hoole and Cecile, Godmother: Catherine Lavallee (signed), Collignon o.m.i.p. (page 222)

Houle, Melanie: B-5, Melanie Houle, baptized 19 February 1872, age 4 days, legitimate daughter of Charles Houle and Francoise Decoine, Godfather: Paul Decoine, Godmother: Marguerite Fosseneuve, V. Vegreville p.o.m.i. (page 127)

Houle, Veronique: B-12, Veronique Hool, baptized 26 May 1870, born yesterday, legitimate daughter of Charles Hool and Josephte Decoin, Godfather: Isidore Decoin, Godmother: Catherine, wife of. Decoin, M. R. Remas p.m.a.o.m.i. (page 112)

Houle, Veronique: S-6, Veronique Houle, buried 30 August 1881, age 11 years, daughter of Charles Houle and Francoise Decoine, Witnesses: Julien Cardinal and William Houle, E. Grouard p.o.m.i. (page 210)

Houle, William: B-108, William Houle, baptized 14 January 1857, born 11 January 1857, of the legitimate marriage of Charles Houle and Ester Bruneau, Godfather: Frederic Frank Johnston, Godmother: Lisette Bruneau, Tissot Jn priest o.m.i. (page 21)

House, Alexandre: B-28, Alexandre House, baptized 23 September 1879, age three days, legitimate son of Charles House and Emilie Bruneau, Godfather: Alec Johnston, Godmother: Pelagie Laventure, Collignon o.m.i. (page 191)

House, Charles and Emelie Bruneau: M-1, Charles House, minor son of the late Piyesiwitakusiw and Josephte Chalifou, married 9 April 1872, Emelie Bruneau, minor daughter of Michel Bruneau and Catherine Ladouceur, Present: Paul Bruneau and Victor Lalican, V. Vegreville p.o.m.i. (page 128)

House, Edouard: B-5, Edouard House, baptized 26 March 1874, born today, legitimate son of Charles House and Emelie Bruneau, Godfather: Pierre Auger, Godmother: Sylvie Bruneau, V. Vegreville p.m.a.o.m.i. (page 142)

House, Edouard: S-6, Edouard House, buried 17 April 1874, age one month, Witnesses: Charles House and Augustin Auger, E. Petitot priest o.m.i. (page 143)

House, Marie: B-5, Marie Housse, baptized 12 February 1882, age 10 days, legitimate daughter of Charles Housse Mustatip and Emilie, Godfather: Thomas, Godmother: Julie Auger (signed Julie), Collignon o.m.i.p. (page 215)

Hupe, Marie-Albertine: B-33, Marie-Albertine Hupe, 3 December 1875, born 1 December 1875, legitimate daughter of Thomas Hupe and Louise Decoin, Godfather: Raphael Tremblay, Godmother: Sister Marie Tisseur (signed), M. R. Remas priest o.m.i. (page 157)

Hupe, Thomas and Louise Decoine: M-2, Thomas Hupe, adult son of Joseph Hupe and Josephte Cyr, married 17 June 1872, Louise Decoine, adult daughter of the late Francois Decoine and Josephte Desjarlais, Present: Paul Decoine and Charles House, V. Vegreville p.m.a.o.m.i. (page 130)

Lac la Biche Baptisms, Marriages and Burials 1853-1884

Huppe, Adelaide: B-39, Adelaide Huppe, baptized 22 December 1883, born yesterday of the legitimate marriage of Thomy Huppe and La Louise Decoine, Godfather: Louison Fosseneuve, Godmother: Julie Decoine, Collignon o.m.i.p. (page 233)

Huppe, Adolphe: B-10, Adolphe Hupe, baptized 23 April 1879, born the same day of the legitimate marriage of Thomy Hupe and Louise Decouanne, Godfather: Narcisse Boucher, Godmother: Catherine L'Esperance, E. Grouard priest o.m.i. (page 187)

Huppe, Johny: B-30, Johny Huppe, baptized 6 September 1877, born of the legitimate marriage of Thomy Huppe and Louise Decouanne, Godfather: Louis Lavallee, Godmother: Francoise wife of Charles Houle, E. Grouard, priest o.m.i. (page 172)

Huppe, Thomas: B-29, Thomas Huppe, baptized 15 July 1881, born today, legitimate son of Thomy Huppe and Louise Desjarlais, Godfather: Pierre Auger, Godmother: Julia Rivet, Collignon o.m.i. p. (page 207)

Ikeline, Angele: B-433, Angele Ikeline, baptized 6 June 1868, age 8 months, legitimate daughter of Julien Ikeline and Francoise Ilickwez, Godfather: Francois Bisson, Godmother: Isakale, V. Vegreville p.m.a.o.m.i. (page 91)

Iliyekitson, Marie; See Francois Enouleille and Marie Iliyekitson

Iroquois, Josephte; See Charles Bourgard and Josephte Iroquois

Isakale, Catherine; See Francois Bisson and Catherine Isakale

Iskwesis, Catherine: S-14, Catherine Iskwesis, buried 22 October 1861, died 20 October 1861, age about 25 years, Present: Francois Decoin and P. Bones [?], Tissot Jn. priest o.m.i. (page 44)

Iyasasis, Lucie: B-60, Lucie Iyasasis, baptized 15 December 1854, age about 6 years, daughter of Iyasasis and Apisik, Godmother: Agathe Ladouceur, M. R. Remas p.o.m.i. (page 11)

Iyatisskamikswew, Stanislas: B-56, Stanislas Iyatisskamikswew, baptized 9 October 1854, age about 3 months, son of Iyatisskamikswew and Iakitshitshewish, Godmother: Eugenie Ladouceur, M. R. Remas p.o.m.i. (page 10)

Iyeze Kas'la, Johny: B-14, Johny Iyeze Kas'la, baptized 31 March 1876, age 5 months, legitimate son of Andre Iyeze Kas'la and Charlotte Shorayusse, Godfather: Gilles Csinnayazegaw, Godmother: Marie Buteau, E. Grouard priest o.m.i. (page 168-169)

Izickcenyose, Angelique: B-9, Angelique Izickcenyose, baptized 16 April 1870, age 9 months, legitimate daughter of Francois Izickcenyose and Adele Piche, Godfather: Fabien Bisson, Godmother: Marie Gladu, M. R. Remas priest o.m.i. (page 111)

Janvier, Jean Baptiste Ouldaye: B-73, Jean_Baptiste Ouldaye Janvier, baptized 15 July 1855, age over 8 months, son of Mathias Ouldaye Janvier and Louise Elowalthia, Godmother: Marcelline Beroyini, Tissot Jn. priest o.m.i. (page 13)

Janvier, Marie: B-118, Marie Janvier, baptized 26 May 1857, age about 6 months, daughter of Jean-Marie Janvier and Sara Neuoskiwan, Godmother: Angelique Janvier, Maisonneuve A. priest o.m.i. (page 23)

Jim, Marie; See Xavier Cardinal and Marie Jim

Johnson, Alexis (Jantson): B-228, Alexis Janston (Johnson), baptized 22 June 1861, born today, of the legitimate marriage of Charly Jantson and Lisette Bruneau, Godfather: Michel Bruneau, Godmother: Isabelle Bruneau, Maisonneuve A. priest o.m.i. (page 42-43)

Johnson, Caroline: B-108, Caroline Johnson, baptized 16 November 1856, born 6 November 1856, of the marriage of Charly Johnson and Lisette Bruneau, Godmother: Henriette Montagnaise, Jn. Tissot priest o.m.i. (page 20)

Johnson, Henriette: B-1, Henriette Johnson, baptized 27 January 1876, born 3 days of the legitimate marriage of John Johnson and Marie Quintal, Godfather: Etienne Quintal, Godmother: Euphrosine Mustatip, H. Leduc priest o.m.i. (page 158)

Johnson, John: B-64, John Johnson, baptized 4 April 1855, age 3 months, son of Charles Johnson and Lisette Bruneau, Godfather: Charles Houlle, Godmother: Esther Bruno, M. R. Remas p.o.m.i. (page 12)

Johnson, Johny and Isabelle Quintal: M-2, Johny Johnson, minor son of Charly Johnson and Elise Bruneau, married 21 March 1875, Isabelle Quintal, minor daughter of Charly Quintal and Euphrosine Cardinal, Present: Pierre Ladouceur and Charly Quintal, H. Leduc priest o.m.i. (page 150)

Johnson, Mathilde: B-379, Mathilde Johnson, baptized 7 May 1866, born today, legitimate daughter of John [Charles Johnston] Johnson and Agathe Auger, Godmother: Isabelle Quintal, V. Vegreville priest mis. o.m.i. (page 74)

Johnson, Nancy: B-28, Nancy Johnson, baptized 31 August 1880, born 2 days, legitimate daughter of Charly Johnson and Agathe Mustatip, Godfather: Jean-Baptiste Moutatip, Godmother: Josette Jolifaux, Collignon o.m.i. priest. (page 198)

Johnson, Robert: B-27, Robert Johnson, baptized 4 August 1877, legitimate son of Charly Johnson and Agathe Mustatip, Godfather: Narcisse Boucher, Godmother: Pelagie Laventure (signed), E. Grouard priest o.m.i. (page 171)

Johnson, Venant (Jantson): B-172, Venant Jantson (Johnson), baptized 24 December 1858, age born 15 December 1858, of the legitimate marriage of Charles Jantson and Lisette Bruneau, Godfather: Louis Leveille, Godmother: Magdeleine Deschamps, Tissot Jn. priest o.m.i. (page 31)

Johnston, Alec: B-5, Alec Johnston, baptized 25 February 1883, born yesterday of the legitimate marriage of Johny Johnston and Maria Quintel, Godfather: Louis Lavallee, Godmother: Agathe Auger, E. Grouard priest o.m.i. (page 225)

Lac la Biche Baptisms, Marriages and Burials 1853-1884

Johnston, Alex and Melanie Lavallee: M-1, Alex Johnston married 24 January 1882 Melanie Lavallee, Witnesses: Milsens (signed) and Baptiste Desjarlais (x), Collignon o.m.i.p. (page 215)

Johnston, Charly and Agathe Auger: M-38, Charly Johnston married 7 June 1864 Agathe Auger,, Present: Francois Decoin and J. Baptiste Amiskiyinisis, Tissot priest o.m.i. (page 57-58)

Johnston, Emma-Cleophee: B-30, Emma-Cleophee Johnston, baptized 18 October 1882, born this morning of the legitimate marriage of Alec Johnston and Melanie Lavallee, Godfather: Alexandre Hamelin (signed), Godmother: Catherine Lavallee (signed), Collignon o.m.i.p. (page 222)

Johnston, Eulalie: B-36, Eulalie Johnston, baptized 11 December 1883, age 2 days, legitimate daughter of Charly Johnston and Agathe Cayatius, Godmother: Eulalie Hamelin (signed), Collignon o.m.i.p. (page 232)

Johnston, Marie Adelphine: B-5, Marie Adelphine Johnston, baptized 29 March 1871, born today, legitimate daughter of Charles Johnston and Agathe Auge, Godfather: Antoine Jackson, Godmother: Caroline Johnston, M. R. Remas priest (page 120)

Johnston, Caroline; See Francois Kakikekamik and Caroline Johnston

Johnston, Marie: B-14, Marie Johnston, baptized 14 August 1874, born yesterday, legitimate daughter of Charles Johnston and Agathe, Godfather: Raphael Tremblay, Godmother: Catherine McDougall, Alb. Pascal p.o.m.i. (page 144)

Johnston, Marie: B-15, Marie Johnston, baptized 19 June 1869, born today, legitimate daughter of Charles Johnston and Agathe Oger, Godfather: Norbert Sauve, Godmother: Angelique Sauve, V. Vegreville p.m.a.o.m.i. (page 101-102)

Johnston, Marie: S-2, Marie Johnston, buried 12 July 1869, died yesterday, daughter of Charles Johnston and Agathe Oger, age 23 days, Present: Eugene Wawiyenam and Pierre Cardinal, V. Vegreville p.m.a.o.m.i. (page 102)

Johnston, Marie-Marguerite: B-29, Marie-Marguerite Johnston, baptized 5 September 1880, born 27 August 1880, of the legitimate marriage of Johny Johnston and Maria Quintal, Godfather: Charley Johnston (signed Chrles Johnstone), Godmother: Marie McGillis, E. Grouard priest o.m.i. (page 198-199)

Johnston, Sophie: B-37, Sophie Johnston, baptized 28 December 1884, born day before yesterday, of the legitimate marriage of Alec Johnston and Melanie Lavallee, Godfather: Duncan Tremblay, Godmother: Sophia St.Sauveur, Collignon o.m.i.p. (page 245)

Johnston, Venance: B-19, Venance Johnston, baptized 28 Jul1878, age 2 days, legitimate son of Johny Johnston and Maria Grand Charles, Godfather: Venance Johnston, Godmother: Sylvie, E. Grouard priest o.m.i. (page 179-180)

Johnston, Venance: S-1, Venance Johnston, buried 24 February 1882, died yesterday, age 24 years, Witnesses: Petit Louis Lavallee and Raphael Tremblay, Collignon o.m.i.p. (page 216)

Lac la Biche Baptisms, Marriages and Burials 1853-1884

Joseph, Aloiza: B-70, Aloiza Joseph, baptized 17 May 1855, age about 6 months, daughter of Joseph and Marie, Godfather: Jerome Laurent, Godmother: Angelique, M. R. Remas p.o.m.i. (page 13)

Joseph, Betsy: B-37, Betsy Joseph, baptized 18 September 1869, age 3 weeks, legitimate daughter of Joseph and Louise, Godfather: Narcisse Morin, Godmother: Marie Laliberte, V. Vegreville p.m.a.o.m.i. (page 107-108)

Kaapisisik, Baptiste: B-131, Baptiste Kaapisisik, baptized 17 May 1857, age 10 months, son of Kaapisisik and Kiskapatsak, Godfather: Joseph Parisien, Godmother: Angelique Desjarlais, Tissot priest (page 25)

Kadikev, Jacob: B-21, Jacob Kadikev, baptized 4 November 1873, age 2 years, illegitimate son of Michel Kadikev and Marguerite Nakhedheaze, Godfather: Damase, Godmother: Marie Bethune, E. Petitot priest o.m.i. (page 139)

Kakanaponokek, Joseph: B-28 Joseph Kakanaponokek, baptized 3 September 1878, age about 8 months, son of the deceased Kekanaponkek and Meskanikonapiw, Godfather: Benjamin Mustatip, Godmother: Catherine Mustatip, Collignon o.m.i. (page 181)

Kakekamik, Catherine: B-403, Catherine Kakekamik, baptized 4 May 1867, born yesterday, legitimate daughter of Jean-Baptiste Kakekamik and Therese Alayokan, Godfather: Joseph Ladouceur, Godmother: Therese Ladouceur, V. Vegreville p.m.a.o.m.i. (page 80)

Kakekamik, Isabelle; See Paul Bruneau and Isabelle Kakekamik

Kakikakamik, Christine; See Thomas Oskijik (Sauteuse) and Christine Kakikakamik

Kakikamik, Agnes: B-33, Agnes Kakikamik, baptized 28 September 1880, age a few days, legitimate daughter of J. B. Kakikamik and Angelique Ducharme, Godmother: Catherine Kakikamik, E. Grouard priest o.m.i. (page 200)

Kakikamik, Emilia: B-36, Emilia Khakikamik, baptized 29 December 1878, age two days, born of the legitimate marriage of Francis Kakikamik and Caroline Johnston, Godfather: Paul Montagnais, Godmother: Peggy Auger, E. Grouard, priest o.m.i. (psge 184)

Kakikekamik, Angelique: B-101, Angelique Kakikekamik, baptized 6 September 1856, age about 4 weeks, legitimate daughter of Baptiste Kakikekamik and Magdeleine Weskipasiku, Godmother: Angelique Tissier, Maisonneuve A. priest o.m.i. (page 19)

Kakikekamik, Angelique: B-182, Angelique Kakikekamik, baptized 27 February 1859, age 17 days, daughter of Baptiste Kakikekamik and Magdeleine Weskifrasiku, Godfather: Louis Leveille, Godmother: Nanncey Quintal, Tissot Jn priest o.m.i. (page 33)

Kakikekamik, Angelique; See Joseph Cardinal and Angelique Kakikekamik

Kakikekamik, Anonyme: S-8, Anonyme Kakikekamik, buried 18 October 1874, born and died today, legitimate son of Jean-Baptiste Kakikekamik and Emilie, Witnesses: Francois Kakikekamik and Basile Cardinal, V. Vegreville p.m.a.o.m.i. (page 146)

Lac la Biche Baptisms, Marriages and Burials 1853-1884

Kakikekamik, Augustin: B-32, Augustin Kakikekamik, baptized 7 November 1884, age 2 days, legitimate son of J. Baptiste Kakikekamik and Angelique Ducharme, Godfather: Francois Kakikekamik, Godmother: Caroline Johnston, Collignon o.m.i.p. (page 242)

Kakikekamik, Baptiste and Magdeleine Weskipaskn: M-13, Baptiste Kakikekamik married 14 July 1856 Magdeleine Wekipaskn, Present: Abraham Lariviere and Robert Tselyons, Tissot Jn. priest o.m.i. (page 18)

Kakikekamik, Christine: B-271, Christine Kakikekamik, baptized 9 November 1862, born 7 November 1862, daughter of Baptiste Kakikekamik and Weskipasiku, Godfather: Baptiste Amiskuiymisis, Godmother: Nancy Quintal, Tissot Jn. priest o.m.i. (page 51)

Kakikekamik, Francois and Caroline Johnston: M-1, Francois Kakikekamik, minor son of Jean Baptiste Kakikekamik and Charlotte, married 15 May 1874, Caroline Johnston, minor daughter of Charles Johnston and Lisette Bruneau, Present: Joseph Boucher and Narcisse Boucher, V. Vegreville, p.m.a.o.m.i. (page 143)

Kakikekamik, Francois: B-4, Francois Kakikekamik, baptized 4 October 1853, son of the legitimate marriage of Baptiste Kakikekamik and Charlotte Kanitaviniok, Godfather: Louis Katipemimikut, Godmother: Tshimiakits, M. R. Remas p.o.m.i. (page 2)

Kakikekamik, J. B. and Angelique Ducharme: M-2, J. B. Kakikekamik married 3 February 1880 Angelique Ducharme, in the presence of witnesses, Collignon o.m.i. (page 194)

Kakikekamik, Jean Baptiste and Therese Atoyokan: M-49, Jean-Baptiste Kakikekamik, adult son of Moyse Makesis and Susanne Osawamik, and widower of Magdeleine Weskiposiku, married 8 June 1866, Therese Atoyokan, minor daughter of Abraham Atoyokan and Sale, Present: Joseph Sisawapas and Theodore Decoine, V. Vegreville priest mis. o.m.i. (page 74)

Kakikekamik, Jean-Baptiste and Emilie: M-2, Jean-Baptiste Kakikekamik, widower of Therese Atoyokan, married 30 March 1869 Emilie, of unknown parents, Present: Louis Sisawapas and Eugene Kakikekakmik, V. Vegrevillle, p.m.a.o.m.i. (page 99)

Kakikekamik, Marie-Julie: B-20, Marie_Julie Kakikekamik, baptized 19 May 1876, born today, legitimate daughter of Francois Kakikekamik and Caroline Johnstone, Godmother: Julie Auge, Godfather: Pierre Auge, Husson p.o.m.i. (page 161)

Kakikekamik, William John: S-3, William John Kakikekamik, buried 10 February 1874, died yesterday, age 24 days, son of Jean Baptiste Kakikekamik and Emelie, Witnesses: Charles Johnston and Francois Kakikekamik, V. Vegreville p.m.a.o.m.i. (page 141)

Kakikekamik, William John: B-1, William John Kakikekamik, baptized 18 January 1874, born day before yesterday, legitimate son of Jean Baptiste Kakikekamik and Emelie, Godfather: Joseph Sisawapas, Godmother: Euphrosine Lamire, V. Vegreville p.m.a.o.m.i. (page 140)

Kakikikamik, Rosalie; See John Landmore and Rosalie Kakikikamik

Lac la Biche Baptisms, Marriages and Burials 1853-1884

Kakinos, Johny: B-69, Johny Kakinos, baptized 17 May 1855, age 2 years, son of Kakinos and Marguerite, Godfather: Theodore Decoin, Godmother: Esther Bruno, M. R. Remas p.o.m.i. (page 13)

Kakiskamikawiyinimuw, Agathe: B-418, Agathe Kakiskamikawiyinimuw, baptized 6 October 1867, age 7 months, legitimate daughter of Jean-Baptiste Kakiskamikawiyinimuw and Atsinakawiwisk, Godfather: Georges Bourque, Godmother: Agathe Ladouceur, V. Vegreville p.m.a.o.m.i. (page 85)

Kakitomastus, Therese: B-104, Therese Kakitomastus, baptized 9 October 1856, age about 3 months, daughter of Kakitomastus and Marie Berland, Godfather: Louis Batoche, Godmother: Julie Auge, Tissot Jn. priest o.m.i. (page 19)

Kakitomostus, Henriette: B-105, Henriette Kakitomostus, baptized 9 October 1856, age about 3 months, daughter of Kakitomostus and Osiyikats, Godfather: Louis Batoche, Godmother: Henriette, Tissot Jn. priest o.m.i. (page 20)

Kakitomustus, Paul: B-167, Paul Kakitomustus, baptized 31 October 1858, age one month, son of Kakitomustus and Marie Berland, Godfather: Francois Lafreniere, Godmother: Julie Lavallee, Tissot Jn. priest o.m.i. (page 31)

Kakitowimessthouhs, Andre: B-15, Andre Kakitowimessthouhs, baptized 9 November 1853, son of Kakitowimessthouhs and Marie Berland, Godfather: Joseph Ladouceur, Godmother: Julie Augee, R. M. Remas p.o.m.i. (page 4)

Kakkikekamik, Angelique: S-1, Angelique Kakkikekamik, buried 26 July 1876, age 6 years, daughter of Jean-Baptiste Kakkikekamik, L. Dupire priest (page 163)

Kakpetuskumikew, David and Angelique: B-10 and B-11, baptized 4 March 1869, David Kakpetuskumikew, age 8 years, Godfather: David Ladouceur, Godmother: Agathe Ladouceur; Angelique Kakpetuskumikew, age 10 years, Godfather: Augustin Ladouceur, Godmother: Therese Larocque, the father of the children is Kakpetuskumikew, the mother is Isabelle Kasipwekutokin, + Vital J. Ev. De Satala o.m.i. (page 100)

Kakwenam, Jean-Baptiste: B-36, Jean-Baptiste Kakwenam, baptized 13 November 1877, age about 6 months, son of Kakwenam and Marie, Godfather: Sandy, Godmother: Isabelle, Collignon p.o.m.i. (page 173)

Kakwenan, Albert: B-11, Albert Kakwenan, baptized 31 March 1872, age about 3 months, legitimate son of Kakwenan and Marie Iyatowatam, Godmother: Marie St.Sauveur, Collignon o.m.i. (page 128)

Kakwetsitaw, Susanne: B-278, Susanne Kakwetsitaw, baptized 7 May 1863, age over one year, daughter of Kakwetsitaw and Rosalie LeBlanc, Godmother: Angelique Cardinal, Tissot Jn. priest o.m.i. (page 52)

Kakwinam, Joseph: B-17, Joseph Kakwinam, baptized 3 April 1881, age about 45 years, Godfather: Nazaire Martel, Godmother: Celina Tremblay, E. Grouard priest o.m.i. (page 205)

Kakwonam, Baptiste: B-4, Baptiste Kakwonam, baptized 22 January 1880, age about one month, son of Kakwenam and Marie Sakatsiwes, Godmother: Marie Siwepitun, Collignon o.m.i. (page 193)

Lac la Biche Baptisms, Marriages and Burials 1853-1884

Kamikouskwanok, Ignace: B-53, Ignace Kamikouskwanok, baptized 2 September 1854, age about 3 months, son of Kamikouskwanok and Iskwenak, Godmother: Nancy Collin, M. R. Remas p.o.m.i. (page 9)

Kamiskietawamiwew, Catherine: B-23, Catherine Kamiskietawamiwew, baptized 25 July 1884, age about 3 years, daughter of the deceased Kamiskietawamiwew and Marie, Godmother: Sister St.Pierre, Lecorre priest o.m.i. (page 239-240)

Kamiskietawamiwew, Charles: B-21, Charles Kamiskietwamiwew, baptized 25 July 1884, age about one year, son of the deceased Kamiskietawamiwew and Marie, Godmother: Sister St.Pierre, Lecorre priest o.m.i. (page 239)

Kamiskietawamiwew, Mathurine: B-22, Mathurine Kamiskietawamiwew, baptized 25 July 1884, age about 6 years, daughter of the deceased Kamiskietawamiwew and Marie, Godmother: Sister St.Pierre, Lecorre priest o.m.i. (page 239)

Kamistaimopekiskwet, Angelique: B-141, Angelique Kamistaimopekiskwet, baptized 7 October 1857, age 8 months, daughter of Kamistaimopekiskwet and Josephte Crise, Godfather: John Nollin, Tissot Jn. priest o.m.i. (page 27)

Kamistaimopekiskwet, John: B-140, John Kamistaimopekiskwet, baptized 7 October 1857, age 4 years, son of Kamistaimopekiskwet and Josephte Crise, Godfather: John Nollin, Tissot Jn. priest o.m.i. (page 26-27)

Kamiyawakimakew, William: B-18, William Kamiyawakimakew, baptized 25 June 1872, age one year, legitimate son of Alexis Kamiyawakimakew and Charlotte Sawatinam, Godfather: Guillaume Desjarlais, Godmother: Louise Decoine, V. Vegreville p.m.a.o.m.i. (page 130)

Kamiyawatan, Lalouise: B-113, Lalouise Kamiyawatan, baptized 18 January 1857, age about 5 years, daughter of Kamiyawatan and Kiyapatowapu, Godmother: Angelique Berland, Maisonneuve A. priest o.m.i. (page 22)

Kanawawasuw, Christina: B-28, Christina Kanawawasuw, baptized 10 October 1870, age about 20 years, Godfather: Charles Cardinal, M. R. Remas priest o.m.i. (page 115)

Kanawawasuw, Christina; See Joseph Wabanikapaw and Christina Kanawawasuw

Kangeli, Angelique: B-52, baptized 1 September 1854, at Fort Pitt, age 2 months, of Kaneli and Aytoweitam, Godmother: Sophie Chatelain, M. R. Remas p.o.m.i. (page 9)

Kanisowatsapew, Josette: B-31, Josette Kanisowatsapew, baptized 4 September 1878, age about 4 months, daughter of Kanisowatsapew and Marguerite, Godmother: Justine Kakikamik, E. Grouard priest o.m.i. (page 182)

Kapahut, Daniel: B-175, Daniel Kapahut, baptized 15 December 1858, born 2 May 1858, son of Kapahut and Tchitawapun, Godfather: Francois Lafreniere, Godmother: Angelique Wabistikay, Maisonneuve A. priest o.m.i. (page 32)

Lac la Biche Baptisms, Marriages and Burials 1853-1884

Kapettakusiwin, Suzanne: B-36, Suzanne Kapettakusiwin, baptized 26 November 1876, age about 55 years, Godmother: Sister M. Carroll (signed), Collignon o.m.i. (page 165)

Kapitikwatma, Pierre: B-124, Pierre Kapitikwatma, baptized 23 April 1857, age about 60 years, Tissot Jn. priest o.m.i. (page 24)

Kapitikwatma, Pierre: S-9, Pierre Kapitikwatma, buried 25 April 1857, died in the evening, Present: Cuthbert McGillis and William McGillis, Tissot Jn. priest o.m.i. (page 24)

Kasiweskaw, Angelique: B-10, Angelique Kasiweskaw, baptized 19 February 1881, age about 5 months, daughter of Kasiweskaw and Lisette, the priest served as godfather, Collignon o.m.i. p. (page 204)

Kasiwiskam, George: B-30, George Kasiwiskam, baptized 4 September 1878, age about 3 months, legitimate son of Pierre Kasiwiskam and Lizette Ayik of Lac Castor, Godfather: Waweyinam Eugene, Godmother: Eliza, E. Grouard priest o.m.i. (page 181-182)

Kasiwiskam, Marguerite: B-33, Marguerite Kasiwiskam, baptized 24 September 1883, daughter of Kasiwiskam and Ayik, Godmother: Marguerite Tremblay, Collignon o.m.i.p. (page 231)

Kaskawan, Angeline: B-3, Angeline Kaskawan, baptized 6 February 1876, age about 3 years, born of the union of Kaskawan and of Gladu parents non-infidels, Godfather: J. Bte. Cardinal (dit Kayatus), H. Leduc priest o.m.i. (page 158)

Kaskawan, Eugenie-Pauline: B-6, Eugenie-Pauline Kaskawan, baptized 20 February 1876, age about 18 years, daughter of Kaskawan and Constance Gladu, Godfather: Joseph L'orfeuvse, Godmother: Sister St. Michel, L. Dupire priest (page 159)

Kaskawan, Maggy: S-8, Maggy Kaskawan, buried 18 October 1881, age about 16 years, daughter of the deceased Kaskawan and Constance, Witnesses: Antoine Ducharme and Baptiste, E. Grouard priest o.m.i. (page 212)

Kaskawan, Raphael: B-5, Raphael Kaskawan, baptized 10 February 1876, age about 4 years, born of the union of Kaskawan and of Gladu, infidel parents, Godfather: Raphael Tremblay, Godmother: Catherine MacDougall, M. R. Remas pret o.m.i. (page 159)

Katetwekamikinaw, Suzane: B-43, Suzane Katetwekamikinaw, baptized 28 May 1854, age a few months, daughter of Katetwekamikinaw and Kepetwekamikinaw, Godfather: Decoine, M. R. Remas p.o.m.i. (page 8)

Katomin, Angelique: B-178, Angelique Katomin, baptized 19 December 1858, age 5 years and 11 months, daughter of Katomin and Kamiyunotukew, Godmother: Angelique Mustuskapeyakut, Maisonneuve A. priest o.m.i. (page 32)

Kawatskupis, Marie: B-2, Marie Kwataskupis, baptized 24 August 1853, at Fort la Montee (Carlton), daughter of Kwataskupis and __ Beaudry, Godfather: Henri Paquette, M. R. Remas p.o.m.i. (page 2)

Lac la Biche Baptisms, Marriages and Burials 1853-1884

Kekekwatam, Josephte: B-34, Josephte Kekekwatam, baptized 8 May 1854, age about 7 years, daughter of Kekekwatam and Pekwayanitwin, Godmother: Catherine Ladouceur, M. R. Remas p.o.m.i. (page 6)

Kekenittawikin, Isabelle; See Basile Cardinal and Isabelle Kekenittawikin

Kekikowatam (Collon), Philippe: B-33, Philippe Kekikowatam, baptized 30 April 1854, age about 2 months, son of Kekikowatam and Iskwetshih, Godmother: Jany Ladouceur, M. R. Remas p.o.m.i. (page 6)

Kekwatsitsak, Catherine: B-120, Catherine Kekwatsitsak, baptized 20 April 1857, age over 3 years, daughter of Kekwatsitsak and Rosalie Leblanc, Godfather: Cuthbert McGillis, Godmother: Marguerite Delorme, Tissot Jn. priest o.m.i. (page 23)

Kekwatsitsak, Magdeleine: B-121, Magdeleine Kekwatsitsak, baptized 20 April 1857, age 4 months, daughter of Kekwatsitsak and Rosalie Leblanc, Godfather: Cuthbert McGillis, Godmother: Marguerite Delorme, Tissot Jn. priest o.m.i. (page 23)

Kekwetuiwepinis, Angelique: B-119, Angelique Kekwetuiwepinis, baptized 13 June 1857, born today, daughter of Kekwetuiwepinis and Sakasawewis, Godmother: Julie Auger, Maisonneuve A. priest o.m.i. (page 23)

Keyiwin, Julie Marie: B-138, Julie Marie Keyiwin, baptized 7 October 1857, age 8 years, daughter of Keyiwin and Weskinapite, Godfather: John Nollin, Godmother: Julie Lavallee, Tissot Jn. priest o.m.i. (page 26)

Keyiwin, Marguerite Susanne: B-139, Marguerite Susanne Keyiwin, baptized 7 October 1857, age 4 years, daughter of Keyiwin and Wekinapite, Godfather: Louis Leveille, Godmother: Marguerite Gervais, Tissot Jn. priest o.m.i. (page 26)

Kijikawasis, Therese and Josephte: B-371 and B-372, Therese Kijikawasis, age 6 years, and Josephte Kijikawasis, age 3 years, baptized 11 February 1866, daughters of Kijikawasis and Kamyuskwatawetpiw, Godmother: of Therese, Marie Cardinal, and of Josephte, Josephte Desjaralais, Maisonneuve A. priest o.m.i. (page 72)

Kikikuwatam, Marguerite: B-34, Marguerite Kikikuwatam, baptized 21 October 1877, age about 17 years, daughter of Kikikuwatam, Godmother: Betsy Tsimanaskat, Collignon o.m.i. (page 172-173)

Kikikuwatam, Marguerite; See Antoine Desjarlais and Marguerite Kikikuwatam

Kinohwaneytam, Marie: B-13, Marie Kinohwaneytam, baptized 1 March 1880, age about 7 years, illegitimate daughter of Kinohwaneytam and Catherine Pisakwanewasuw, Godmother: Marie Mustatip, Collignon o.m.i. priest. (page 195)

Kipitaskunikew, Henry: B-4, Henry Kipitaskunikew, baptized 6 February 1869, age 4 months, legitimate son of Kipitaskunikew and Isabelle Casipewehutsin, Godmother: Matsanine, V. Vegrevillle, p.m.a.o.m.i. (page 98)

Kisikawikutsin, Rosalie; See Francois Cardinal and Rosalie Kisikawikutsin

Lac la Biche Baptisms, Marriages and Burials 1853-1884

Kisikowasis, Jean Baptiste: B-30, Jean Baptiste Kisikowasis, baptized 29 April 1854, age about 2 years, son of Kisikowasis and Ekamaskipiew, Godfather: Joseph Ladouceur, Godmother: Julie Auge, M. R. Remas p.o.m.i. (page 6)

Kiskaskamikuwapiw, Marie-Louise: B-3, Marie-Louise Kiskaskamikuwapiw, baptized 15 January 1882, age about 28 years, Godfather: Claude Gonnet (signed Gonat), Godmother: Sister Beliveau (signed), Collignon priest o.m.i. (page 215)

Kiskinamakew, Joseph: B-28, Joseph Kiskinamakew, baptized 16 July 1876, age one year, son of Nanimis dit Chatelain and Wapasakaye, Godfather: brother Lecomte (signed H. Lecomte o.m.i.), Godmother: Catherine Simpson, E. Petitot priest o.m.i. (page 163)

Kiskiwinagusiw, Matthieu: B-281, Matthieu Kiskiwinagusiw, baptized 13 May 1863, age 10 days, son of Pierre Kiskiwinagusiw and Marie Montagnaise, Godmother: Isabelle Crise, Tissot Jn. priest o.m.i. (page 53)

Kiyatshikaskwew, Jean and Rosalie Wabamukamik: M-8, Jean Kiyatshikaskwew married 4 October 1870 Rosalie Wabamukamik, Witnesses: Johnny Piyestawakinam and Angele Wiyepitshitsheb, M. R. Remas priest o.m.i. (page 115)

Kiyatshikaskwew, Jean: B-25, Jean Kiyatshikaskwew, baptized 4 October 1870, age about 25 years, Godfather: Johnny Piyestawakinam, M. R. Remas priest o.m.i. (page 115)

Kwetabanokew, Rosalie: S-4, Rosalie Kwetabanokew buried 26 April 1882, age 6 years, daughter of the deceased Kwetabanokew and Marie-Louise Kistoskawapiw, Witnesses: Narcisse Boucher and Jean-Baptiste Laroque, E. Grouard priest o.m.i. (page 217-218)

Kwetapanukow, Rosalie: B-4, Rosalie Kwetapanukow, baptized 6 February 1881, age about 5 years, son of the deceased Kwetapanukow and Kistaskamokwapiw, Godmother: Lisa wife of Siyafiokyikwepiew, E. Grouard priest o.m.i. (page 203)

L'Assiniboine, Louis: B-48, Louis L'Assiniboine, baptized 1 September 1854 at Fort Pitt, age 24 days, of Louis L'Assiniboine and Catherine Wapawis, Godmother: Sophie Chatelain, M. R. Remas p.o.m.i. (page 8)

Labatoche, Celina: B-35, Celina Labatoche, baptized 14 August 1881, age 3 months, legitimate daughter of Joseph Labatoche Wikwepan and Liza Desjarlais, Godfather: Antoine Laliberte, Godmother: Sophie Ladouceur, Collignon o.m.i.p. (page 209)

LaBatoche, Joseph and Eliza Desjarlais: M-5, Joseph LaBatoche, adult son of Gabriel Labatoche and Marie Bruneau, married 5 August 1878, Eliza Desjarlais, minor daughter of Francois Desjarlais and the deceased Euphrosine Auger, Witnesses: fr. Larfevre and Napesis Desjarlais, Collignon o.m.i. (page 180)

Labonne, Angele (Beaudoin): B-308, Angele Labonne (Beaudoin), baptized 10 June 1864, age 26 days, daughter of Pierre Labonne (Beaudoin) and Julie Iyakwawiyepiw, Godmother: Nannecy Quintal, Tissot Jn. priest o.m.i. (page 58)

Labonne, Cecile: See Aubichon John and Cecile Labonne

Lac la Biche Baptisms, Marriages and Burials 1853-1884

Labonne, Fortunee: B-309, Fortunee Labonne (Beaudoin), baptized 10 June 1864, age 26 days, daughter of Pierre Labonne (Beaudoin) and Julie Iyakwawiyepiw, Godmother: Silvie Bruneau, Tissot Jn. priest o.m.i. (page 58)

Labonne, Jean Philippe (Beaudoin): B-168, Jean-Philippe Labonne (Beaudoin), baptized 31 October 1858, age 4 or 5 months, son of Pierre Labonne and his Crise wife, Godfather: Francois Lafreniere, Godmother: Henriette Montagnaise, Tissot Jn. priest o.m.i. (page 31)

Labonne, Joseph: B-23, Joseph Labonne (Beaudoin), baptized 23 April 1854, age 7 months, son of Pierre Labonne and Iyakwawiyepiw, Godfather: Joseph Gray, Alex Ev. de St.Boniface o.m.i. (page 5)

Labonne, Josephte (Beaudoin): B-242, Josephte Labonne (Beaudoin), baptized 1 November 1861, age 4 months, daughter of Pierre Labonne and a Crise (Julie Iyakwawiyepiw), Godfather: Joachim Bruneau, Godmother: Catherine Ladouceur, Tissot Jn. priest o.m.i. (page 45)

Labonne, Pierre (Beaudoin): S-26, Pierre Labonne (Beaudoin), buried 26 April 1865, died 24 April 1864, age about 35 years, Present: Francois Decoin and Moise Larocque, Masionneuve, A. priest o.m.i. (page 66)

Ladebauche, Isidore: B-65, Isidore Ladebauche, baptized 6 April 1855, age 2 months, illegitimate son of Betshy femme Ladebauche, Godfather: Isidore Decoin, Godmother: Louise Dejarlais, M. R. Remas p.o.m.i. (page 12)

Ladouceur, Absalom: B-373, Absalom Ladouceur, baptized 25 March 1873, born 12 March 1873, of the legitimate marriage of Joseph Ladouceur and Marguerite Frysher, Godmother: Isabelle Bruneau, Maisonneuve A. priest o.m.i. (page 72)

Ladouceur, Absalon and Marianne Cardinal: M-5, Absalon Ladouceur married 5 August 1884 Marianne Cardinal, A. Desmarais priest o.m.i. (page 238)

Ladouceur, Adam and Marguerite Desmarais: M-5, Adam Ladouceur, adult son of Joseph Ladouceur and Julie Auger, married 12 November 1872, Marguerite Desmarais, minor daughter of Johnny Desmarais and Marie Deschamps, Present: Joseph Ladouceur and Francois Larocque, V. Vegreville p.m.a.o.m.i. (page 132)

Ladouceur, Adele: B-9, Adele Ladouceur, baptized 9 April 1876, age 23 days, legitimate d/o Adam Ladouceur and Marguerite Desmarais, Godfather: Joseph Ladouceur, Godmother: Genevieve Ladouceur, M. R. Remas, priest o.m.i (page 159)

Ladouceur, Agathe: B-35, Agathe Ladouceur, baptized 6 November 1879, age 2 days in danger of death, by her father Adam Ladouceur, E. Grouard priest o.m.i. (page 192)

Ladouceur, Agathe: S-11, Agathe Ladouceur, buried 7 November 1879, age 3 days and christened by her father Adam Ladouceur, Present: Louison Fosseneuve and Joseph Ladouceur, E. Grouard priest o.m.i. (page 192)

Ladouceur, Agathe; See Georges Burk and Agathe Ladouceur

Ladouceur, Agnes Martine: B-66, Agnes-Martine Ladouceur, baptized 7 April 1855, age 16 days, daughter of Joseph Ladouceur and Julie Auge, Godfather: Michel Picsayit, Godmother: Marguerite Cilgysi, M. R. Remas p.o.m.i. (page 12)

Ladouceur, Albert: B-31, Albert Ladouceur, baptized 4 December 1882, age 5 days, legitimate son of Adam Ladouceur and Marguerite Desmarais, Godfather: Gilbert Comtois, Godmother: Marguerite Crin his wife, Collignon o.m.i.p. (page 222-223)

Ladouceur, Alexandrine: B-14, Alexandrine Ladouceur, baptized 10 June 1879, born yesterday, of the legitimate marriage of Pierre Ladouceur and Marguerite Fraser, Godfather: Narcisse Boucher, Godmother: Caroline Ladouceur, Collignon o.m.i. (page 188)

Ladouceur, Augustin: B-150, Augustin Ladouceur, baptized 12 April 1858, born today, of the legitimate marriage of Joseph Ladocueur and Julie Auger, Godfather: Joseph Roy, Godmother: Julie Lavallee, Tissot Jn priest o.m.i. (page 28)

Ladouceur, Caroline: B-252, Caroline Ladouceur, baptized 21 March 1862, age 2 months, legitimate daughter of Pierre Ladouceur and Marguerite Fraser, Godfather: Antoine Plante, Godmother: Scholastique Vivier, Tissot Jn. priest o.m.i. (page 47)

Ladouceur, Caroline; See Narcisse Boucher and Caroline Ladouceur

Ladouceur, Damien: B-23, Damien Ladouceur, baptized 19 October 1871, born yesterday, legitimate son of Agapit Ladouceur and Marguerite Fraser, Godfather: Mare Cage, Godmother: Agathe Oger, V. Vegreville p.m.a.o.m.i. (page 124)

Ladouceur, Damien: S-4, Damien Ladouceur, buried 31 August 1884, died 2 days, age about 12 years, Witnesses: Abasalon Ladouceur and Moise Boucher, + Henri Ev. D'Anamour o.m.i. (page 241)

Ladouceur, David: B-205, David Ladouceur, baptized 8 May 1860, born yesterday, of the legitimate marriage of Joseph Ladouceur and Julie Auger, Godfather: Baptiste Lafreniere, Godmother: Ursule St.Germain, Tissot Jn priest (page 38)

Ladouceur, Elisa; See Julien Cardinal and Elisa Ladouceur

Ladouceur, Elisabeth: B-36, Elisabeth Ladouceur, baptized 28 November 1880, age 20 days, legitimate daughter of Adam Ladouceur and Marguerite Desmarais, Godfather: Augustin Ladouceur, Godmother: Marguerite Desjarlais, Collignon o.m.i.p. (page 201)

Ladouceur, Fabien: B-7, Fabien Ladouceur, baptized 12 March 1883, born today of the legitimate marriage of Pierre Ladouceur and Marguerite Fraser, Godfather: Julien Cardinal, Godmother: Caroline Ladouceur, Collignon o.m.i.p. (page 225)

Ladouceur, Felicie: B-14, Felicie Ladouceur, baptized 5 July 1884, born today of the legitimate marriage of Narcisse Ladouceur and Julie Auger, Godfather: Pierre Auger, Godmother: Silvie Bruneau, Collignon o.m.i.p. (page 237)

Lac la Biche Baptisms, Marriages and Burials 1853-1884

Ladouceur, Felicie Narcisse: S-5, Felicie Narcisse Ladouceur, buried 26 November 1884, died day before yesterday, age 5 months, Witnesses: Joseph Bourque and Pierre Auger, Collignon o.m.i.p. (page 242)

Ladouceur, Felix: B-283, Felix Ladouceur, baptized 30 May 1863, born today, of the legitmate marriage of Joseph Ladouceur and Julie Auger, Godfather: George Burk, Godmother: Agathe Ladouceur, Tissot Jn. priest o.m.i. (page 53)

Ladouceur, Felix: S-19, Felix Ladouceur, buried 24 June 1863, died yesterday, Present: Joseph Ladouceur and Paulette Desjarlais, Tissot Jn. priest o.m.i. (page 53)

Ladouceur, Florence: B-311, Florence Ladouceur, baptized 31 July 1864, age 15 days, legitimate daughter of Pierre Ladouceur and Marguerite Fraser, Godfather: Joachim Bruneau, Godmother: Catherine Ladouceur, Tissot Jn. priest o.m.i. (page 58)

Ladouceur, Florestine; See Thomas Taylor and Florestine Ladouceur

Ladouceur, Henriette: B-13, Henriette Ladouceur, baptized 14 August 1874, born yesterday, legitimate daughter of Agapit Ladouceur and Marguerite Fraser, Godfather: Francois Laroque, Godmother: Marianne Pattenaude, Collignon o.m.i. (page 144)

Ladouceur, Henriette: B-34, Henriette Lacouceur, baptized 8 November 1876, born yesterday, legitimate daughter of Pierre Ladouceur and Marguerite Fraser, Godmother: Sister St. Michel (signed) and Liza Ladouceur, Collignon o.m.i. (page 164)

Ladouceur, Henriette: S-3, Henriette Ladouceur, buried 28 April 1875, age about 8 months, daughter of Agapit Ladouceur and Marguerite Fraser, Present: Julien William and many others, J. V. Fourmond priest o.m.i. (page 151-152)

Ladouceur, Jane; See Olivier Courte-oreille and Jane Ladouceur

Ladouceur, Joseph and Veronique Osisis: M-7, Joseph Ladouceur, widower of Julie Auger, married 2 November 1878, Veronique Osisis, widow of Narvis, Witnesses: E. Grouard priest o.m.i. (signed) and C. Racette (signed), Collignon o.m.i. (page 182-183)

Ladouceur, Joseph: B-11, Joseph Ladouceur, baptized 12 October 1853, born 25 June, son of the legitimate marriage of Joseph Ladouceur and Julie Auge, Godfather: Paul Paulette, Godmother: Frosine Auge, M. R. Remas p.o.m.i. (page 3)

Ladouceur, Josephine Alice: B-4, Josephine Alice Ladouceur, baptized 9 March 1884, age 12 days, legitimate daughter of Joseph Ladouceur dit Osisis, Godmother: Sister Youville, Collignon o.m.i.p. (page 235)

Ladouceur, Lia: B-5, Lia Ladouceur, baptized 30 March 1884, age 16 days, legitimate daughter of Adam Ladouceur and Marguerite Desmarais, Godfather: Edouard Villeneuve, Godmother: Adelaide Decoine, Collignon o.m.i.p. (page 235)

Lac la Biche Baptisms, Marriages and Burials 1853-1884

Ladouceur, Louis: B-449, Louis Ladouceur, baptized 11 October 1868, born yesterday, legitimate son of Pierre Ladouceur and Marguerite Fraser, Godfather: Louis Larocque, Godmother: Catherine Cardinal, V. Vegreville, p.m.a.o.m.i. (page 96)

Ladouceur, Marie-Alexandrine: B-19, Alexandrine Ladouceur, baptized 29 June 1879, age 10 days, legitimate d/o Joseph Ladouceur and Veronique Osisis, Godfather: Cayatius Cardinal, Godmother: Marie McDelis, Collignon o.m.i. (page 189)

Ladouceur, Marie-Marguerite: B-7, Marie_Marguerite Ladouceur, baptized 4 April 1874, age 10 days, legitimate daughter of Adam Ladouceur and Marguerite Desjarlais, Godmother: Marie Ducharme, wife of Pierre Pruden, E. Petitot priest o.m.i. (page 142)

Ladouceur, Maxime: B-21, Maxime Ladouceur, baptized 29 July 1883, age two months, legitimate son of Augustin Ladouceur and Betsy, Godmother: Sophie Ladouceur, Collignon o.m.i.p. (page 228-229)

Ladouceur, Melanie: B-44, Melanie Ladouceur, baptized 14 October 1881, age about 3 weeks, legitimate daughter of Joseph Ladouceur and Veronique Osisis, Godfather: Joseph Ladouceur Jr., Godmother: Agnes Ladouceur, E. Grouard priest o.m.i. (page 211-212)

Ladouceur, Narcisse and Julie Auger: M-1, Narcisse Ladouceur married 30 January 1883 Julie Auger, Present: Pierre Ladouceur (x) and Antoine Ducharme (x), Collignon o.m.i.p. (page 224)

Ladouceur, Narcisse: B-307, Narcisse Ladouceur, baptized 8 June 1864, born today, of the legitimate marriage of Joseph Ladouceur and Julie Auger, Godfather: Paulette Auger, Godmother: Genevieve Ladouceur, Tissot Jn. priest o.m.i. (page 58)

Ladouceur, Olivier: S-15, Olivier Ladouceur, buried 13 July 1862, drowned 6 November 1861 and found yesterday, Present: Augustin Auger and Baptiste Kakikekamik, Tissot Jn. priest o.m.i. (page 49)

Ladouceur, Salomon: B-33, Salomon Ladouceur, baptized 16 November 1884, age 5 weeks, legitimate son of Augustin Ladouceur and Betsy, Godfather: David Ladouceur, Godmother: Marie-Rose Vandale, Collignon o.m.i.p. (page 242)

Ladouceur, Sophie: B-9, Sophie Ladouceur, baptized 1 April 1878, age 2 days, legitimate d/o Adam Ladouceur and Marguerite Desmarais, Godfather: Oliver Courte_oreille, Godmother: Sophie Ladouceur, E. Grouard priest o.m.i. (page 176_177)

Ladouceur, Sophie; See Antoine Ducharme and Sophie Ladouceur

Ladouceur, Sophie; See Louis Daze and Sophie Ladouceur

Ladouceur, Therese; See Louison Fosseneuve and Therese Ladouceur

Lafond, Marie Eulalie: B-413, Marie Eulalie Lafond, baptized 28 June 1867, born 1 February 1867, of the legitimate marriage of Cyrille Lafond and Agathe Pepin, Godfather: Charles Houl, Godmother: Marie Atukukup, Maisonneuve A. priest o.m.i. (page 84)

Lac la Biche Baptisms, Marriages and Burials 1853-1884

Lafont, Salomon: B-38, Salomon Lafont, baptized 26 September 1869, age 6 months, legitimate son of Jean Baptiste Lafont and Therese Arcan, Godfather: Cyrille Lafont, Godmother: Agathe Pepin, V. Vegreville p.m.a.o.m.i. (page 108)

Lafreniere, Marie: B-202, Marie Lafreiniere, baptized 26 February 1860, born yesterday, of the legitimate marriage of Baptiste Lafreiniere and Ursule St.Germain, Godmother: Eugenie Ladouceur, Tissot Jn priest (page 37)

Lagrosse-tete: Caroline: B-445, Caroline Lagrosse-tete, baptized 20 September 1868, age over 3 months, legitimate daughter of Pierre Lagrosse-tete and Angelique Ethalerda, Godfather: Laurent Izonke, V. Vegreville, p.m.a.o.m.i. (page 94-95)

Lagrossetete: B-9, __ Lagrossetete, baptized 1 June 1874, age over 2 months, legitimate son of St.Pierre Lagrossetete and Judule Dzintchede, Godmother: Marie Gladu, V. Vegreville, p.m.a.o.m.i. (page 143)

Lagrossetete, Marguerite; See Fabien Bisson and Marguerite Lagrossetete

Lagrossetete, Marianne: B-436, Marianne Lagrossetete, baptized 6 June 1868, age 5 months, natural daughter of Antoine Lagrossetete and Marguerite Nakethyaze, Godfather: Francois Bisson, Godmother: Catherine Isakale, V. Vegreville p.m.a.o.m.i. (page 91)

Lagrossetete, Pierre and Judith Dzinlchule: M-4, Pierre Lagrossetete, adult son of Lagrossetete, widower of Louise Eloi, married 8 October 1871, Judith Dzinlchule, minor daughter of Dzinlchule and Sharoulgone, Present: Francois Bisson and Fabien Bisson, V. Vegreville p.m.a.o.m.i. (page 123)

Lagrossetete, William: B-20, William Lagrossetete, baptized 8 October 1871, age 15 months, son of St. Pierre Lagrossetete and Judith Dzintehede, Godmother: Marie Gladu, V. Vegreville p.m.a.o.m.i. (page 123)

Laliberte, Pierre-Clement: B-33, Pierre-Clement Laliberte, baptized 23 December 1882, age about 9 days, natural son of Antoine Clement and Mathilde Collin, no godparents, E. Grouard priest o.m.i. (page 223)

Landmore, John and Rosalie Kakikikamik: M-1, John Landmore married [about 6 February 1869] Rosalie Kakikikamik, Present: Joseph Duquette and Louis Daze (signed), M. R. Remas priest o.m.i. (page 97-98)

Landry, Marguerite: B-412, Marguerite Landry, baptized 28 June 1867, christened by Monseigneur Grandin on the 23 March 1867, born 30 November 1866, legitimate infant of Alexandre Landry and Marie Castawis, Godfather: Isidore Boucher, Godmother: Marie Landry, Maisonneuve A. priest o.m.i. (page 84)

Landry, Marie; See Henry Pruden and Marie Landry

Lapoudre, Ambroise: B-2, Ambroise Lapoudre, baptized 22 January 1880, age about one month, legitimate son of Pierre Lapoudre and Rosalie Naud, Godmother: Isabelle, wife of Paul Montagnaise, E. Grouard priest o.m.i. (page 193)

Lapoudre, Arsene Abe: B-38, Arsene Abe Lapoudre, baptized 18 December 1883, age about one month, legitimate son of Abe Lepoudre and Catherine, Godmother: Eulalie Hamelin (signed), Collignon o.m.i.p. (page 233)

Lapoudre, Eulalie: B-34, Eulalie Lapoudre, baptized 6 October 1880, age about one month, legitimate daughter of Abel Lapoudre and Catherine, Godfather: Thomas, Godmother: Eulalie Hamelin, E. Grouard priest o.m.i. (page 200)

Lapoudre, Felix: B-33, Felix Lapoudre, baptized 23 November 1878, age about one month, son of Paul Lapoudre and Christine Bews, Godfather: Francois Decouanne, Godmother: Honorine Lapoudre, E. Grouard priest o.m.i. (page 182)

Lapoudre, Francis: B-19, Francis Lapoudre, baptized 10 April 1881, age one month, legitiamte son of Paul Lapoudre and Christine Bews, Godfather: Thomy Hupe, Godmother: Marie Decouanne (Isidore), E. Grouard priest o.m.i. (page 205)

Lapoudre, Francois: B-43, Francois Lapoudre, baptized 30 December 1883, age 6 days, legitimate son of Eric Lapoudre and Christine Vivier, Godfather: Julien Cardinal, Godmother: Marie Mustatip, Collignon o.m.i.p. (page 233)

Lapoudre, Frederic-Arthur: B-15, Frederic-Arthur Lapoudre, baptized 30 June 1883, age about 2 months, legitimate son of Paulis Lapoudre and Christine Bews (Hughes), Godfather: Alec Johnston, Godmother: Melanie Lavallee (signed), Collignon o.m.i.p. (page 227)

Lapoudre, Henry: B-6, Henry Lapoudre, baptized 12 April 1884, age about one month, legitimate son of Pierre Lapoudre and Rosalie, Godfather: Louis Lavallee, Godmother: Catherine L'Esperance (signed), Collignon o.m.i.p. (page 236)

Lapoudre, Honorine; See Thomas Aputsan and Honorine Lapoudre

Lapoudre, Julien and Madeleine Decoine: M-3, Julien Lapoudre married 19 February 1884 Madeleine Decoine, Present: Absalom Ladouceur (x) and George Martin (signed), Collignon o.m.i.p. (page 234)

Lapoudre, Marguerite: B-8, Marguerite Lapoudre, baptized 13 April 1879 at Lac de Coeur, age about one month, legitimate daughter of Henri Lapoudre and Christine, Godfather: Gilbert Comtois, Godmother: Marguerite Cayen, wife of Comtois, E. Grouard priest o.m.i. (page 187)

Lapoudre, Paul (Decoin): B-6, Paul Lapoudre (Decoin), baptized 6 March 1875, age 10 days, of Pierre Lapoudre and Rosalie, Godfather: Jules Desjarlais, Godmother: Marie Quintal, J. V. Fourmond priest o.m.i. (page 149)

Lapoudre, Paul and Christine Bews: M-8, Paul Lapoudre, adult son of the late Lapoudre and Therese, married 2 December 1878, Christine Bews, minor daughter of the deceased Bews and Catherine, Witnesses: Andre Fortier (signed) and Isidore Decoine (x), Collignon o.m.i. (page 183)

Lac la Biche Baptisms, Marriages and Burials 1853-1884

Lapoudre, Venance: B-32, Venance Lapoudre, baptized 31 July 1881, age about 3 weeks, legitimate son of Essie [?] Lapoudre and Christine Vivier, Godfather: Alec Johnston, Godmother: Liza Moustatip, Collignon o.m.i.p. (page 208)

Lariviere, Francois: B-87, Francois Lariviere, baptized 30 January 1856, born yesterday, of the legitimate marriage of Abraham Lariviere and Marie, Godfather: Baptiste Beaudry, Godmother: Nannecy Quintal, Tissot Jn. priest o.m.i. (page 16)

Larocque, Marguerite; See Louison Sisawapas and Marguerite Larocque

Larocque, Melanie: B-282, Melanie Larocque, baptized 19 May 1863, age 10 days, daughter of Moise Larocque and Ursule Beauregard, Godmother: Esther Bruneau, Tissot Jn. priest o.m.i. (page 53)

Larocque, Romain: B-341, Romain Larocque, baptized 23 April 1865, born the same days, of the legitimate marriage of Moise Larocque and Ursule Beaugrand, Godmother: Catherine Ladouceur, Godfather: Joachim Bruneau, Masionneuve, A. priest o.m.i. (page 65)

Laroque, Agnes: B-40, Agnes Laroque, baptized 6 September 1881, born 2 September 1881, legitimate daughter of Francois Laroque and Marianne Paquenaude, Godmother: Elise Laroque, E. Grouard p.o.m.i. (page 210)

Laroque, Florestine: B-6, Florestine Laroque, baptized 22 February 1872, born yesterday, legitimate daughter of Louis Laroque and Angelique Sauve, Godfather: Francois Laroque, Godmother: Josephtte St.Pierre, M. R. Remas priest o.m.i. (page 127)

Laroque, Julie Marie: B-7, Julie_Marie Laroque, baptized 28 March 1878, b. 27 March 1878, of the legitimate marriage of Francois Laroque and Marie_Anne Paguenaude, Godfather: Francois Decouanne, Godmother: Julie Decouanne, E. Grouard, priest o.m.i. (page 176)

Laroque, Leon: B-4, Leon Laroque, baptized 4 April 1870, born yesterday, legitimate son of Francois Laroque and Angelique Sais, Godfather: Leon Desjarlais, Godmother: Marie Laroque, M. R. Remas priest o.m.i. (page 110)

Laroque, Louis and Angelique Sauve: M-1, Louis Laroque, minor son of Francois Laroque and Angelique Salois, married 10 January 1871, Angelique Sauve, minor daughter of Norbert Sauve and Josephte Saint-Pierre, Present: Francois Laroque and Robert Jackson, V. Vegreville priest o.m.i. (page 117)

Laroque, Marquerite: B-9, Marguerite Laroque, baptized 14 March 1875, born today, of the legitimate marriage of Francois Laroque and Marianne, Godfather: Julien Cardinal, Godmother: Elisa Ladouceur, M. R. Remas priest o.m.i. (page 149)

Laroque, Moise and Ursule Beauregard: M-24, Moise Laroque married 8 April 1861 Ursule Beauregard, Present: Louis Chatelain and Alfred Smith, Tissot Jn. priest o.m.i. (page 42)

Lavallee, Alfred-Napoleon: B-29, Alfred-Napoleon Lavallee, baptized 29 August 1883, born yesterday of the legitimate marriage of Petit Louis Lavallee and Catherine L'Esperance, Godfather: Alec Johnston, Godmother: Melanie Lavallee, Collignon o.m.i.p. (page 230)

Lac la Biche Baptisms, Marriages and Burials 1853-1884

Lavallee, Frederic-Arthur: B-26, Frederic_Arthur Lavallee, baptized 16 September 1879, born the same day, of the legitimate marriage of Louis Martel Lavallee and Catherine Lesperance, Godfather: Georges Bourke (signed Georges Bourque), Godmother: Agathe Lacouceur, wife of Bourke, E. Grouard priest o.m.i. (page 190)

Lavallee, Joseph-Emile: B-43, Joseph-Emile Lavallee, baptized 24 September 1881, born yesterday, of the legitimate marriage of Louis Lavallee and Catherine L'Esperance, Godfather: Pierre Ladouceur, Godmother: Sister Youville (signed), Collignon o.m.i.p. (page 211)

Lavallee, Martin: B-38, Martin Lavallee, baptized 21 November 1877, born yesterday, legitimate son of Louis Lavallee and Catherine L'Esperance, Godmother: Louise Decoigne, Collignon o.m.i. (page 173-174)

Lavallee, Melanie; See Alex Johnston and Melanie Lavallee

Lavallee, Patrice: S-6, Patrice Lavallee, buried 18 November 1880, age about 8 years, son of Louis Lavallee and Catherine Lesperance, Witnesses: Pierre Ladouceur and Georges Bourque, E. Grouard priest o.m.i. (page 200)

Lavallee, Veronique (Otakinatikway): B-7, Veronique Otakinatikway (Lavallee), baptized 27 March 1869, age 40 years, Godfather: Joseph Ladouceur, Godmother: Marie Mognon, + Vital J Ev. De Satala o.m.i. (page 99)

Laventure, Marie-Claire: B-21, Marie-Claire Laventure, baptized 1 July 1877, born of the legitimate marriage of Charles Laventure and Amelie, Godfather: Charles Johnson, Godmother: Pelagie Laventure, F. Le Serrec priest o.m.i. (page 170)

Lefrance, Isabelle: B-12, Isabelle Lefrance, baptized 31 March 1877, age over one month, legitimate daughter of Paul Lefrance and Therese Redharil'an, Godmother: Delima Asselin, E. Grouard priest o.m.i. (page 168)

Leman, Judith: B-30, Judith Leman, baptized 5 October 1875, age 18 months, of the legitimate marriage of Joseph Leman and Francoise Antwan, Godmother: Angelique Antwan, Husson At. Priest m.o.m.i. (page 156)

Louis, Marie-Pelagie: B-32, Marie-Pelagie Louis, baptized 6 September 1875, born 3 or 4 January 1875, daughter of Louis and Julie, M. R. Remas priest o.m.i. (page 156-157)

Makimutaw, Catherine: B-298, Catherine Makimutaw, bt, 27 March 1864, age 13 days, daughter of Louis Makimutaw and Josephte Cardinal, Godfather: Paulette, Godmother: Euphrosine Cardinal, Tissot Jn. priest o.m.i. (page 56)

Malaterre, Gregoire and Marisis Duquet: M-2, Gregoire Malaterre married 20 February 1882, Marisis Duqet, Present: Petit Louis Lavallee (x) and Peter Pruden (signed), Collignon o.m.i.p. (page 215-216)

Mallet, Joseph and Marie Bellanger: M-19, Joseph Mallett married 22 January 1860 Marie Bellanger, Present: Louis Chatelain and Johny Rolland, Tissot Jn. priest o.m.i. (page 37)

Manotewop, Pierre: B-112, Pierre Manotewop, baptized 18 January 1857, age about 7 years, son of Manotewop and Kiyapwetewapu, Godfather: Paschal Berland, Maisonneuve A. priest o.m.i. (page 22)

Lac la Biche Baptisms, Marriages and Burials 1853-1884

Martel, Catherine: B-25, Catherine Martel, baptized 28 August 1879, born the same day, legitimate daughter of Nazaire Martel and Celina Tremblay, Godfather: Raphael Tremblay, Godmother: Catherine McDougall, E. Grouard priest o.m.i. (page 190)

Martin dit Cisip, Josephine; See Jean-Baptiste Cardinal and Josephine Martin dit Cisip

Martin, Scholastique: S-47, Scholastique Martin, buired 18 January 1868, died 16 January 1868, age about 22 years, daughter of Martin dit Cisip, Present: Joseph Cardinal and Francois Cardinal, Maisonneuve A. priest o.m.i. (page 88)

Maskawanis, Catherine; See Albert Decoine and Catherine Maskawanis

Maskek, Marie: B-407, Marie Maskek, baptized 30 June 1867, age 6 months, legitimate daughter of Jean-Baptiste Maskek and Sophie Petapanesimew, Godmother: Julie Decoine, V. Vegreville, p.m.a.o.m.i. (page 82)

Maskekaskapo, Jean: B-265, Jean Maskekaskapo, baptized 21 September 1862, age about 2 years, son of Baptiste Maskekaskapo and Sophie Petapanesimo, Godmother: Agathe Ladouceur, Tissot Jn. priest o.m.i. (page 50)

Maskekwatik, Rosalie: B-200, Rosalie Maskekwatik, baptized 16 December 1859, age about one year, daughter of Maskekwatik and Marie Crise, Godmother: Marie Nipissing, Maisonneuve A. priest o.m.i. (page 37)

Masson dit Mulot, Melanie: B-32, Melanie Masson dit Mulot, baptized 11 December 1882, born yesterday, of the legitimate marriage of Francois Masson dit Mulot and Elise Ocanes, Godfather: Alexandre Hamelin (signed), Godmother: Eleonore Desjarlais, Collignon o.m.i.p. (page 223)

Matatutun, James: B-17, James Matatutun, baptized 15 April 1876, age 4 months, legitimate son of Joseph Matatutun and Marianne Witiwisham, Godmother: Catherine, Husson p.o.m.i. (page 160-161)

Matoimuttaw, Caroline: S-5, Caroline Matoimuttaw, buried 16 June 1882, died yesterday, age one year, daughter of (Baptiste) Matsimuttaw and Josephte Cardinal, Witnesses: Jerome Cardinal and F. Boisrame, Collignon o.m.i.p. (page 219)

Matsimutaw, Caroline: B-30, Caroline Matsimutaw, baptized 12 September 1880, born 15 days, legitimate daughter of Matsimutaw and Josephte, Godfather: Duncan Tremblay, Godmother: Lisette Mustatip, Collignon o.m.i. p. (page 199)

Matsimutaw, Jean-Baptiste: B-408, Jean-Baptiste Matsimutaw, baptized 7 July 1867, age 22 days, legitimate son of Louison Matsimutaw and Josephte Cardinal, Godfather: Charles Quintal, Godmother: Euphrosine Cardinal, V. Vegreville, p.m.a.o.m.i. (page 82)

Matsimutaw, Johny: B-8, Johny Matsimutaw, baptized 25 March 1872, born today, legitimate son of Matsimutaw and Josephte Cardinal, Godfather: Johny Johnston, Godmother: Caroline Johnston, V. Vegreville priest o.m.i. (page 127-128)

Lac la Biche Baptisms, Marriages and Burials 1853-1884

Matsimutaw, Marguerite: B-1, Marguerite Matsimutaw, baptized 4 January 1870, born today, legitimate daughter of Louison Matsimutaw and Josephte Cardinal, Godmother: Bethsy Kistinawataw, V. Vegreville p.m.a.o.m.i. (page 108)

Matsimutaw, Raphael: B-37, Raphael Matsimutaw, baptized 18 November 1877, legitimate son of Louison Matsimutaw and Josette, Godfather: Paul Cardinal, Godmother: Olive Tremblay (signed), E. Grouard priest o.m.i. (page 173)

Matsimuttau: S-5, Matsimuttau, buried 2 February 1873, Collignon o.m.i. (page 135)

Matsimuttaw, Catherine; See Pierre Paulette Desjarlais and Catherine Matsimuttaw

Matsimuttaw, Maria-Lasa: B-18, Maria-Lasa Matsimuttaw, baptized 15 July 1883, age one month, legitimate daughter of Jean-Baptiste Matsimuttaw and Josephte Mustatip, Godmother: Marie Cardinal Mustatip, Collignon o.m.i.p. (page 227-228)

Matsunta, Louis and Josephte Cardinal: M-25, Louis Matsunta married 27 May 1861 Josephte Cardinal, Present: Jacques Cardinal and Maisonneuve, Tissot Jn. priest o.m.i. (page 42)

Mayinaknois, Pierre: B-333, Pierre Mayinaknois, baptized 11 January 1865, age over 5 months, son of Mayinaknois and Kwekin [?], Godfather: Abraham Simard, Godmother: Marie Bellanger, Tissot Jn. priest o.m.i. (page 63-64)

Mayistikwan, Charles: B-20, Charles Mayistikwan, baptized 18 July 1883, age about two months, son of Louis Mayistikwan and Nancy, Godmother: Marianne Nipitahan, Collignon o.m.i.p. (page 228)

Mayotakus, Simeon: B-10, Simeon Mayotakus, baptized 12 March 1880, age about 5 months, legitimate son of Baptiste Mayotakus and Marie Matsinokohunis, Godfather: Theophile Boucher, Godmother: Adelaide Pitikuwinis, Collignon o.m.i. priest. (page 195)

McDonald, Bethsy: B-368, Bethsy McDonald, baptized 26 November 1865, born day before yesterday, legitimate daughter of Kenneth McDonald and Emma Rowland, Godfather: Joseph Chatelain, Godmother: Sophie Chatelain, V. Vegreville priest o.m.i. (page 71-72)

McGillis, Elise; See Michel Sisawapas and Elise McGillis

McGillis, Urbain: S-28, Urbain McGillis, buried 6 July 1865, died yesterday, age 2 months, legitimate son of Corbett McGillis and Marguerite Delorme, Present: William McGillis and Johny McGillis, V. Vegreville priest o.m.i. (page 67)

Meiskinak, Jamy: B-17, Jamy Meiskinak, baptized 28 September 1871, age 2 years, child of Miskinak and Mimikunakus, Godmother: Marguerite Desjarlais, M. R. Remas priest o.m.i. (page 122)

Meiyotakus, Susanne: B-235, Susanne Meiyotakus, baptized 20 September 1861, age about one year, daughter of Meiyotakus and Osamikisikwewisk, Godmother: Susanne Eitipiakawekesin, Tissot Jn. priest o.m.i. (page 43-44)

Mekwanep, Paulette: B-14, Paulette Mekwanep, baptized 27 March 1881, age about 3 years, son of Mekwanep and Oskipakaw, Godfather: Guillaume Villebrun, Godmother: Silvie Quintal, Collignon o.m.i. p. (page 205)

Mesinikunem, Michel: B-268, Michel Mesinikunem, baptized 26 October 1862, age 5 months, son of Baptiste Mesinikunem and Marie Kowikin, Godfather: Joachim Bruneau, Godmother: Catherine Ladouceur, Tissot Jn. priest o.m.i. (page 50)

Meyotakus, Vital: B-32, Vital Meyotakus, baptized 29 April 1854, age about 2 years, son of Meyotakus and Siamkisikweuok, Godfather: Louis St. Arnaud, M. R. Remas p.o.m.i. (page 6)

Meyotaskus, Jeannette: B-10, Jeannette Meyotaskus, baptized 31 March 1872, age about 8 days, daughter of Baptiste Meyotaskus and Atsinakubuwis, Godmother: Silvy Bruneau, M. R. Remas priest o.m.i. (page 128)

Michel, Cesar: B-22, Cesar Michel, baptized 11 July 1880, age about 20 days, legitimate son of Louis Michel and Julie, Godfather: Alexandre, E. Grouard priest o.m.i. (page 197)

Michel, Francois: B-9, Francois (Michel), baptized 21 March 1877, age 10 months, son of Michel ___, F. Le Serrec priest o.m.i. (page 168)

Michel, Louise: B-4, Louise Michel, baptized 3 April 1873, age over 7 months, legitimate daughter of Louis Michel and Julie Bisson, Godfather: Fabien Bisson, Godmother:Francoise Tielros, V. Vegreville p.m.a.o.m.i. (page 135)

Michel, Mathilde: B-23, Mathilde, baptized 9 November 1873, age 3 months, legitimate daughter of Michel and Emma Piwastakut, Godmother: Mathilde Tremblay, E. Petitot priest o.m.i. (page 139-140)

Mikku, Pierre: B-25, Pierre Mikku, baptized 5 August 1883, age about one month, son of Mikku and Angelique, Godmother: Elise Loiuson Sisawapas, Collignon o.m.i.p. (page 229)

Minahikusis, Josephte: B-222, Josephte Minahikusis, baptized 24 February 1861, age 4 years, daughter of Minahikusis and Matowitam, Godmother: Magdeleine Deschamps, Tissot Jn. priest o.m.i. (page 41)

Miskinak, Anne: B-37, Anne Miskinak, baptized 26 November 1876, age about 35 years, Godmother: Georgina Hudon, Collignon o.m.i. (page 165)

Miskinak, Anne: S-6, Anne Miskinak, buried 23 February 1879, age 38 years, Witnesses: Louis Lavallee and Alexandre Hamelin, E. Grouard priest o.m.i. (page 185-186)

Mistahepiweyan, Bethsy: B-279, Bethsy Mistahepiweyan, baptized 7 May 1863, age 8 months, daughter of Angelique Cardinal and Mistahepiweyan, Godmother: Genevieve Ladouceur, Tissot Jn. priest o.m.i. (page 52)

Mistahipeweyan, Moise: B-123, Moise Mistahipeweyan, baptized 23 April 1857, age 14 days, son of Mistahipeweyan and Angelique Cardinal, Godfather: Moise St.Denis, Godmother: Scholastique Versaille, Tissot Jn. priest o.m.i. (page 23-24)

Lac la Biche Baptisms, Marriages and Burials 1853-1884

Miyaweyiniw, Josephte: B-117, Josephte Miyaweyiniw, baptized 19 January 1857, age one year, daughter of Miyaweyiniw and Marguerite Piyetta, Godmother: Lalouise Cardinal, Maisonneuve A. priest o.m.i. (page 22)

Miyosaskamikutew dit Opiwitew, Jacques and Catherine Cardinal: M-59, Jacques Miyosaskamikutew dit Opiwitew, adult son of Pierre Miyosaskamikutew and Charlotte Kwasiwisit, married 24 September 1867, Catherine Cardinal, minor daughter of Jacques Cardinal and Pelagie Samaskekapaw, Present: Louis Daze and Joseph Ladoceur, V. Vegreville p.m.a.o.m.i. (page 85)

Miyoseskamikutew (dit Opiwitew), Marianne: B-439, Marianne Miyoseskamikutew (dit Opiwitew), baptized 4 July 1868, age 48 days, daughter of Jacques Miyoseskamikutew (dit Opiwitew) and Catherine Cardinal, Godmother: Bethsy, V. Vegreville p.m.a.o.m.i. (page 93)

Miyosipisiw and Emma Piwastimow: M-5, Miyosipisiw married 3 April 1875 Emma Piwastimow, Present; Joseph Nipiteham and Therese, J. V. Fourmond priest o.m.i. (page 151)

Miyoskipis, Liza: B-21, Liza Miyoskipis, baptized 9 September 1882, age 5 days, legitimate daughter of Miyoskipis and Emma, Godfather: Baptiste Laroque, Godmother: Angelique Hoole, Collignon o.m.i.p. (page 220)

Miyoskipisin, Agathe: B-19, Agathe Miyoskipisin, baptized 19 May 1876, age 10 days, legitimate daughter of Pierre Miyoskipisin and Emma Kakitomustus, Godmother: Pelagie Cardinal, Husson, p.o.m.i. (page 161)

Miyotakus, Justine: B-236, Justine Miyotakus, baptized 20 September 1861, age about 5 years, daughter of Miyotakus and Osamikisikwewisk, Godmother: Candide Ouwabiskokumaniwit, Tissot Jn. priest o.m.i. (page 44)

Moberly, Franck-Arthur: B-17, Franck-Arthur Moberly, baptized 18 June 1872, age one month, legitimate son of Henry Moberly and Francoise, Godfather: Thomas Hupe, Godmother: Louise Decoine, V. Vegreville p.m.a.o.m.i. (page 130)

Mognon, Augustin and Marie Sisawapas: M-7, Augustin Mognon, minor son of Joseph Mognon and Kinisknokwe, married 13 November 1871, Marie Sisawapas, minor daughter of Pierre Sisawapas and Agnes Batoche, Present: Pierre Sisawapas and Agnes Batoche, the father and mother of the bride, M. R. Remas priest o.m.i. (page 124-125)

Mognon, Joseph: B-316, Joseph Mognon, baptized 20 September 1864, age one year, son of Michel Mognon and Oskweyaw, Godfather: Joseph Deschamp, Maisonneuve A. priest o.m.i. (page 60)

Mognon, Narcisse and Elise Deschamp: M-41, Narcisse Mognon, married 20 September 1864, Elise Deschamp, daughter of Joseph Deschamps and Larose Berger, Present: Baptiste Pelletier and Norbert Morisset, Maisonneuve A. priest o.m.i. (page 60)

Molligan, Henriette; See Maxime Fidler and Henriette Molligan

Mongrin, Francois: B-27, Francois Mongrin, baptized 26 August 1875, born the beginning of July last, legitimate son of Michel Mongrin and Angele, Godmother: Mary Cleary (signed), Husson Ate. Priest o.m.i. (page 156)

Lac la Biche Baptisms, Marriages and Burials 1853-1884

Monias, Felix: B-350, Felix Monias, baptized 6 August 1865, age 8 months, son of Monias and Siwiyaskew, Godmother: Sophie Chatelain, V. Vegreville priest o.m.i. (page 67)

Monias, Pierre: B-24, Pierre Monias, baptized 14 July 1877, born of the legitimate marriage of Michel Monias and Wapasun, Godfather: Edouard Cunningham (signed), Godmother: Susanne, + Vital J. Ev. de St. Albert o.m.i. (page 171)

Montagnais, Alec: B-16, Alec Montagnais, baptized 2 July 1883, age about one month, legitimate son of Alec and Madeleine Montagnais, Godfather: Alec, Godmother: Julie, Collignon o.m.i.p. (page 227)

Montagnais, Angele; See Pascal Charles and Angele Montagnais

Montagnais, Catholique: B-24, Catholique baptized 30 August 1878, age about 3 months, legitimate son of Andre and Marie, Godfather: Charles T'el'aileru, E. Grouard priest o.m.i. (page 180-181)

Montagnais, Daniel: B-22, Daniel Montagnais [Bruneau], baptized 15 July 1877, born 14 May, of the legitimate marriage of Paul Montagnais and Isabelle [Kaketiamik], Godfather: Pierre Auger, Godmother: Caroline, H. Leduc priest o.m.i. (page 170_171)

Montagnais, Eugenie: S-8, Eugenie Montagnais, buried 24 September 1882, age about 9 years, daughter of Charles and Marie Montagnais, Witnesses: Thomas and St.Pierre (Montagnais), E. Grouard priest o.m.i. (page 220-221)

Montagnais, Joseph: B-22, Joseph Montagnais, baptized 17 April 1881, age over 2 months, legitimate son of Andre and Marie Montagnais (of lac de Coeur, no godparents, E. Grouard priest o.m.i. (page 206)

Montagnais, Laurent: B-22, Laurent, baptized 10 August 1879, age about 2 months, legitimate son of Jean-Baptiste (Montagnais) and Catherine K'attla, Godfather: Francois Piche, E. Grouard priest o.m.i. (page 190)

Montagnais, Marie-Julie: B-10, Marie-Julie (Montagnais), baptized 29 May 1884, age about 5 months, daughter of Alexandre and Madeleine, Godfather: Damien Ladouceur, Godmother: Florestine Ladouceur, Collignon o.m.i.p. (page 236-237)

Montagnais, Mary: B-38, Mary Montagnais, baptized 13 December 1880, age about 4 months, illegitimate daughter of Andre and Charlotte (Montagnais of Lac de Coeur), Godmother: Marie wife of Francois, E. Grouard priest o.m.i. (page 201)

Montagnais, Thomas-Charles: S-3, Thomas-Charles Montagnais, buried 15 September 1883, died yesterday, age about 30 years, Witnesses: Charles (Montagnais) and Thomas, Collignon o.m.i.p. (page 230-231)

Montagnaise, Alice: B-5, Alice Montagnaise, baptized 24 March 1879, age about 7 days, legitimate daughter of St. Pierre and Judith, Godfather: Pascal, E. Grouard priest o.m.i. (page 186)

Montagnaise, Lucia: B-4, Lucia Montagnaise, baptized 24 March 1879, age about 5 months, legitimate daughter of Paul and Sophie, Godmother: Marie, E. Grouard priest o.m.i. (page 186)

Lac la Biche Baptisms, Marriages and Burials 1853-1884

Montagnaise, Marianne; See Antoine Buisson [Bisson] and Marianne Montagnaise

Montagnaise, Marie: B-300, Marie Montagnaise, baptized 27 March 1864, age 5 months, daughter of Iyekatlesha and Marie Montagnaise, Godmother: Marie Castor, Tissot Jn. priest o.m.i. (page 56)

Montagnaise, Pierre: B-6, Pierre Montagnaise, baptized 24 March 1879, age about 5 months, legitimate daughter of St. Pierre and Judith, Godfather: Pascal, E. Grouard priest o.m.i. (page 186)
Morin, Maria: B-35, Maria Morin, baptized 18 September 1869, age 9 days, legitimate daughter of Alexandre Morin and Angelique, Godmother: Julie McGillis, V. Vegreville p.m.a.o.m.i. (page 107)

Mouillion, Constant dit Kamakwe: B-41, Constant Mouillion dit Kamakwe, baptized 28 May 1854, age 5 years, daughter of Mouillion dit Makwe and Suzane, Godfather: Francois Decoing, M. R. Remas p.o.m.i. (page 8)

Moustatip, Pelagie; See Francois Decoin and Pelagie Moustatip

Moyon, Catherine; See James Simpson and Catherine Moyon

Mustatip (Cardinal), Marie Pelagie: B-11, Marie-Pelagie Mustatip (Cardinal), baptized 23 May 1879, age about one month, legitimate daughter of Olivier Laventure (Kayatius Cardinal dit Mustatip) and Adelaide Siyapukyikwepiw, Godfather: Venance Johnston, Godmother: Pelagie Laventure Cardinal, E. Grouard priest o.m.i. (page 187)

Mustatip, Angelique: S-3, Angelique St.Pierre Mustatip, baptized 22 March 1877, died yesterday, age 9 years, Witnesses: Etienne Quintal and Francois Decoin, H. Leduc priest o.m.i. (page 169)

Mustatip, Baptiste: S-9, Baptiste Mustatip, buried 2 September 1879, age about one year, son of Xavier Louison Mustatip and Mary Jane, Witness: Louison Sisawapas, E. Grouard, priest o.m.i. (page 190)

Mustatip, Benjamin: S-2, Benjamin Mustatip, buried 30 March 1884, died 8 days, age about 28 years, Witnesses: Petit Louis Lavallee and Duncan Tremblay, Collignon o.m.i.p. (page 236)

Mustatip, Catherine: B-8, Catherine Mustatip, baptized 26 February 1880, age about one year, legitimate daughter of Jospeh Mustatip and Angelique Kakikekamik, Godmother: Christine Kakikekamik, Collignon o.m.i. (page 194)

Mustatip, Cecile: B-7, Cecile Mustatip, baptized 13 April 1884, age about one month, legitimate daughter of Francois Mustatip and Angele, Godfather: Olivier Cayatius, Godmother: Elise Mustatip, Collignon o.m.i.p. (page 236)

Mustatip, Jean-Baptiste: B-56, Jean-Baptiste Mustatip, baptized 25 December 1881, about about 8 days, legitimate son of Francois Mustatip and Adele, Godfather: Jean-Baptiste Laventure, Godmother: Josette Joly, E. Grouard priest o.m.i. (page 214)

Mustatip, Joseph-Emile: B-17, Joseph_Emile Mustatip, baptized 15 June 1879, age about 5 months, legitimate son of Joseph Mustatip and __, Godmother: Marie Landry, E. Grouard priest o.m.i. (page 188)

Mustatip, Louis: B-21, Louis Mustatip, baptized 21 July 1879, age about 12 days, legitimate son of Francois Mustatip and Adele, Godfather: LouiS-Martin Lavallee, Godmother: Pelagie Laventure (signed), E. Grouard priest o.m.i. (page 189)

Mustatip, Maria-Lisette: B-7, Maria-Lisette Mustatip, baptized 28 February 1882, born yesterday, illegitimate daughter of Lisette Mustatip, Godfather: Antoine Ducharme, Godmother: Marguerite Fosseneuve, Collignon o.m.i.p. (page 216)

Mustatip, Marie-Marguerite: B-12, Marie-Marguerite Mustatip, baptized 15 May 1882, age 2 days, illegitimate daughter of Catherine Mustatip dit Apititit, Godfather: Scolastique Mustatip, Collignon o.m.i.p. (page 218)

Mustatip, Melanie: B-17, Melanie Mustatip, baptized 8 July 1878, age about 2 months, legitimate d/o Joseph Mustatip and Mathilde Tremblay, Godfather: Benjamin Mustatip, Godmother: Catherine Mustatip, Collignon p.o.m.i. (page 179)

Mustatip, Rosalie: B-41, Rosalie Mustatip, baptized 28 December 1876, born today of the legitimate marriage of Joseph Mustatip and Catherine Angelique Kakekekamik, Godparents: Marcel Duncan and his wife, H. Leduc priest (page 165)

Mustatip, Theophile: B-23, Theophile Mustatip, baptized 17 April 1881, age about 6 months, illegitimate son of Antoine Mustatip and Marie Keyakiskanepiw, Godfather: Waweyenmon, Godmother: Scholastique Moustatip, Collignon o.m.i. p. (page 206)

Mustatip, Victoire: B-16, Victoire Mustatip, baptized 12 May 1877, age about 20 days, legitimate daughter of Francois Mustatip and Adele, Godfather: Eric Mustatip, Godmother: Christine Lisette, Collignon o.m.i. (page 169)

Mustatip, Victoire: S-6, Victoire Mustatip, buried 11 December 1878, age about one year, Witnesses: Adam Ladouceur and Charles Houle, E. Grouard priest o.m.i. (page 183)

Nabatoche, J.: S-5, J. Nabatoche, buried 18 September 1880, age over one month, legitimate son of Gabriel Nabatoche and Marie of lac Assinikakamut, the infant was christened by his father, Present: Augustin Moyon, E. Grouard priest o.m.i. (page 199)

Nadarenlyeille, Eugenie; See Thomas Eelkelero and Eugenie Nadarenlyeille

Nadlaitu, Josephine: B-432, Josephine Nadlaitu, baptized 6 June 1868, age 5 months, legitimate daughter of Louis Nadlaitu and Julie Bisson, Godfather: Francois Bisson, Godmother:Isakale, V. Vegreville p.m.a.o.m.i. (page 90)

Nadlaitu, Louis and Julie Bisson: M-52, Louis Nadlaitu, minor son of Nadlaitu and Tsokamtsinaha, married 16 September 1866, Julie Bisson, minor daughter of Alexis Bisson and Catherine Netasbae, Present: Alexis Bisson and Pierre Lagrossetete, V. Vegreville o.m.i. (page 75)

Lac la Biche Baptisms, Marriages and Burials 1853-1884

Nanamepekinam, Marie: S-2, Marie Nanamepekinam, buried 3 February 1874, died yesterday, age about 30 years, wife of Joseph Cardinal, Witnesses: Marcel Tremblay and Joseph Boucher, V. Vegreville p.m.a.o.m.i. (page 141)

Nanehotakusiw, Absalom: B-9, Abaslom Nanehotakusiw, baptized 27 April 1871, age a few weeks, legitimate child of Joseph Nanehotakusiw and Lisette Cardinal, Godmother: Elaiza Ladouceur, M. R. Remas priest (page 120-121)

Nanehotakusiw, Joseph and Lisette Cardinal: M-9, Joseph Nanehotakusiw married 3 October 1869 Nanehotakusiw, Present: Baptiste Pepin and Angelqiue Sauve, M. R. Remas priest o.m.i. (page 106)

Nanehotakusiw, Joseph: B-30, Joseph Nanehotakusiw, baptized 3 October 1869, age about 30 years, Godfather: Baptiste Pepin, Godmother: Angelique Sauve, M. R. Remas priest o.m.i. (page 106)

Nanetehan, Charlotte; See Jean Gane and Charlotte Nanetehan

Naneyotakusiw, Joseph: B-266, Joseph Naneyotakusiw, baptized 26 September 1862, born yesterday, of the legitimate marriage of Naneyotakusiw and Lisette Cardinal, Godmother: Josephte Cardinal, Tissot Jn. priest o.m.i. (page 50)

Naniskit dit Siyapotawikiwam, Jean Baptiste: B-440, Jean Baptiste Naniskit dit Siyapotawikiwam, baptized 4 July 1868, age 3 years and 4 months, legitimate son of Naniskit (dit Siyapotawikiwam) and Nikspaw, Godfather: Alexis Naniskit (dit Siyapotawikiwam), V. Vegreville p.m.a.o.m.i. (page 93)

Naniwotakusiw, Albine: B-204, Albine Naniwotakusiw, baptized 4 May 1860, age 12 days, daughter of Naniwotakusiw and Lisette Cardinal, Godmother: Genevieve Cardinal, Tissot Jn priest (page 38)

Naniwotakusiw; See Lisette Cardinal and Naniwotakusiw

Nanyutagusiw, Francois: B-347, Francois Nanyutagusiw, baptized 2 August 1865, born 21 July 1865, son of Nanyutagusiw and Lisette Cardinal, Godfather: Antoine Cardinal, Godmother: Catherine Decoin, Masionneuve, A. priest o.m.i. (page 67)

Napel, Alexandre: B-151, Alexandre Napel [Narel), baptized 25 April 1858, age over one year, son of Antoine Napel (Narel) and Tsimatowe, Godmother: Marie Desjarlais, Tissot Jn priest o.m.i. (page 28)

Napesis, Jean-Baptiste: B-20, Jean-Baptiste Napesis, baptized 7 June 1880, age about one month, legitimate son of Joseph Napesis and Mathilde Tremblay, Godfather: Raphael Tremblay, Godmother: Lisette Moustatip, E. Grouard priest o.m.i. (page 197)

Napesis, Jean-Marie: B-25, Jean-Marie Napesis, baptized 25 July 1884, age about 2 years, son of Napesis and Osawupiwapiskawew, Godmother: Marie Anne Dreau, Lecorre priest o.m.i. (page 239)

Napesis, Marie Josephine: B-26, Marie Josephine Napesis, baptized 25 July 1884, age about 3 weeks, daughter of Napesis and Osawupiwapiskawew, Godmother: Marie Anne Dreau, Lecorre priest o.m.i. (page 239)

Lac la Biche Baptisms, Marriages and Burials 1853-1884

Natakam, Alphonse; B:32, Alphonse Natakam, baptized 29 September 1878, born yesterday, of the legitimate marriage of Joseph Natakam and __, Godfather: Duncan Marcel Tremblay, Godmother: Marie Maggilis, wife of Louis Hamelin, E. Grouard priest o.m.i. (page 182)

Natakam, Francoise Sisawapas: B-12, Francoise Sisawapas Natakam, bapatized 11 May 1883, age 2 days, of the legitimate marriage of Joseph S. Natakam Sisawapas and Euphronsine, Godfather: Raphael Tremblay, Godmother: Elise Louison, Collignon o.m.i.p. (page 226-227)

Natakam, Marie-Marguerite: B-25, Marie-Marguerite Natakam, baptized 19 July 1880, born yesterday, of the legitimate marriage of Joseph Natakam and Euphrosine, Godfather: Alec Johnston, Godmother: Marguerite Laroque, Collignon. (page 198)

Natakam, Marie-Marguerite: S-11, Marie-Marguerite Natakam, buried 31 May 1881, died 29 May 1881, age 6 months, Witnesses: Petit Louis Hamelin and Francois Kakikekamik, Collignon o.m.i. p. (page 206)

Natselshel, Genevieve: B-29, Genevieve Natselshel, baptized 5 October 1875, age 5 months, daughter of Gregoire Natselshel and Francoise Tsckwitseze, Godmother: Emilie Chekkess, Husson p.o.m.i. (page 156)

Natselthed, Josephine: B-5, Josephine Natselthed, baptized 3 April 1873, age over 7 months, legitimate daughter of Naselthed and Francoise Tsekwitsez, Godfather: Fabien Bisson, Godmother: Francoise Tielros, V. Vegreville p.m.a.o.m.i. (page 135-136)

Natselthel, Louis: B-211, Louis Natselthel, baptized 3 October 1860, age 6 months, son of Natselthel and Francoise Tsekwitsethe, Godmother: Marguerite Intoyaze, Tissot Jn priest o.m.i. (page 39)

Natselthet, Elisa: B-21, Elisa Natselthet, baptized 2 September 1869, age 8 months, daughter of Natselthet and Francoise Tsekwitsoze, Godmother: Marguerite Edoeyaze, V. Vegreville p.m.a.o.m.i. (page 104)

Natsetthel, Gregoire: B-240, Gregoire Natsetthel, baptized 25 October 1861, age about 25 years, son of Andre Yeseogalra, Tissot Jn. priest o.m.i. (page 44)

Natsetthel, Sophie: B-152, Sophie Natsetthel, baptized 25 April 1858, daughter of Natsetthel and Tschwitocthe Francoise, Godmother: Genevieve Cardinal, Tissot Jn priest o.m.i. (page 28)

Natslthed, Marie: S-33, Marie Natslthed, buried 5 April 1866, died yesterday, age over 11 years, daughter of Gregoire Natslthed and Francois Tschwitseze, Witnesses: Pierre Lagrossetet and St.Pierre Lagrossetete, V. Vegreville priest mis. o.m.i. (page 73)

Nawis, Joseph: B-6, Joseph Nawis, baptized 29 March 1874, age 2 months, legitimate son of Joseph Nawis and Veronique Osisis, Godfather: Francois Castor, Godmother: Sophie Daze nee Ladouceur, E. Petitot priest o.m.i. (page 142)

Neheyan, Rosalie: B-146, Rosalie Neheyan, baptized 2 December 1857, age about 2 months, daughter of Neheyan (Cris) and Cecile Batauche, Godmother: Rosalie Batoche, Maisonneuve Jn. priest o.m.i. (page 27)

Lac la Biche Baptisms, Marriages and Burials 1853-1884

Nekateki, Augustin: B-94, Augustin Nekateki, baptized 20 July 1856, age about 9 months, legitimate son of Pierre Nekateki and Therese Cardinal, Godfather: Isidore Decoin, Godmother: Marie Decoin, Tissot Jn. priest o.m.i. (page 18)

Nekateki, Honorine: B-318, Honorine Nekateki, baptized 13 October 1864, born today, of the legitimate marriage of Pierre Nekateki and Therese Cardinal, Godmother: Genevieve Cardinal, Tissot Jn. priest o.m.i. (page 60)

Nekateki, Paul: B-170, Paul Nekateki, baptized 2 December 1858, age 5 months, son of Nekateki and Therese Cardinal, Godmother: Genevieve Cardinal, Tissot Jn. priest o.m.i. (page 31)

Nekateki, Pierre: S-27, Pierre Nekateki, buried 30 April 1865, died 28 April 1865, age about 45 years, Present: Georges Bourk and Johnston, Masionneuve, A. priest o.m.i. (page 66)

Nekatiki, Jules: B-255, Jules Nekatiki, baptized 18 April 1862, age 2 months, of the legitimate marriage of Pierre Nekatiki and Therese Cardinal, Godmother: Josephte Desjarlais, Tissot Jn. priest o.m.i. (page 48)

Nepiteam, Marianne: B-422, Marianne Nepiteam, baptized 29 December 1867, age one month, natural daughter of Joseph Nepiteam (dite Sesowikaskwep) and Therese Okimawasis, Godmother: Marianne Matsamin, V. Vegreville p.m.a.o.m.i. (page 87)

Nettanikamuw, Edouard: B-32, Edouard Nettanikamuw, baptized 23 September 1877, legitimate son of Francois Nettanikamuw and Marguerite Desjarlais, Godfather: Pierre Auger, Godmother: Julia Rivet (signed), E. Grouard priest o.m.i. (page 172)

Neyo, Agnes: B-28, Agnes Neyo, baptized 24 April 1854, age 2 years, daughter of Neyo and Kasotshi, Godfather: Joseph Gray, M. R. Remas p.o.m.i. (page 5)

Neyo, John: B-27, John Neyo, baptized 24 April 1854, age 4 years, son of Neyo and Kasotshi, Godfather: Joseph Gray, M. R. Remas p.o.m.i. (page 5)

Nikateki, Pierre and Rosalie Sisawikaskwep: M-54, Pierre Nikateki, minor son of the late Pierre Nikateki and Therese Cardinal, married 21 May 1867, Rosalie Sisawikaskwep, daughter of Sisawikaskwep and Wiyesikwepewisk, Present: Jean Baptiste Kakekamik and Isidore Decoine, V. Vegreville p.m.a.o.m.i. (page 80-81)

Nimihitowin, Julien and Alexis: B-396 and B-397, Julien and Alexis Nimihitowin, baptized 13 January 1867, age 15 months, infants of Nimihitowin and Okisikoawasis, Godmother: of Julien, Rosalie Kakekamik, and of Alexis, Philomene Cardinal, V. Vegreville, priest mis. o.m.i. (page 78)

Nipitcham, Julien: B-42, Julien Nipitcham, baptized 24 December 1877, age three months, legitimate son of Joseph Nipitcham and Therese, Godfather: Julien Cardinal, Godmother: Isabelle, wife of Paul Montagnais, E. Grouard priest o.m.i. (page 174)

Lac la Biche Baptisms, Marriages and Burials 1853-1884

Nipiteham, Caroline: B-2, Caroline Nipiteham, baptized 14 January 1872, age 8 days, legitimate daughter of Joseph Nipiteham and Therese, Godfather: Louison Cardinal, Godmother: Judith Desjarlais, Collignon o.m.i. (page 126)

Nipiteham, Florence: B-10, Florence Nipiteham, baptized 2 April 1875, age one month, son of Joseph Nipiteham and Therese, Godfather: Jerome Vilbrun, Godmother: Florence Hope, J. V. Fourmond priest o.m.i. (page 150)

Nipiteham, Joseph and Therese: M-4, Joseph Nipiteham married 3 April 1875 Therese, Present: Miyosipiw and Emma O'Piwas, J. V. Fourmond priest o.m.i. (page 150)

Nisowatsapiw, Emile: B-5, Emile Nisowatsapiw, baptized 22 January 1880, age about 4 months, son of Nisowatsapiw and Marguerite, Collignon o.m.i. (page 193)

Nisto, Joseph and Mathilde Tremblay: M-2, Joseph Nisto, adult son of Louison Nisto and Cecile Boucher, married 18 August 1874, Matilde Tremblay, adult daughter of Raphael Tremblay and Catherine McDougall, Present: Raphael Tremblay and Marcel Tremblay, V. Vegreville, p.m.a.o.m.i. (page 144_145)

Nisto, Olive (Nabisis): B-23, Olive Nabisis (Nisto), baptized 12 August 1875, legitimate daughter of Nabisis (Joseph Nisto) and Mathilde Tremblay, Godfather: Narcisse Boucher, Godmother: Sophie St.Sauveur, Alexis G. B. Brunet priest (page 154)

Nitanikamuw, Francis and Marguerite Desjarlais: M-2, Francois Nitanikamuw, adult son of Nitanikamuw and Angelique, married 22 April 1873, Marguerite Desjarlais, minor daughter of Francois Desjarlais and Euphrosine Oger, Present: Raphael Tremblay and Marcel Tremblay, V. Vegreville p.m.a.o.m.i. (page 137)

Nitzitsam, Pierre: B-27, Pierre Nitzitsam, baptized 10 July 1878, age about one year, son of Andre Nitzitsam and Marie Enazhune, no godfather, E. Grouard priest o.m.i. (page 181)

Niyanampekinam, Modeste: B-326, Modeste Niyanampekinam, baptized 10 November 1864, age about 25 years, Godmother: Marguerite Larocque, Tissot Jn. priest o.m.i. (page 62)

Niyanampekinam, Modeste; See Joseph Cardinal and Modeste Niyanampekinam

Niyanampekinam; See Joseph Cardinal and Niyanampekinam

Niyananyekapo, Rosalie: B-389, Rosalie Niyananyekapo, baptized 14 October 1866, age 3 months, daughter of Baptiste Niyananyekapo and Julie Kawapassamwipiw, Godmother: Julie Decoin, Maisonneuve A. priest o.m.i. (page 76)

Niyawakapaw, Marie; Ord. 1, Marie Niyawakapaw, christened 4 October 1866 at Fort Pitt, age about 6 years, legitimate daughter of Niyawakapaw and Nikoukapawiwisk, Godmother: Archange Kekik, V. Vegreville o.m.i. (page 77)

Niyawakapaw, Marie: S-34, Marie Niyawakapaw, buried 5 October 1866 at Fort Pitt, died yesterday, age about 6 years, daughter of Niyawakapaw and Nikoukapawiwisk, Witnesses: Louis Schmidt and Louis Viviers, V. Vegreville o.m.i. (page 77)

Nodlorelew, Leon: B-7, Leon Nodlorelew, baptized 16 April 1870, age 3 months, legitimate son of Louis Nodlorelew and Julie Bisson, Godfather: Fabien Bisson, Godmother: Marie Gladu, M. R. Remas priest o.m.i. (page 110)

Nolin, Melanie: B-181, Melanie Nollin, baptized 20 February 1859, born yesterday of the legitimate marriage of Johnny Nollin and Julie Lavallee, Godfather: Baptiste Lafarienere, Godmother: Ursule St.Germain, Tissot Jn priest o.m.i. (page 33)

Nolin, Rose: B-134, Rose Nollin, baptized 23 September 1857, born yesterday of the legitimate marriage of John Nollin and Julie Lavallee, Godfather: Louis Lavallee, Godmother: Marguerite Gervais, Tissot, Jn priest o.m.i. (page 26)

Norris, Elisa: B-221, Elisa Norris, baptized 22 February 1861, born yesterday, of the marriage of Johny Norris and Marie Katowe, Godfather: Alfred Smith, Godmother: Sophie Chatelain, Tissot Jn. priest o.m.i. (page 41)

Norris, Johny: B-163, Johny Norris, baptized 3 September 1858, age about 3 months, son of Johny Norris and Marie Katoes, Godmother: Genevieve Savoyard, Maisonneuve A. priest o.m.i. (page 30)

Norris, Marguerite: B-335, Marguerite Norris, baptized 20 January 1865, age 10 years, daughter of John Norris and Marie Katowe., Godmother: Genevieve Savoyard, Tissot Jn. priest o.m.i. (page 65)

Ntsatock, Rosalie; See Joseph Okistot and Rosalie Ntsatock

Nule, Simon: B-6, Simon Nule, montagnais, baptized 15 February 1880, age about one month, legitimate son of Alexandre Nule and Marie, Godfather: Charles, E. Grouard priest o.m.i. (page 194)

Okanes, Julienne: B-1, Julienne Okanes, baptized 31 January 1881, age 2 years, daughter of Saint Paul Okanes and Iskwesensis, Godfather: Alexandre Hamelin (signed), Godmother: Angelique Hoole wife of Hamelin, E. Grouard priest o.m.i. (page 202)

Okanes, Patrice: B-13, Patrice Okanes, baptized 16 May 1882, age about 3 months, legitimate son of Saint Paul Okanes and Iskwesis, Godmother: Louisa Hamelin (signed), E. Grouard priest o.m.i. (page 218)

Okanes, Pierrish: S-1, Pierrish Okanes, buried 19 February 1881, died 17 February 1881, age 16 years, son of Pierre Okanes and ___, Witnesses: Pierre Okanes and Johny Johnston, E. Grouard priest o.m.i. (page 203)

Okimawasis, Isabelle: S-1, Isabelle Okimawasis, buried 26 February 1872, died on the prairie, age about 18 or 20 years, Witnesses: Julien Cardinal and Jacques Piwitew, M. R. Remas priest o.m.i. (page 127)

Okimawaskanikinam, Marguerite; See Louis Batoche and Marie Okimawaskanikinam

Okimawawasis, Marie; See Pierre Quintal and Marie Okimawawasis

Okisto, Paul: B-7, Paul Okisto, baptized 8 April 1871, born 26 March 1871, illegitimate child of Marie Okisto, Godmother: Cecile Boucher, M. R. Remas priest (page 120)

Okistot, Joseph and Rosalie Ntsatock;M-68, Joseph Okistot, adult son of Okistot and Cecile Boucher, married 12 September 1868, Rosalie Ntsatock, minor daughter of Alexis Ntsatock and Louise Kiwekop, Present: Cecile Boucher and Louise Kiwekop, V. Vegreville, p.m.a.o.m.i. (page 94)

Okistut, Marie-Josephine: B-13, Marie-Josephine Okistut, baptized 14 April 1876, age 3 months, illegitimate daughter of Marie Okistut, Godmother: Marie Ladouceur, Husson p.o.m.i. (page 160)

Okkakew, Catherine: B-18, Catherine Okkakew, baptized 5 August 1870, born 3 August 1870, daughter of Jean-Baptiste Okkakew and Adelaide Yatuwatam, Godfather: Yatuwatam, Godmother: Kutshistam, M. R. Remas priest o.m.i. (page 113)

Okkakew, Jean Baptiste and Catherine Yatuwatam: M-7, Jean-Baptiste Okkakew married 5 August 1870 Catherine Yatuwatam, Witnesses: Yatuwatam and Kutshistam, father and mother of the bride, M. R. Remas priest o.m.i. (page 113)

Okkakew; Jean-Baptiste: B-17, Jean-Baptiste Okkakew, baptized 5 August 1870, age about 25 or 30 years, Godfather: Martin Canard, M. R. Remas priest o.m.i. (page 113)

Olivier, Dolphis-Augustin: B-3, Dolphis-Augustin Olivier, baptized 5 September 1853, age about one month, son of the legitimate marriage of Olivier and Louise Vallette, Godfather: Antoine Brazeau, Godmother: Nancisse Colin, M. R. Remas p.o.m.i. (page 2)

Onahouwatam, Silvie: B-53, Silvie Onahouwatam, baptized 24 December 1881, age about three months, of the legitimate marriage of William Onahouwatam and Betsy Quintal, Godmother: Silvie Quintal, J. M. A. Blanchet priest o.m.i. (page 213-214)

Onahuwatam, David: B-16, David Onahuwatam, baptized 19 July 1884, born yesterday of the marriage of Onahuwatam and Betsy Mustatip, Godmother: Scholastique Mustatip, Collignon o.m.i.p. (page 238)

Onahuwatam, Maria: B-8, Maria Onahuwatam, baptized 5 March 1882, age about 8 years, legitimate daughter of Onahuwatam and Betsy Quintal, Godfather: Guillaume Villebrun, Godmother: Silvie Quintal, Collignon o.m.i.p. (page 216)

Onahuwatam, Paul: B-24, Paul Onahuwatam, baptized 19 September 1870, age 20 years, Godfather: Paul Yatumwatam, M. R. Remas priest o.m.i. (page 114)

Onanhatam, Louis: B-19, Louis Onanhatam, baptized 5 August 1884, age 6 years, of the legitimate marriage of Onanhatam and Elisabeth Cardinal, A. Desmarais priest o.m.i. (page 239)

Opishin, Alexis: B-276, Alexis Opishin, baptized 5 April 1863, age 4 months, son of Opishin and Marie Sakatsiwes, Godmother: Rosalie Kakikekamik, Tissot Jn. priest o.m.i. (page 52)

Opistew, Joseph: B-354, Joseph Opistew, baptized 8 October 1865, born 6 October 1865, son of Opistew and Sakatsiwes, Godmother: Marguerite Larocque, Maisonneuve A. priest o.m.i. (page 68)

Lac la Biche Baptisms, Marriages and Burials 1853-1884

Opiway, Marguerite: B-201, Marguerite Opiway, baptized 19 December 1859, age over one month, daughter of Opiway and Angelique Cardinal, Godmother: Marguerite, Maisonneuve A. priest o.m.i. (page 37)

Osisis, Isabelle; See Francis Isidore Decoine and Isabelle Osisis

Osisis, Veronique: B-6, Veronique Osisis, baptized 8 April 1871, age 28 years, Godfather: __ Fosseneuve, Godmother: Jane Ladouceur, V. Vegreville p.m.a.o.m.i. (page 120)

Osisis, Veronique; See Joseph Ladouceur and Veronique Osisis

Oskijik, Thomas (Sauteuse) and Christine Kakikakamik: M-4, Thomas Oskijik (Sauteuse) married 1 August 1882 Christine Kakikakamik, Witnesses, brother Boisrame (signed F. Boisrqme), + Henri Eveque d'Anemour o.m.i. (page 220)

Otenaskamikapiw, Rose: B-12, Rose Otenaskamikapiw, baptized 14 April 1875, Godfather: Brother Gesante, Godmother: Sister St.Michel (signed), A. Brunet priest o.m.i. (page 151)

Otsebes, Noe and Angelique Derez: M-3, Noe Otsebes, legitimate son of the late Jean-Marie Nannetson, married 6 November 1873, Angelique Derez, minor daughter of Antoine Derez and Marie Aytize, Present: Gregoire Natsinildhien and Marguerite Intoreaze, E. Petitot priest o.m.i. (page 139)

Pakwatsawas, Joseph: B-351, Joseph Pakwatsawas, baptized 6 August 1865, age one year, son of Pakwatsawas and Angelique ..., Godmother: Genevieve Savoyard, V. Vegreville priest o.m.i. (page 68)

Pambrun, Alexandre: B-393, Alexandre Pambrun, baptized 25 November 1866, age 2 months, son of Pierre Chrysologue Pambrun and Bethsy Quintal, Godfather: Joseph Ladouceur, Godmother: Julie Auger, V. Vegreville, priest mis. o.m.i. (page 77)

Pambrun, Alexandre: S-40, Alexandre Pambrun, buried 30 March 1867, died yesterday, age 6 months, son of Pierre Chrysologue Pambrun and Bethsy Quintal, Present: Louis Dase and Louis Charland, V. Vegreville priest mis. o.m.i. (page 79)

Pambrun, Eleonore: B-30, Eleonore Pambrun, baptized 27 November 1870, age one month, natural child of Pierre Chrysologue Pambrun and Bethsy Quintal, Godfather: Isidore Pambrun (signed), Godmother: Sister Catherine Quinette (signed), V. Vegreville priest o.m.i. (page 116)

Pambrun, Francois: B-243, Francois Pambrin, baptized 10 November 1861, born 31 Octobert, illegitimate son of Peter Pambruin and Bethsy Quintal, Godfather: Francois Desjarlais, Godmother: Isabelle Quintal, Tissot Jn. priest o.m.i. (page 45)

Pambrun, Frederic: B-27, Frederic Pambrun, baptized 8 December 1872, age one month, son of Pierre Chrysologue Pambrun and Bethsy Quintal, Godfather: Guillaume Vilbrun, V. Vegreville priest omi. (page 133)

Pambrun, Henriette: B-444, Henriette Pambrun, baptized 9 August 1868, natural daughter of Pierre Chrysologue Pambrun and Bethsy Quintal, Godfather: Michel Sisawapas, Godmother: Judith Desjarlais, V. Vegreville, p.m.a.o.m.i. (page 94)

Lac la Biche Baptisms, Marriages and Burials 1853-1884

Pambrun, Isidore and Isabelle Dufresne: M-7, Isidore Pambrun married 13 June 1875 Isabelle Dufresne, Present: Johnny Pambrun and James Pruden, M. R. Remas priest om.i. (page 153)

Pambrun, John: B-107, Jean [John Pambrun] Quintal, baptized 9 November 1856, age 9 days, illegitimate son of Bethsy Quintal, Godfather: Joseph Pepamowew, Godmother: Josephte Cardinal, Tissot Jn. priest o.m.i. (page 20)

Pambrun, Magdeleine: B-18, Magdeleine Pambrun, baptized 3 May 1876, age 2 days, legitimate daughter of Isidore Pambrun and Isabelle Dufresne, Godfather: Johnny Pambrun, Husson p.o.m.i. (page 161)

Pambrun, Marie: B-195, Marie Pambrun, baptized 28 August 1859, illegitimate daughter of Peter Pambrun and Bethsy Quintal, Godmother: Nancy Quintal, Tissot Jn. priest o.m.i. (page 35)

Pambrun, Pierre: B-294, Pierre Pambrin, baptized 20 December 1863, born 12 December 1863, son of Peter Pambrin and Bethsy Quintal, Godfather: Pierre Quintal, Godmother: Bethsy Cardinal, Tissot Jn. priest o.m.i. (page 55)

Pambrun, Pierre Chrysologue and Elisabeth Quintal: M-3, Pierre Chrysologue Pambrun (signed) married 10 March 1871 Elisabeth Quintal (x), Witnesses: Reverend Father Remas (signed) and Clement Cullen (signed), M. R. Remas priest (page 119)

Papamatsimuw, Joseph: B-36, Joseph Papamatsimuw, baptized 18 September 1869, age one month, son of an unknown father and Papamatsimuw, Godfather: Narcisse Morin, Godmother: Marie Lalibierte, V. Vegreville p.m.a.o.m.i. (page 107)

Paquette, Antoine: B-100, Antoine Paquette, baptized 6 September 1856, born 2 January 1856, legitimate son of Henri Paquette and Cecile Durand, Godfather: Antoine Goin, Godmother: Francoise Boucher, Maisonneuve A. priest o.m.i. (page 19)

Paquette, Joseph and Magdeleine Desrocher: M-40, Joseph Paquette son of Jean Paquette and Ursule Premont of the St.Roch, Quebec parish, married 20 September 1864, Magdeleine Desrocher, minor daughter of Philippe Desrocher and Catherine Parant, Present: Louis Chatelain and Olivier Bellerose, Maisonneuve A. priest o.m.i. (page 60)

Paquette, Joseph: B-160, Joseph Paquette, baptized 3 September 1858, born 18 July 1858, of the legitimate marriage of Henri Paquette and Cecile Durand, Godfather: Joseph Roy, Godmother: Marguerite Haineau, Maisonneuve A. priest o.m.i. (page 30)

Paquette, Louis: B-81, Louis Paquette, baptized 31 August 1855, age 22 months, legitimate son of Henri Paquette and Cecile Decoine at Fort Carlton, Maissoneuve A. priest o.m.i. (page 15)

Paquette, Norbert: B-34, Norbert Paquette, baptized 18 September 1869, born yesterday, legitimate son of Joseph Paquette and Magdeleine Brillant (Desrochers), Godmother: Marie Laliberte, V. Vegreville p.m.a.o.m.i. (page 107)

Paskawakaw, Angelique: B-51, Angelique Paskawakaw, baptized 1 September 1854 at Fort Pitt, age about one year, of Paskawakaw and Kamesitetawat, Godfather: George Adsthon (Hudson), M. R. Remas p.o.m.i. (page 9)

Paskawakaw, Julie: B-49, Julie Paskawakaw, baptized 1 September 1854 at Fort Pitt, age 5 months (years), of Paskawakaw and Kamesitetawat, Godfather: George Hudson, M. R. Remas p.o.m.i. (page 9)

Paskawakaw, Marie: B-50, Marie Paskawakaw, baptized 1 September 1854 at Fort Pitt, age 2 years, of Paskawakaw and Kamesitetawat, Godfather: George Adsthon (Hudson), M. R. Remas p.o.m.i. (page 9)

Passam, Bethsy: B-296, Bethsy Passam, baptized 17 January 1864, born 10 January 1864, daughter of Michel Passam and Elise McGillis, Godfather: Joseph Natakam, Godmother: Angelique Desjarlais, Tissot Jn. priest o.m.i. (page 56)

Passam, Bethsy: S-24, Bethsy Passam, buried 28 February 1865, died 5 days, age one year and 5 days, Present: Pierre Nekateki and Cyrille Lafont, Maisonneuve A. Priest o.m.i. (page 64)

Passam, Daniel: B-248, Daniel Passam, baptized 19 January 1862, born 17 January 1862, son of Michel Passam and Elisa McGillis, Godfather: Adam Sisawapas, Godmother: Silvie Bruneau, Tissot Jn. priest o.m.i. (page 47)

Passam, Daniel: S-16, Daniel Passam, buried 11 March 1863, died in the evening, age about one year, Present: Charles Houle and Paul Desjarlais, Tissot Jn. priest o.m.i. (page 51-52)

Pastew, Maria-Julia: B-12, Maria-Julia Pastew, baptized 9 April 1876, age about one year, daughter of an infidel Pastew and an infidel Gladu, Godmother: Julia Rivet, Husson p.o.m.i. (page 160)

Pastew, Philomene-Augustine: B-11, Philomene-Augustine Pastew, baptized 9 April 1876, age 3 years, daughter of an infidel Pastew and an infidel Gladu, Godmother: Philomene Gendron, Husson p.o.m.i. (page 159-160)

Pastew, Rosalie: B-12, Rosalie Pastew, baptized 14 March 1880, age about 14 months, daughter of Alexandre Pastew and Sale Houle, Godmother: Catherine Matsimuttaw, Collignon o.m.i. priest. (page 195)

Patrice, Angele: B-20, Angele Patrice, baptized 30 August 1874, legitimate daughter of Patrice and Marie, Godmother: Elisa, Godfather: Alphonse Pradier, X. G. Ducot o.m.i. (page 146)

Pattenode, Maria: B-27, Maria Pattenode, baptized 16 July 1876, age 6 months, legitimate daughter of Benjamin Pattenode and Marguerite Donald, Godmother: Maria Pambrun, E. Petitot priest o.m.i. (page 163)

Paydeze, Marie: B-74, Marie Paydeze, baptized 16 July 1855, age about 23 years, daughter of Iza Kaple and Marcelline Beroyini, Godmother: Elisabeth Tsaither, Tissot Jn. priest o.m.i. (page 13)

Paydeze, Marie; See Antoine Deprez and Marie Paydeze

Pelletier, Cuthbert: B-314, Cuthbert Pelletier, baptized 20 September 1865, age over 2 months, son of Baptiste Pelletier and Madeleine Deschamps, Godfather: Norbert Morissett, Godmother: Marie Kayatowe, Masisonneuve A. priest o.m.i. (page 59)

Pelletier, Helene: B-233, Helene Pelletier, baptized 16 September 1861, born 6 May 1861, of the legitimate marriage of Baptiste Pelletier and Magdeleine Deschamps, Godfather: Charles Houle, Godmother: Henriette Cayen, Maisonneuve A. priest o.m.i. (page 44)

Pelletier, Louis: B-98, Louis Pelletier, baptized 6 September 1856, born 20 December 1855, of the legitimate marriage of Baptiste Pelletier and Madeleine Deschamps, Godmother: Genevieve Savoyard, Maisonneuve A. priest o.m.i. (page 18-19)

Pelletier, Marie: B-162, Marie Pelletier, baptized 3 September 1858, born 1 February 1858, of the legitimate marriage of Baptiste Pelletier and Magdeleine Deschamps, Godfather: Francois Lafrynier, Godmother: Sophie Chatlain, Maisonneuve A. priest o.m.i. (page 30)

Pepamhapiw, Hizabel: B-40, Hizabel Pepamhapiw, baptized 26 May 1854, age 7 years, daughter of Pepamhapiw and Kiyakis, Godmother: Eljenie Ladouceur, M. R. Remas p.o.m.i. (page 7)

Pepamikapo, Marie: B-323, Marie Pepamikapo, baptized 23 October 1864, age about 18 months, daughter of Pepamikapo and Julie Gladu dit Janvier, Godfather: Baptiste Kakikekamik, Maisonneuve A. priest o.m.i. (page 61)

Pepamowew, Eugenie: B-207, Eugenie Papamowew, baptized 28 May 1860, age about 3 years, daughter of Jean-Baptiste Pepamowew and Marguerite Janvier, Godmother: Cecile Labonne, Tissot Jn priest o.m.i. (page 38)

Pepamowew, Eugenie: S-25, Eugenie Pepamowew, buried 7 March 1865, died 26 February 1865, age about 8 years, Present: Pierre Nakateki and Paulette Auger, Maisonneuve A. Priest o.m.i. (page 64)

Pepamowew, Felix: B-97, Felix Papamowew, baptized 1 September 1856, born 9 August 1856, of the legitimate marriage of Joseph Pepamowew and Susanne Desjarlais, Godmother: Julie Auge, Tissot Jn priest o.m.i. (page 18)

Petikuwiynis, Agnes: B-17, Agnes Petikuwiynis, baptized 14 June 1882, age about one month, daughter of Petikuwiynis and Liza Auger, Godmother: Catherine L'Esperance (signed Catherine), Collignon o.m.i.p. (page 219)

Petit-Castor, Sophie: S-1, Sophie Petit-Castor, buried 13 January 1875, age about 2 years, daughter of Baptiste Petit-Castor and Nancy Cardinal, J. V. Fourmond priest o.m.i. (page 148)

Petwewitam, Baptiste: S-2, Baptiste Petwewitam, buried 20 November 1876, age about 70 years, Witnesses: brother Lorfeuvre, brother Milsons, Collignon o.m.i. (page 164)

Petwiwitam, Baptiste and Rosalie Wiskipapamuttew: M-3, Baptiste Petwiwitam, married 22 July 1876, Rosalie Wiskipapamuttew, Present: Paul Cardinal and Sister Youville (signed), M. R. Remas priest o.m.i. (page 162)

Petwiwitam, Baptiste: B-22, Baptiste Petwiwitam, baptized 22 July 1876, age about 72 years, Godfather: Paul Cardinal, Godmother: Sister Youville (signed Sr. Youville Sr. de. la B., Mr. R. Remas, priest o.m.i. (page 162)

Piche, Anne: B-27, Anne Piche, baptized 12 October 1882, age about 9 months, legitimate daughter of Francois Piche and ___, Godmother: Marie, wife of Antoine, E. Grouard priest o.m.i. (page 221-222)

Piche, Augustin: S-10, Augustin Piche, buried 6 August 1859, died about 4 days, age about 30 yeares, Present: Baptiste Lafreniere and Louis Leveille, Tissot Jn. priest o.m.i. (page 34)

Piche, Lisette Piyetta: B-116, Lisette Piyetta (Piche), baptized 19 January 1857, age 4 months, daughter of Piyetta and Lalouise Cardinal, Godmother: Marguerite Piyetta, Maisonneuve A. priest o.m.i. (page 22)

Piche, Marie: B-184, Marie Piche, baptized 27 March 1859, age 7 months, daughter of Augustin Piche and Clodilther, Godfather: Baptiste Pelletier, Godmother: Magdeleine Deschamps, Tissot Jn priest o.m.i. (page 33)

Piche, Marie; See Andre Ek'elthene and Marie Piche

Piche, William: B-17, William Piche, baptized 4 June 1877, age about 4 months, legitimate son of Francois Piche and Marie, Godfather: Alick, Godmother: Marguerite, E. Grouard priest o.m.i. (page 169)

Pichon, Abraham: B-30, Abraham Pichon, baptized 8 July 1881, age about 5 months, legitimate son of Paul Pichon and Sophie Grosse-Tete, Godfather: Antoine Pichon, E. Grouard priest o.m.i. (page 207-208)

Picimakawikuniat, Joseph: B-176, Joseph Picimakawikuniatm bt, 18 December 1858, born 1 January 1858, son of Pierre Picimakawikuniat and Marie Mustuskpeyakut, Godmother: Marguerite Mustuskpeyakut, Maisonneuve A. priest o.m.i. (page 32)

Pikkayinis, Augustin: B-15, Augustin Pikkaynis, baptized 13 July 1884, age 15 days, of the legitimate marriage of Pikkayinis and Liza Auger, Godfather: Olivier Cayatius, Godmother: Adelaide Pikkayinis, A. Desmarais priest o.m.i. (page 237-238)

Pinakay, Jean Baptiste: B-218,. Jean Baptiste Pinakay, baptized 4 January 1861, age nine months, son of Pinakay and Angelique Batauche, Godfather: Baptiste Kakikekamik, Godmother: Marie Batauche, Maisonneuve A. priest o.m.i. (page 41)

Pinakay, Joseph and Angelique Batoche: M-42, Joseph Pinakay married 30 October 1864, Angelique Batoche, Present: Eugene Wawiyamam and Moise Larocque, Tissot Jn. priest o.m.i. (page 61)

Pinakay, Joseph: B-322, Joseph Pinakay, baptized 30 October 1864, age about 30 years, Godfather: Eugene Wawiyenam, Tissot Jn. priest o.m.i. (page 61)

Pinakay, Paul and Angelique Batoche: M-28, Paul Pinakay married 22 June 1861 Angelique Batoche, Witnesses: Jacob and Louis Batoche, Tissot Jn. priest o.m.i. (page 46)

Pinakay, Sophie: B-78, Sophie Pinakay, baptized 12 October 1855, age 4 months, daughter of Pinakay and Cecile Batoche, Godmother: Rosalie Batoche, Tissot Jn. priest o.m.i. (page 14)

Lac la Biche Baptisms, Marriages and Burials 1853-1884

Piochon, Hyacinthe: B-15, Hyacinthe Pioch0n, baptized 6 April 1880, born 4 April 1880, of the legitimate marriage of Paul Piochon and Marguerite Fosseneuve, Godfather: Louison Fosseneuve, Godmother: Therese Ladouceur, Collignon o.m.i. priest. (page 195-196)

Piochon, Hyacinthe: S-2, Hyacinthe Piochon, buried 13 April 1880, died yesterday, age 13 days, Witnesses: Louison Fosseneuve and Petit Castor, Collignon o.m.i. priest. (page 196)

Pipamikapiw, Anacelt: B-11, Anaclet Pipamikapiw, baptized 13 July 1871, age 2 months, legitimate child of Jean Pipamikapiw and Charlotte Gladu, Godmother: Sophie Kakikamik, + Henri Ev. D'Anomour o.m.i. (page 121)

Pitikiwinis, Magloire: B-23, Magloire Pitikiwinis, baptized 16 July 1877, age 8 days, of the legitimate marriage of Pitikiwinis and Elisa Auger, Godfather: Charles Johnson Jr., Godmother: wife of Augustin Auger, F. LeSerrec priest o.m.i. (page 171)

Pitikuwinis, Louis: B-9, Louis Pitikuwinis, baptized 29 February 1880, age about 4 months, son of Pitikuwinis and Liza Auger, Godmother: Marie Auger, Collignon o.m.i. (page 194)

Piwapiskapaw, Marie; See Gabriel Cardinal and Marie Piwapiskapaw

Piwastimow, Emma; See Miyosipisiw and Emma Piwastimow

Piwitew, Jamy: B-5, Jamy Piwitew, baptized 7 April 1870, legitimate son of Jacques Piwitew and Catherine Cardinal, Godfather: Charles Cardinal, Godmother: Christine Viviers, M. R. Remas priest o.m.i. (page 110)

Piwitew, Jamy: S-2, Jamy Piwitew, buried 8 February 1877, age about 7 years, Present: the mother and the sister of the infant, H. Leduc priest o.m.i. (page 167)

Piyeseskaw, Catherine: B-7, Catherine Piyeseskaw, baptized 19 February 1881, age about 6 weeks, daughter of Piyeseskaw and Therese Memesis, the priest served as godfather, Collignon o.m.i. p. (page 203)

Piyeseskaw, Felix: B-5, Felix Piyeseskaw, baptized 19 February 1881, age about 6 years, son of Piyeseskaw and Therese Memesis, the priest served as godfather, Collignon o.m.i. p. (page 203)

Piyeseskaw, Isabelle: B-6, Isabelle Piyeseskaw, baptized 19 February 1881, age about 3 years, daughter of Piyeseskaw and Therese Memesis, the priest served as godfather, Collignon o.m.i. p. (page 203)

Piyesiwikimaw, Emelie: B-40, Emelie Piyesiwikimaw, baptized 29 September 1869, age 16 years, daughter of Piyesiwikimaw and Habasiw, Godfather: Julien Genereux, Godmother: Marie Tastawits, V. Vegreville p.m.a.o.m.i. (page 108)

Pokakew, Jean-Baptiste: S-3, Jean-Baptiste Pokakew, buried 23 February 1881, died a few days ago, age about 45 years, Witnesses: Johny Johnston and Thomas, E. Grouard priest o.m.i. (page 204)

Pokakew, William: B-8, William Pokakew, baptized 19 February 1881, age about 4 months, son of Pokokew and Iskwesis, the priest served as godfather, Collignon o.m.i. p. (page 203-204)

Pokakew, William: S-2, William Pokakew, buried 2 March 1882, age about one years, Witnesses: Alexandre Hamelin and Andre Fortier, Collignon o.m.i.p. (page 216)

Pruden, Alexandre: B-3, Alexandre Pruden, baptized 14 January 1872, age 8 days, legitimate son of Patrick Pruden and Elisabeth Bruneau, Godfather: James Tag, Godmother: Emelie Bruneau, V. Vegreville p.o.m.i. (page 126)

Pruden, Charlie: B-54, Charlie Prudent, baptized 25 December 1881, age about 3 months, legitimate son of Patrick Prudent and Isabelle Bruneau, Godfather: Alex Johnston, Godmother: Louisa Hamelin, Collignon o.m.i.p. (page 214)

Pruden, Charlotte: B-2, Charlotte Pruden, baptized 9 January 1870, age 4 days, legitimate daughter of Patrick Pruden and Isabelle Bruneau, Godfather: Agapit Ladouceur, Godmother: Marie Ducharme, V. Vegreville p.m.a.o.m.i. (page 109)

Pruden, Charlotte: B-23, Charlotte Pruden, baptized 24 December 1874, age about 80 yearse, Godmother: Sister Youville, H. Leduc priest o.m.i. (page 147)

Pruden, Elisa: B-334, Elisa Pruden, baptized 16 January 1865, born 26 December 1864, daughter of Cornelius Pruden and Jane Rollen, Godfather: Louis Chatelain, Godmother: Genevieve Savoyard, + Alex Tache Eveque. (page 64)

Pruden, Frederic: B-12, Frederic Pruden, baptized 27 July 1874, born yesterday, legitimate son of Patrick Pruden and Isabelle Bruneau, Godfather: Francois Kakikekamik, Godmother: Elisa Ladouceur, V. Vegreville p.m.a.o.m.i. (page 144)

Pruden, Henry and Marie Landry: M-6, Henry Pruden (signed), married 1 August 1869, Marie Landry, Present: Patrick Pruden (signed) and Peter Pruden (signed), M. R. Remas priest o.m.i. (page 103_104)

Pruden, Henry: B-410, Henry Pruden, baptized 14 July 1867, born day before yesterday, legitimate son of Patrick Pruden and Isabelle Bruneau, Godfather: Augustin Auger, Godmother: Silvy Bruneau, V. Vegreville, p.m.a.o.m.i. (page 83)

Pruden, James Edward: B-3, James Edward Pruden, baptized 6 February 1881, born 12 days, legitimate son of Charles Pruden and Rosalie Vandale, Godfather: James Pruden, Godmother: his wife, Collignon o.m.i.p. (page 202-203)

Pruden, Jeanne: B-52, Jeanne Prudent, baptized 23 November 1881, age about two months, legitimate daughter of James Prudent and Genevieve Desjarlais, no godparents, Collignon o.m.i.p. (page 213)

Pruden, John: B-14, John Prudent, baptized 12 June 1883, age about 10 days, illegitimate son of Rose James Pruden, [no godparents], Collignon o.m.i.p. (page 227)

Pruden, John: B-17, John Pruden, baptized 26 July 1869, born 17 September 1868, son of Henry Pruden and Marie Landry, Godmother: Marie Ducharme, M. R. Remas priest o.m.i. (page 102)

Pruden, Louis: B-16, Louis Pruden, baptized 15 June 1879, age 4 days, legitimate son of Patrick Pruden and Isabelle Bruneau, Godfather: Louis Hamelin, Godmother: Marie McGillis, E. Grouard priest o.m.i. (page 188)

Pruden, Marie-Jeanne; See Samuel Whiteford and Marie-Jeanne Pruden

Pruden, Marie-Louise: B-3, Marie-Louise Pruden, baptized 10 January 1877, born of the legitimate marriage of Patrick Pruden and Isabelle Montagnais, Godfather: Pierre Auger, Godmother: Julia Rivet, F. Le Serrec priest o.m.i. (page 166)

Pruden, Mary Jane: B-352, Mary Jane Pruden, baptized 18 August 1865, born 16 August 1865, of the legitimate marriage of Patrick Pruden and Isabelle Bruneau, Godfather: Georges Bourque, Godmother: Esther Bruneau, V. Vegreville priest o.m.i. (page 68)

Pruden, Patrick and Isabelle Bruneau: M-44, Patrick Pruden (signed) married 5 November 1864 Isabelle Bruneau, Present: Joachim Bruneau and Monsigneur Tache (signed + Alex. Eveque de St.Boniface O.M.I., Tissot Jn. priest o.m.i. (page 62)

Pyezkalla, Joseph: B-434, Joseph Pyezkalla, baptized 6 June 1868, age over 13 months, legitimate son of Andre Pyezkalla and Charlotte Tsayus, Godfather: Francois Bisson, Godmother: Kay Deze, V. Vegreville p.m.a.o.m.i. (page 91)

Quintal, Alexandre: B-25, Alexandre Quintal, baptized 10 October 1872, age 6 days, son of Charles Quintal and Euphrosine, Godfather: Narcisse Ladouceur, Godmother: Pelagie Samaskekapiw, V. Vegreville, p.m.a.o.m.i. (page 132)

Quintal, Andre: B-369, Andre Quintal, baptized 10 January 1866, born 1 Jan1866, legitimate son of Saint Pierre Quintal and Marie, Godfather: Joseph Ladouceur, Godmother: Isabelle Quintal, V. Vegreville priest o.m.i. (page 72)

Quintal, Andre: B-18, Andre Quintal, baptized 25 July 1869, born today, legitimate son of Charles Quintal and Euphrosine Cardinal, Godfather: Joseph Duquet, Godmother: Philomene Cardinal, M. R. Remas, priest o.m.i. (page 102)

Quintal, Charles and Euphrosine Cardinal: M-14, Charles Quintal married 12 December 1856 Euphrosine Cardinal, Present: Abraham Lariviere and Jean Marie Auger, Tissot Jn priest o.m.i. (page 21)

Quintal, Charles: B-219, Charles Quintal, baptized 24 February 1861, b. 2 Feb, of the legitimate marriage of Charles Quintal and Froisine Cardinal, Godfather: Georges Bourk, Godmother, Marguerite Fraser, Maisonneuve A. priest o.m.i. (page 41)

Quintal, Edouard: B-13, Edouard Quintal, baptized 20 March 1881, age 3 days, legitimate son of Etienne Quintal and Marie ____, Godfather: Jules Desjarlais, Godmother: Marie wife of St.Pierre Quintal, E. Grouard priest o.m.i. (page 204)

Quintal, Elisabeth; See Pierre Chrysologue Pambrun and Elisabeth Quintal

Quintal, Emma: B-16, Emma Quintal, baptized 18 July 1878, born 10 days, of the legitimate marriage of Etienne Quintal and Marie, Godfather: Guillaume Villebrun, Godmother: Mathilde Collin, Collignon o.m.i. (page 179)

Quintal, Etienne and Marie Cardinal: M-67, Etienne Quintal, minor son of the late Quintal and the late Charlotte Ladouceur, m. 17 September 1868, Marie Cardinal, minor d/o Pierre Cardinal and Angelique Apistiskwesis, Present: Joseph Duquette and Nancy Quintal, V. Vegreville p.m.a.o.m.i. (page 94)

Quintal, Isabelle; See Johny Johnson and Isabelle Quintal

Quintal, Jean Baptiste: S-1, Jean-Baptiste Quintal, buried last July 1854, age about 10 years, Present: Joseph Ladouceur and James Hope, M. R. Remas p.o.m.i. (page 11)

Quintal, Julie: B-19, Julie Quintal, baptized 7 August 1870, born 5 August 1870, of the legitimate marriage of Etienne Quintal and Marie Cardinal, Godmother: Betsay Cardinal, M. R. Remas priest o.m.i. (page 113-114)

Quintal, Justine: B-18, Justine Quintal, baptized 14 June 1871, age 5 days, legitimate daughter of Pierre Quintal and Marie, Godmother: Francoise Hope, V. Vegreville priest o.m.i. (page 122)

Quintal, Lalouise: B-16, Lalouise Quintal, baptized 27 March 1881, born yesterday, legitimate daughter of St.Pierre Quintal and Marie, Godfather: Nefriteham, Godmother: Therese, Collignon o.m.i. p. (page 205)

Quintal, LaLouise: S-7, LaLouise Quintal, buried 5 August 1882, age about one year, Witness: R. P. Collignon o.m.i.p. (signed), + Henri Eveque d'Anemour o.m.i. (page 220)

Quintal, Madeleine: B-15, Madeleine Quintal, baptized 27 July 1873, age about 11 days, legitimate son of Etienne Quintal and Marie Cardinal, Godfather: Guillaume Cardinal, Godmother: Nancy Quintal, M. R. Remas priest o.m.i. (page 138)

Quintal, Marie: B-145, Marie Quintal, baptized 27 December 1857, age 12 days, legitimate daughter of Charles Quintal and Euphrosine Cardinal, Godmother: Isabelle Quintal, Tissot Jn. priest o.m.i. (page 27)

Quintal, Marie Caroline: B-3, Marie Caroline Cardinal (Quintal), baptized 24 January 1875, legitimate daughter of Etienne Cardinal (Quintal) and Marie St.Pierre, Godfather: Isidore Lecomte, Godmother:; Julie Decoin, J. V. Fourmond priest o.m.i. (page 148)

Quintal, Marie-Jany: B-16, Marie-Jany Quintal, baptized 23 August 1874, age 8 days, legitimate daughter of Pierre Quintal and Marie Gladu, Godfather: Georges Bourque, Godmother: Agathe Ladouceur, Alb. Pascal priest o.m.i. (page 145)

Quintal, Michel Jules: B-34, Michel Jules Quintal, baptized 20 December 1879, age 10 days, legitimate son of Jules Quintal and ____, Godfather: Ayayasiw Joseph, Godmother: Nokwestakay, E. Grouard priest o.m.i. (page 192)

Quintal, Nancy; See Jean Baptiste Amiskuiynisis and Nancy Quintal

Lac la Biche Baptisms, Marriages and Burials 1853-1884

Quintal, Oliver: B-6, Olivier Quintal, baptized 10 March 1878, age about 5 days, legitimate son of Pierre Quintal and Marie Gladu, Godfather: Jean-Baptiste Bellecourt, Godmother: Isabelle, Collignon o.m.i. (page 176)

Quintal, Philomene: B-380, Philomene Quintal, baptized 17 July 1866, age 12 days, legitimate child of Charles Quintal and Euphrosine Cardinal, Godmother: Sophie Ladouceur, Maisonneuve priest mis. o.m.i. (page 74)

Quintal, Philomene: S-51, Philomene Quintal, buried 20 June 1868, died yesterday, daughter of Charles Quintal and Euphrosine Cardinal, Witnesses: Charles Quintal and Joseph Duquette, V. Vegreville p.m.a.o.m.i. (page 92)

Quintal, Pierre and Marie Okimawawasis: M-36, Pierre Quintal married 17 October 1863 Marie Okimawawasis dit Gilet, Present: Augustin Auger and Charles Quintal, Tissot Jn. priest o.m.i. (page 54)

Quintal, Pierre: B-312, Pierre Quintal, baptized 14 August 1864, born 12 August 1864, of the legitimate marriage of Pierre Quintal and Marie Okimaunasis, Godmother: Nannecy Quintal, Tissot Jn. priest o.m.i. (page 58-59)

Quintal, Pierre: S-22, Pierre Quintal, buried 1 September 1864, died in the evening, Present: Charles Quintal and Joseph Courte-oreille, Tissot Jn. priest o.m.i. (page 59)

Quintal, Silvie: B-287, Silvie Quintal, baptized 30 July 1863, born 27 July 1863, daughter of Charles Quintal and Euphrosine Cardina, Godmother: Silvie Bruneau, Tissot Jr., priest o.m.i. (page 53_54)

Quintal, Theophile: B-2, Theophile Quintal, baptized 8 March 1884, age 18 days, legitimate son of Etienne Quintal and Marie St.Pierre Mustatip, Godfather: Theophile Boucher, Godmother: Maria Joseph Mustatip, Collignon o.m.i.p. (page 235)

Quintal, Vital: B-431, Vital Quintal, baptized 30 May 1868, age 8 days, legitimate son of Pierre Quintal and Marie, Godmother: Nancy Quintal, V. Vegreville p.m.a.o.m.i. (page 90)

Rassette, Elise: B-197, Elise Rassette, baptized 12 September 1859, born 4 September 1859, daughter of Charles Rassette and Wihipit Crise, Godfather: Francois Deschamp, Godmother: Henriette Cayen, Maisonneuve A. priest o.m.i. (page 36)

Rassette, Isabelle: B-135, Isabelle Rassette, baptized 24 September 1857, age 5 days, daughter of Joseph Rassette and Mikukakakiwapi, Godfather: Louis Leveille, Tissot, Jn priest o.m.i. (page 26)

Rassette, Marguerite: B-83, Marguerite Rassette, baptized 12 September 1855, age 3 months, natural child of Joseph Rassette and Mikukokakinmpi, infidel crise, Maisonneuve priest o.m.i. (page 15)

Rassette, Marguerite; C.B., Marguerite Rassette, baptized 29 July 1856, daughter of Joseph Rassette and Mikukakokiwapi, Godmother: Abraham Lariviere, Godmother: Marie, Tissot Jn. priest o.m.i. (page 18)

Reed, William James: B-365, William James Reed, baptized 2 November 1865, born day before yesterday, legitimate son of William Reed and Mary Mordoux, Godfather: Johny Rowland, Godmother: Sophie Chatelain, V. Vegreville priest o.m.i. (page 71)

Lac la Biche Baptisms, Marriages and Burials 1853-1884

Reid, George: B-18, George Reid, baptized 24 April 1880, age about 15 days, legitimate son of William Reid and Mary Setter, Godfather: Nazaire Martel, Godmother: Celina Tremblay wife of Martel, E. Grouard priest o.m.i.. (page 196)

Reid, George: S-3, George Reid, buried 26 May 1880 at the mission, age 2 [sic] days [and one month], Witnesses: Nazaire Martel (signed N. Martel) and Benjamin Bellecourt (signed B. Bellecour), Collignon o.m.i. priest. (page 197)

Reynard, Alexis: S-6, Alexis Reynard, buried 5 September 1875, died July last, Witnesses: Reverend Fathers Leduc (signed) and Huson (signed), + Henri T. Ev. D'Anemour o.m.i. (page 155)

Riguidel, Louis and Rosalie Temblay: M-1, Louis Riguidel married 10 January 1881 Rosalie Tremblay, Present: Louis Lavallee (x), Collignon o.m.i.p. (page 202)

Rivet, Julia; See Pierre Auger and Julia Rivet

Robillard, Catherine: See John Simpson and Catherine Robillard

Rowland, Albert John Louis: B-136, Albert John Louis Rollen (Rowland), baptized 4 October 1857, son of John Rollen (Rowland) and Sophie Chastelain, Godmother: Genevieve Savoyard, Tissot, Jn priest o.m.i. (page 26)

Rowland, Flora: B-196, Flora Rolland, baptized 12 September 1859, born 1 July 1859, daughter of Johny Rolland and Sophie Chatelain, Godfather: Charles Houle, Godmother: Genevieve Savoyard, Maisonneuve A. priest o.m.i. (page 36)

Rowland, Isabelle: B-237, Isabelle Rolland, baptized 16 September 1861, born 1 May 1861, of the legitimate marriage of Johny Rolland and Sophie Chatelain, Godmother: Marie Bellanger, Tissot Jn. priest o.m.i. (page 44)

Rowland, James Samuel: B-348, James Samuel Rowland, baptized 2 August 1865 at Fort Pitt, legitimate son of John Rowland and Sophie Chatelain, Godfather: William McGillis, Godmother: Marie Campbell, V. Vegreville priest o.m.i. (page 67)

Rowland ,John and Sophie Chatelain: M-10, John Rowland, adult son of William Rowland and Elisabeth Ballington, married 25 July 1855, Sophie Chatlain, minor daughter of Louis Chatelain and Genevieve Savoyard, Present: Louis Chatelain, father of the bride, William Rowland, brother, and Antoine Goin, Maisonneuve A. priest o.m.i. (page 15)

Rowland, Mary: B-367, Mary Rowland, baptized 22 November 1865, born day before yesterday, legitimate daughter of William Rowland and Helene Beauregard, Godfather: Henry Leblanc, Godmother: Rosille Beauregard, V. Vegreville priest o.m.i. (page 71)

Roy, Louis: B-224, Louis Roy, baptized 25 March 1861, born today of the legitimate marriage of Joseph Roy and Henriette Montagnaise, Godfather: Louis Chatelain, Godmother: Sophie Chatelain, Tissot Jn. priest o.m.i. (page 42)

Lac la Biche Baptisms, Marriages and Burials 1853-1884

Roy, Marie: B-153, Marie Roy, baptized 10 May 1858, born today, of the legitimate marriage of Joseph Roy and Henriette Mantagnaise, Godfather: John Nollin, Godmother: Julie Auger, Tissot Jn priest o.m.i. (page 29)

Sacob, Jeanne: B-122, Jeanne Sacob, baptized 20 April 1857, age 3 months, daughter of Pierre Sacob and Agnes Batoche, Godfather: William McGillis, Godmother: Marie Cambel, Tissot Jn. priest o.m.i. (page 23)

Sacop, Marie: B-79, Marie Sacop, baptized 18 October 1855, age over 5 months, daughter of Pierre Sacop and Agnes Batoche, Godfather: Abraham Lariviere, Godmother: Marie, Tissot Jn. o.m.i. (page 14)

Sakutohin, Dominic: B-6, Dominic Sakutohin, baptized 8 March 1869, age 35 years, Godfather: Dominic Cardinal, + Vital J Ev. De Satala o.m.i. (page 99)

Samaskekabo, Pelagie: B-260, Pelagie Samaskekabo, baptized 19 June 1862, age about 30 years, Godmother: Josephte Desjarlais, Tissot Jn. priest o.m.i. (page 49)

Samaskekabo, Pelagie; See Jacques Cardinal and Pelagie Samaskekabo

Sandy, Alix: B-38, Alix Sandy, baptized 24 August 1881, age about one month, daughter of Sandy and Isabelle, Godmother: Anna Hamelin (signed), E. Grouard p.o.m.i. (page 209)

Sandy, Marguerite: B-24, Marguerite Sandy, baptized 25 December 1873, age 8 days, legitimate daughter of Sandy and Isabelle Iyatuwatam, Godmother: Marguerite Desjarlais, wife of Castor, E. Petitot priest o.m.i. (page 140)

Sapokisikwepiw, Marguerite: B-31, Marguerite Sapokisikwepiw, baptized 23 December 1872, age 4 days, legitimate daughter of Sapokisikwepiw and Elsa Oger, Godfather: Pierre Oger, Godmother: Marguerite Desmarais, V. Vegreville p.m.a.o.m.i. (page 134)

Sapokyikyepiw, Julie: B-388, Julie Sapokyikyepiw, baptized 1 October 1866, age about 5 months, daughter of Sapokyikyepiw and Etsakopwew, Godmother: Marguerite Fosseneuve, Maisonneuve A. priest o.m.i. (page 76)

Sasawakonop, Baptiste: B-115, Baptiste Sasawakonop, baptized 18 January 1857, age about 3 months, son of Sasawakonop and Nanette Kisiman, Godfather: James McGuay, Maisonneuve A. priest o.m.i. (page 22)

Sasawakonop, Catherine: B-114, Catherine Sasawakonop, baptized 18 January 1857, age about 6 years, daughter of Sasawakonop and Nanette Kisiman, Godmother: Catherine Berland, Maisonneuve A. priest o.m.i. (page 22)

Sauteuse, Marie and Tsimanoskats: M-29, Marie Sauteuse married 10 September 1861, Witnesses: George Adam and the brother of Tsimanoskats, Tissot Jn. priest o.m.i. (page 46)

Sauteuse, Marie: B-416, Marie Sauteuse, buried 8 September 1867, died 6 September 1867, age 22 years, daughter of Angelique Desjarlais, Present: Georges Adam and Joseph Cardinal, Maisonneuve A. priest o.m.i. (page 84)

Sauve, Angelique; See Louis Laroque and Angelique Sauve

Lac la Biche Baptisms, Marriages and Burials 1853-1884

Sauve, Marguerite; See Guillaume Desjarlais and Marguerite Sauve

Sauve, Norbert and Isabelle Bellehumeur: M-6, Norbert Sauve, adult son of Norbert Sauve and Josephte St.Pierre, married 6 November 1871, Isabelle Bellehumeur, minor daughter of Michel Bellehumeur and Louise Gonneville, Present: Norbert Sauve and Victor Sulivan, V. Vegreville p.m.a.o.m.i. (page 124)

Sawan, Joseph: B-313, Joseph Sawan, baptized 6 September 1864, born yesterday, son of Sawan and __, Godfather: Paulette Auger, Godmother: Marguerite Laroque, Tissot Jn. priest o.m.i. (page 59)

Sawan, Pierre: B-24, Pierre Sawan, baptized 23 April 1854, age 2 months, son of Sawan and Nawanokupawik, Godfather: Pierre Morin, Alex Ev. de St.Boniface o.m.i. (page 5)

Sawapas, Johny: B-209, Johny Sawapas, baptized 16 September 1860, born 5 August 1860, son of Michel Sawapas and Louisa McGillis, Godfather: Charles Houl, Godmother: Julie McGillis, Maisonneuve A. priest o.m.i. (page 39)

Sesawekaskwek, Michel and Rozalie: B-12 and B-13, Michel and Rozalie Sesawekaskwek, baptized 13 October 1853, age about 3 years, children of Sesawekaskwek and Wiyasikwapiwisk, Godfather: Joseph Ladouceur, Godmother: Julie Auge, M. R. Remas p.o.m.i. (page 3-4)

Sesowekaskwet, Catherine: B-234, Catherine Sesowekaskwet, baptized 16 September 1861, age 6 years, daughter of Sesowekaskwet and Wiyasikepiwis, Godmother: Catherine Ladouceur, Tissot Jn. priest o.m.i. (page 43)

Seyabotawatinam, Josephte: B-280, Josephte Seyabotawatinam, baptized 13 May 1863, age one year, daughter of Seyabotawatinam and Sakasawisk, Godmother: Angelique Crise, Tissot Jn. priest o.m.i. (page 52)

Seyapukyikwepiw, Adelaide; See Olivier Cardinal and Adelaide Seyapukyikwepiw

Shelkederro, William: B-435, William Skelkederro, baptized 6 June 1868, age 16 months, legitimate son of Charles Shelkederro and Marie Istoile, Godfather: Francois Bisson, Godmother: Isakale, V. Vegreville p.m.a.o.m.i. (page 91)

Simpson, James and Catherine Moyon: M-43, James Simpson (signed), married 21 October 1864 Catherine Moyon, widow of Louis Patenode, Witnesses: Charles Montigne (signed), Fl. Vanden Bergh priest o.m.i. (signed), Maisonneuve A. P. o.m.i. (signed), and Alex. Eveque de St.Boniface o.m.i. (signed). (page 62)

Simpson, John and Catherine Robillard: M-12, John Sympson, adult son of Thomas Sympson and Jeanne Koog, married 17 August 1856 at Fort Cumberland, Catherine Robillard, minor daughter of Baptiste Robillard and Catherine Ducharme, Witnesses: Baptiste Pelletier and Joseph McSellan, Maisonneuve A. priest o.m.i. (page 17)

Sisawapas, Adam: B-21, Adam Sisawapas, buried 26 January 1864, died night before last, age about 20 years, Present: Georges Burk and Eugene Wawiyenam, Tissot Jn. priest o.m.i. (page 56)

Lac la Biche Baptisms, Marriages and Burials 1853-1884

Sisawapas, Alexandre: B-25, Alexandre Sisawapas, baptized 13 December 1871, born yesterday, legitimate son of Louis Sisawapas and Marguerite Laroque, Godfather: Francois Laroque, Godmother: Marianne Pattenaude, M. R. Remas priest o.m.i. (page 126)

Sisawapas, Augustin: B-8, Augustin Sisawapas, baptized 4 April 1869, born today, legitimate son of Louison Sisawapas and Marguerite Laroque, Godfather: Elzear Laroque, Godmother: Marie Laroque, V. Vegrevillle, p.m.a.o.m.i. (page 99)

Sisawapas, Eleonore: B-42, Eleonore Sisawapas, baptized 18 September 1881, age about 8 days, legitimate daughter of Louison Sisawapas and Marguerite Laroque, Godmother: Louise Hamelin (signed), E. Grouard priest o.m.i. (page 211)

Sisawapas, Elisabeth: B-174, Elisabeth Sisawapas, baptized 18 December 1858, age about 3 months, daughter of Pierre Sisawapas and Agnes Batauche, Godfather: Johny Nolin, Godmother: Rosalie Batauche, Maisonneuve A. priest o.m.i. (page 32)

Sisawapas, Elise: B-392, Elise Sisawapas, baptized 17 November 1866, legitimate daughter of Louison Sisawapas and Marguerite Laroque, Gofather: _ Laroque, Godmother: Angelique Sahis, V. Vegreville, priest mis. o.m.i. (page 77)

Sisawapas, Louison and Marguerite Larocque: M-48, Louison Sisawapas, married 28 November 1865, Marguerite Larocque, Present: Francois Larocque and Michel Passam, Maisonneuve A. priest o.m.i. (page 69)

Sisawapas, Marcel: B-38, Marcel Sisawapas, baptized 26 November 1876, born yesterday, legitimate son of Louison Sisawapas and Marguerite Laroque, Godfather: Marcel Tremblay, Godmother: Sophie St.Sauveur, Collignon o.m.i. (page 165)

Sisawapas, Marie Delphine: B-378, Marie-Delphine Sisawapas, baptized 30 April 1866, born yesterday, legitimate daughter of Pierre Sisawapas and Agnes Batoche, Godfather: Julien Cardinal, Godmother: Rosalie Kakikekamik, V. Vegreville priest mis. o.m.i. (page 74)

Sisawapas, Michel: S-5, Michel Sisawapas, buried 24 October 1871, age 35 or 40 years, Witnesses: Louis Sisawapas and Norbert Sauve, M. R. Remas priest o.m.i. (page 124)

Sisawapas, Marie Julie: S-1, Marie Julie Sisawapas, bu. 26 January 1874, died yesterday age over 6 years, daughter of Joseph Sisawapas and Euphrosine Lemire, Witnesses: Theophile Boucher and Joseph Boucher, V. Vegreville p.m.a.o.m.i. (page 141)

Sisawapas, Marie; See Augustin Mognon and Marie Sisawapas

Sisawapas, Michel and Elise McGillis: M-15, Michel Sisawapas married 14 June 1857 Elise McGillis, Present: Augustin Gaudry and Baptiste Surprenant, Tissot priest (page 25)

Sisawapas, Patrice: B-18, Patrice Sisawapas, baptized 13 July 1878, born yesterday, legitimate son of Louison Sisawapas and Marguerite Laroque, Godfather: Farncois Laroque, Godmother: Marie Anne Paguenaude, Collignon o.m.i. (page 179)

Lac la Biche Baptisms, Marriages and Burials 1853-1884

Sisawapas, Patrice: S-3, Patrice Sisawapas, buried 14 July 1884, died 12 July 1884, age about 5 years, Witnesses: Duncan Tremblay and Baptiste Laroque, Collignon o.m.i.p. (page 238)

Sisawapas, Rosalie: B-34, Rosalie Sisawapas, baptized 12 December 1884, born yesterday of the legitimate marriage of Louison Sisawapas and Marguerite Laroque, Godfather: Baptiste Laroque, Godmother: Anna Hamelin, Collignon o.m.i.p. (page 242-243)

Sisawapas: S-4, Sisawapas, buried 10 January 1873, Collignon o.m.i. (page 134-135)

Sisawapas, Sophie: B-198, Sophie Sisawapas, baptized 20 November 1859, age about 6 months, daughter of Michel Siswapas and Elisa McGillis, Godfather: Baptiste Lafreniere, Godmother: Ursule St.Germain, Tissot Jn. priest o.m.i. (page 36)

Sisawapas, Sophie: B-210, Sophie Sisawapas, baptized 16 September 1860, born 15 September 1860, daughter of Pierre Sisawapas and Agnes Batauche, Godfather: Baptiste Kakikekamik, Godmother: Louise McGillis, Maisonneuve, A. priest o.m.i. (page 39)

Sisawapas, Sophie: S-18, Sophie Sisawapas, buried 12 May 1863, died this morning, age 4 years, Present: Joseph Ladouceur and Baptiste Amiskuiyinisis, Tissot Jn. priest o.m.i. (page 52)

Sisawapas, Susanne: B-5, Susanne Sisawapas, baptized 28 March 1871, born yesterday, legitimate child of Joseph Sisawapas and Fraisine Jiousso, Godfather: Johnny Sisawapas, Godmother: Elaiza McGillis, M. R. Remas priest (page 120)

Sisawekaskwet, Alphonse: B-327, Alphonse Sisawekaskwet, baptized 13 December 1864, age about one year, son of Sisawekaskwet and Wisikepewis, Godmother: Pelagie Samaskekabo, Tissot Jn. priest o.m.i. (page 62)

Sisawikaskwep, Peter: B-403, Peter Sisawikaskwep, baptized 8 June 1867, age over 2 months, son of Sisawikaskwep and Wiyesikwepewisk, Godmother: Julie Auger, V. Vegreville, p.m.a.o.m.i. (page 81)

Sisawikaskwep, Rosalie; See Pierre Nikateki and Rosalie Sisawikaskwep

Sisipis, Charles: B-15, Charles Sisispis, baptized 27 March 1881, age about 10 years, son of the deceased Sisipis and Oskipakaw, Godfather: Guillaume Villebrun, Godmother: Silvie Quintal, Collignon o.m.i. p. (page 205)

Sisowitaskwet, Isabelle: B-259, Isabelle Sisowitaskwet, baptized 25 May 1862, are 5 months, daughter of Sisowitaskwet and Wasikopewis, Godmother: Angelique Desjarlais, Tissot Jn. priest o.m.i. (page 49)

Siswapas, Alexandre: S-3, Alexandre Siswapas, buried 29 March 1872, age about 4 months, Witnesses: Francois Laroque and David Ladouceur, M. R. Remas priest o.m.i. (page 128)

Siyabokisiwepayiw, Justine: B-10, Justine Siyabokisiwepayiw, baptized 20 April 1870, abe 11 days, legitimate daughter of Siyabokisiwepayiw and Elisa Auge, Godmother: Genevieve Ladouceur, M. R. Remas priest o.m.i. (page 111)

Lac la Biche Baptisms, Marriages and Burials 1853-1884

Siyapokisikwepiw; See Elise (Oger) Auger and Siyapokisikwepiw

Siyaposikwepo, Josephte: B-320, Josephte Siyaposikwepo, baptized 21 October 1864, age 6 years, daughter of Siyaposikwepo and Etsakapo, Godmother: Josephte Jolifant, Tissot Jn. priest o.m.i. (page 60-61)

Siyaposikwepo, Priscille: B-321, Priscille Siyaposikwepo, baptized 21 October 1864, age 3 years, daughter of Siyaposikwepo and Etsakapo, Godmother: Josephte Desjarlais, Tissot Jn. priest o.m.i. (page 61)

Siyapukisikwepiw, Sophie: B-14, Sophie Siyapukisikwepiw, baptized 25 April 1875, age 20 days, father Siyapukisikwepiw, mother Elisa Auge, Godfather: Pierre Auger, Godmother: Elisa Ladouceur, A. G. B. Brunet p.o.m.i. (page 151)

Smith, Modeste: B-331, Modeste Smith, baptized 8 January 1865, age about one month, illegitimate son of Louis Alfred Smith and Kasewiyasu, Godfather: Honore, Godmother: Bethsy Branconnier, Tissot Jn. Priest o.m.i. (page 63)

St.Luc, Arsene: B-39, Arsene St.Luc, baptized 15 December 1880, age 2 days, illegitimate son of Melanie St.Luc, Godmother: Eleonore St.Luc, Collignon o.m.i.p. (page 201)

St.Paul, Isabelle: B-13, Isabelle St.Paul, baptized 27 July 1871, born yesterday, legitimate daughter of Bruno St.Paul and Isabelle Kakikekamik, Godmother: Angelique, Collignon o.m.i. (page 121)

St.Pierre, Anastasie (Montagnaise): B-55, Anastasie St.Pierre (Montagnaise), baptized 25 December 1881, age about 4 months, daughter of St.Pierre and Judith (Montagnaise), no godparents, Collignon o.m.i.p. (page 214)

St.Pierre, Patrice (Montagnais): B-29, Patrice St.Pierre (Montagnais), baptized 8 October 1884, age 5 weeks, son of St.Pierre and Judith (Montagnais), Godfather: Petit Louis Hamelin, Godmother: Marguerite Desjarlais, Collignon o.m.i.p. (page 241)

St.Sauveur, Sophie: B-47, Sophie St.Sauveur, baptized 1 September 1854 at Fort Pitt, age 8 months, daughter of Pierre St.Sauveur and Marie Wapasthak, Godfather: Goerge Adthon (Hudon), M. R. Remas p.o.m.i. (page 8)

St.Sauveur, Sophie; See Marcel Tremblay and Sophie St.Sauveur

Strengle, Caroline: B-20, Caroline Major, baptized 27 August 1882, age about one month, illegitimate daughter of Major Trondle (Charles Strengle) and Pauline, Godmother: Marie Courte-Oreille, Collignon o.m.i.p. (page 220)

Strengler, Augustin: B-37, Augustin (Strengler), baptized 11 December 1880, age about one year, illegitimate son of Major Chendler (Strengler) and Pauline, the godfather was Father Collignon, Godmother: Lisette Mustatip, Collignon o.m.i.p. (page 201)

Sunday, Marie-Anne: B-21, Marie-Anne Sunday, baptized 9 August 1878, age one month, legitimate daughter of __ Sunday and Isabelle Missinewakop, Godmother: Marie-Anne Cardinal, + Henri, Eveque d'Amonamour, o.m.i. (page 180)

Lac la Biche Baptisms, Marriages and Burials 1853-1884

T'elk'alu, Adelaide: B-16, Adelaide T'elk'alu, baptized 15 April 1876, age 3 months, legitimate daughter of Charles T'elk'alu and Marguerite Othere, Godmother: Angelique, Godfather: Antoine Derez, Husson priest o.m.i. (page 160)

T'elkaileru, Alexis: B-11, Alexis T'elkaileru, baptized 20 April 1878, age about 4 months, legitimate son of Charles T'elkaileru and Marguerite Intoraze, Godfather: Pascal, E. Grouard priest o.m.i. (page 177)

Taetse, Marie: B-85, Marie Taetse, baptized 16 January 1856, age over one month, illegitimate daughter of Marie Taetse, Godfather: Alexis Buisson, Godmother: Marie, Tissot Jn. priest o.m.i. (page 16)

Taetsi, Sophie: B-185, Sophie Taetsi, baptized 3 April 1859, illegitimate daughter of Taetsi, Godfather: Pierre Edelakrone, Godmother: Louise Shahonshi, Tissot Jn priest o.m.i. (page 33-34)

Tahitsi, Magdeleine: B-338, Magdeleine Tahitsi, baptized 12 April 1865, age 4 months, illegitimate daughter of Marie Tahitsi, Godfather: Pierre Grosse-Tete, Godmother: Angelique Ishanada, Tissot Jn. priest o.m.i. (page 65)

Takutchin, Francois: B-29, Francois Takutchin, baptized 15 October 1870, age about one month, son of Dominique Takutchin and Susanne Cardinal, Godmother: Isabelle Kikinittawikiw, M. R. Remas priest o.m.i. (page 116)

Takutchin, Alexandre: B-32, Alexandre Takutchin, baptized 29 October 1879, age one month, legitimate son of Takutchin and Suzanne, Godfather: Absalom Ladouceur, Godmother: Florestine Ladouceur (signed), E. Grouard priest o.m.i. (page 192)

Takutchin, Helene: B-37, Helene Takutchin, baptized 24 August 1881, age about one month, legitimate daughter of Dominique Takutchin and Suzanne Cardinal, Godmother: Eulalie Hamelin (signed), E. Grouard p.o.m.i. (page 209)

Takutchin, Louise: B-4, Louise Takutchin, baptized 31 January 1875, born a few days, of the legitimate marriage of Dominique Takutchin and Susanne Cardinal, Godfather: Johny Pambrun, Godmother: Suzette Cardinal, J. V. Fourmond priest o.m.i. (page 148)

Takutshin, James: B-33, James Takutshin, baptized 23 September 1877, age one month, legitimate son of Takutshin and __, Godfather: Joseph Nipiteham, Godmother: Therese, E. Grouard priest o.m.i. (page 172)

Takutsin, Agathe: B-305, Agathe Takutsin, baptized 8 May 1864, age 10 months, daughter of Takutsin and Susanne Cardinal, Godfather: Eugene Wawispnam [?], Godmother: Genevieve Cardinal, Tissot priest o.m.i. (page 57)

Takutsin, Charlotte; See Ignace Cardinal and Charlotte Takutsin

Takutsin, Pierre: B-31, Pierre Takutsin, baptized 14 September 1883, age about one month, legitimate son of Takutsin and Susanne Cardinal, Godfather: Pierre Lapoudre, Godmother: his wife, Collignon o.m.i.p. (page 231)

Lac la Biche Baptisms, Marriages and Burials 1853-1884

Takutsin, Therese: B-11, Therese Takutsin, baptized 11 May 1873, age about 6 months, legitimate daughter of Dominique Takutsin and Susanne Laurent, Godfather: Louison Fosseneuve, Godmother: Sophie Ladouceur, Collignon o.m.i. (page 137)

Taylor, Thomas and Florestine Ladouceur: M-4, Thomas Taylor married 28 September 1880 Florestine Ladouceur, two bans dispensed, Witnesses: Edward Villeneuve (x) and Narcisse Boucher (x), Collignon o.m.i.p. Declaration by Thomas Taylor (signed with an x) promising he will allow his future wife and children to practice the Catholic faith, Witnesses: Julien Cardinal (signed) and Louis Lavallee (signed). (page 199-200)

Tcipis, Cuthbert: B-165, Cuthbert Tcipis, baptized 19 September 1858, age about 3 months, son of Tcipis and Marie Sisawikunew, Godfather: Baptiste Pelletier, Godmother: Magdeleine Deschamps, Maisonneuve A. priest o.m.i. (page 30)

Telkelero, Julien: B-20, Julien Telkelero, baptized 31 August 1869, age 6 months, legitimate son of Charles Telkelero and Marguerite Edoeyaze, Godmother: Julie Gladu, V. Vegreville p.m.a.o.m.i. (page 104)

Tepwatamakew, Eugenie: B-92, Eugenie Tepwatamakew, baptized 18 May 1856, age over 2 months, daughter of Tepwatamakew and Kiyakikapiw, Godfather: Abraham Lariviere, Godmother: Eugenie Ladouceur, Tissot Jn. priest o.m.i. (page 17)

Teyapetawapiw, Marguerite: B-247, Marguerite Teyapetawapiw, baptized 16 January 1861, age about 2 months, daughter of Teyapetawapiw, Godmother: Marie Kiywin, Maisonneuve, A. priest o.m.i. (page 47)

Theottine, Rosalie: B-23, Rosalie Theottine, baptized 11 July 1880, age about one month, legitimate daughter of Fabien Theottine and Marguerite, Godmother: Marie wife of Andre, E. Grouard priest o.m.i. (page 198)

Theweyan, Mary; B54, Marie Theweyan, baptized 4 September 1854, at Fort Pitt, age about 18 years, daughter of Theweyan, Godfather: Louis Chatelain, M. R. Remas p.o.m.i. (page 9)

Thiottine, Isabelle: B-12, Isabelle Thiottine, baptized 20 April 1878, age about 4 months, legitimate daughter of Fabien Thiottine and Marguerite, Godmother: Angele, E. Grouard priest o.m.i. (page 177)

Thompson, Bethsy: B-364, Bethsy Thomson, baptized 25 October 1865, born 5 October 1865, daughter of Thompson and Tomik, Godmother: Bethsy Braconnier, V. Vegreville priest o.m.i. (page 71)

Tige, James and Mary Fraser: M-2, James Tige, adult son of Michael Tige and Mary Lanian, married 14 May 1872, Mary Fraser, adult daughter of the late Louis Fraser and Cecile Ogden, Present: Alexis Reynard and David Ladouceur, V. Vegreville p.m.a.o.m.i. (page 129-130)

Tige, James: B-11, James Tige, baptized 29 June 1874, born yesterday, legitimate son of James Tige and Marie Fraser, Godfather: Narcisse Boucher, Godmother: Marianne Pattenaude, V. Vegreville p.m.a.o.m.i. (page 143_144)

Tige, James: S-8, James Tige, buried 28 October 1875, age about 7 months, Witnesses: Julien Cardinal and James Tige, M. R. Remas priest o.m.i. (page 157)

Timanaskak, Joseph and Angelique Ducharme: M-3, Joseph Timanaskak married 21 April 1870 Angelique Ducharme, Present: Julie Cardinal and Louis Laroque, M. R. Remas priest o.m.i. (page 111)

Timanaskak, Joseph: B-9, Joseph Timanaskak, baptized 4 March 1869, age 30 years, Godmother: Julie Auge, + Vital J Ev. De Satala o.m.i. (page 100)

Titipowakew, Paul: B-45, Paul Titipowakew, baptized 22 October 1881, age about 55 years, Godfather: Paul Cardinal, Collignon o.m.i.p. (page 212)

Toussaint, Nancy: B-32, Nancy Toussaint, baptized 3 September 1878, age about 5 months, daughter of Toussaint and Angelique, Godfather: St.Luc Mustatip, Godmother: Lisette Mustatip, Collignon o.m.i. (page 181)

Toussaint, William: B-41, William Toussaint, baptized 30 December 1883, age about one month, legitimate son of Toussaint and Angelique, Godmother: Isabelle Osisis, Collignon o.m.i.p. (page 233)

Tremblay, Alexandre: B-29, Alexandre Temblay, baptized 3 October 1879, born today of the legitimate marriage of Marcel Tremblay and Sophie St.Sauveur, Godfather: Joseph Desilets (signed), Godmother: Olive Tremblay (signed), Collignon o.m.i. (page 191)

Tremblay, Emile: B-31, Emile Tremblay, baptized 11 September 1877, born yesterday of the legitimate marriage of Duncan Tremblay and Sophie St. Sauveur, Godfather: Pierre Ladouceur, Godmother: Marguerite Tremblay, Collignon o.m.i. (page 172)

Tremblay, Louis: B-21, Louis Tremblay, baptized 30 July 1875, age about two months, legitimate son of Thomas Tremblay and Sophie St.Sauveur, Godfather: Joseph Nista, Godmother: Mathilde Tremblay, M. R. Remas pret o.m.i. (page 153-154)

Tremblay, Marcel and Sophie St.Sauveur: M-6, Marcel Tremblay, minor son of Raphael Tremblay and Catherine McDougall, married 19 November 1872, Sophie St.Sauveur, Present: Raphael Tremblay and Louison Sisawapas, V. Vegreville priest omi. (page 133)

Tremblay, Marguerite; See Paul Cardinal and Marguerite Tremblay

Tremblay, Marie Victoire: B-3, Marie Victoire Tremblay, baptized 29 January 1874, born yesterday, legitimate daughter of Marcel Treblay and Sophie St.Sauveur, Godfather: Raphael Tremblay, Godmother: Catherine McDougall, V. Vegreville p.m.a.o.m.i. (page 141)

Tremblay, Marie-Angelina-Adele: B-2, Marie-Angelina-Adele Tremblais, baptized 24 January 1875, born yesterday, of the legitimate marriage of Raphael Tremblais and Catherine McDougall, Godfather: Joseph Ladouceur, Godmother: Marie-Angelina Landry, J. V. Fourmond priest o.m.i. (page 148)

Tremblay, Marie-Angelique: S-9, Marie-Angelique Tremblay, baptized 21 November 1875, age 11 [months], Witnesses: Raphael and Duncan Tremblay, H. Leduc priest (page 157)

Lac la Biche Baptisms, Marriages and Burials 1853-1884

Tremblay, Marie-Delphine: B-12, Marie-Delphine Tremblay, baptized 30 May 1884, born today of the legitimate marriage of Marcel Temblay and Sophie St.Sauveur, Godfather: Raphael Tremblay, Godmother: Marguerite Laroque, Collignon o.m.i.p. (page 237)

Tremblay, Marie-Victoire: S-4, Marie-Victoire Tremblay, buried 14 March 1874, died yesterday, age 6 weeks, daughter of Marcel Tremblay and Sophie St.Sauveur, Witnesses: Raphael Tremblay and Narcisse Boucher, V. Vegreville p.m.a.o.m.i. (page 141-142)

Tremblay, Mathilde; See Joseph Nisto and Mathilde Tremblay

Tremblay, Rosalie; See Louis Riguidel and Rosalie Tremblay

Tsak'ale, Francois: B-31, Francois Tsak'ale, baptized 10 September 1876, born 6 August 1876, son of Jean-Baptiste __ and Catherine Tsak'ale, Godmother: Sophie Tsak'ale, F. LeSerrec priest (page 163)

Tsakutsin, Charlotte: B-284, Charlotte Tsakutsin, baptized 31 May 1863, age about 2 years, daughter of Tsakutsin and Susanne Cardinal, Godmother: Marguerite Timakis, Tissot Jn. priest o.m.i. (page 53)

Tscottine, Auguste;B-15, Auguste Tscottine, baptized 15 April 1876, age 2 months, legitimate son of Fabien Tscottine and Marguerite Otthere, Godmother: Sophie Otthere, Husson p.o.m.i. (page 160)

Tsillis, Baptiste: B-239, Baptiste Tsillis, baptized 17 September 1861, age about 5 months, son of Tsillis Cris and Marguerite Crise, Godmother: Marie Cardinal, Maisonneuve A. priest o.m.i. (page 44)

Tsimanaskat, Baptiste: B-343, Baptiste Tsimanaskat, baptized 12 May 1865, age about 6 years, natural son of Tsimanaskat and Kyakikekwanepiw, Godfather: Eugene Waweyonam, Masionneuve, A. priest o.m.i. (page 66)

Tsimanaskat, Baptiste: S-36, Baptiste Tsimanaskat, buried 25 February 1867, died day before yesterday, age about 8 years, natural son of Tsimanaskat and Kyakikekwamepiw, Present: Georges Bourk and Theodore Decoin, Maisonneuve A. priest o.m.i. (page 78-79)

Tsimanaskat, Betsy; See Joseph Desjarlais and Betsy Tsimanaskat

Tsimanaskats, Bethsy: B-272, Bethsy Tsimanaskats, baptized 16 November 1862, age one month, daughter of Tsimanaskats and Marie Sauteuse, Godmother: Bethsy Cardinal, Tissot Jn. priest o.m.i. (page 51)

Tsimanoskats; See Marie Sauteuse and Tsimanoskats

Tsimokits, Josephte: S-1, Josephte Tsimokits, buried 30 May 1869, died yesterday, age about 50 years, Witnesses: Luc Cardinal and Johny Cardinal, V. Vegreville p.m.a.o.m.i. (page 101)

Tsinizegan, Marie; See Louis Woule and Marie Tsinizegan

Tsinnaze, Therese: B-23, Therese Tsinnaze, baptized 5 September 1869, age about 40 years, Godfather: Thomas [...], Godmother: Marguerite [...], V. Vegreville p.m.a.o.m.i. (page 105)

Tsoulyaze, Marie; See Andre Yeskatla and Marie Tsoulyaze

Villebrun, Elise: B-4, Elise Villebrun, baptized 28 January 1872, born 15 January 1872, legitimate daughter of Guillaume Villebrun and Flora Hope, Godmother: Bethsey Quintal, M. R. Remas priest o.m.i. (page 127)

Villebrun, Emma: B-10, Emma Villebrun, baptized 21 June 1874, born day before yesterday, legitimate daughter of Guillaume Vilbrun and Flora Hope, Godfather: Charles Johnston, Godmother: Catherine Hope, V. Vegreville, p.m.a.o.m.i. (page 143)

Villebrun, Flora: B-4, Flora Villebrun, baptized 25 January 1877, born 23 of the same month, of the legitimate marriage of Guillaume Villebrun and Flora Hope, Godfather: Isidore Pambrun, Godmother: Maggy Hope, E. Grouard priest o.m.i. (page 166)

Villebrun, Francois: B-29, FrancoisVillebrun, baptized 14 October 1882, age 4 days, legitimate son of Guillaume Villebrun and Flora Hope, Godmother: Elise, Collignon o.m.i.p. (page 222)

Villebrun, Gilbert: B-17, Gilbert Villebrun, baptized 14 April 1880, born 10 April 1880, of the legitimate marriage of Guillaume Villebrun and Flora Hope, no godparents, E. Grouard priest o.m.i.. (page 196)

Villebrun, Guillaume and Flora Hope: M-58, Guillaume Villebrun, adult son of Louis Villebrun and Louise Collin, married 21 July 1867, Flora Hope, minor daughter of the late James Hope and Judith Desjarlais, Present: Ignace McKay and Louis Lavallee, V. Vegreville p.m.a.o.m.i. (page 83)

Villeneuve, Edward and Adelaide Decoine: M-2, Edward Villeneuve married 10 January 1881 Adelaide Decoine, Present: Isidore Decoine (x) and Pierre Ladouceur (x), Collignon o.m.i.p. (page 202)

Villeneuve, Edward: B-6, Edward Villeneuve, baptized 26 February 1882, born 15 February 1882, legitimate son of Edward Villeneuve and Adelaide Decoine, Godfather: Peter Prudent, Godmother: Marie Ducharme, Collignon o.m.i.p. (page 216)

Vivier, Jonas: B-102, Jonas Viviers, baptized 6 September 1856, age about 11 months, legitimate son of Olivier Viviers and Lalouise Lavallee, Godmother: Scholastique Viviers, Maisonneuve A. priest o.m.i. (page 19)

Viviers, Christianne; See Theodore Decoine and Christianne Viviers

Viviers, Christianne; See Henry Decoin and Christianne Viviers

Viviers, Isidore: B-164, Isidore Viviers, baptized 5 September 1858, age about 9 months, son of Abraham Viviers and Lalouise Vallee, Godmother: Genevieve Savoyard, Maisonneuve A. priest o.m.i. (page 30)

Wabamukamik, Rosalie: B-26, Rosalie Wabamukamik, baptized 4 October 1870, age about 20 years, Godmother: Angele Wiyepitshitsheb, M. R. Remas priest o.m.i. (page 115)

Wabamukamik, Rosalie; See Jean Kiyatshikaskwew and Rosalie Wabamukamik

Lac la Biche Baptisms, Marriages and Burials 1853-1884

Wabanikapaw, Francois: B-27, Francois Wabanikapaw, baptized 9 October 1870, age about one month, son of Joseph Wabanikapaw and Kanawawasuw, Godmother: Angelique Sauve, M. R. Remas priest o.m.i. (page 115)

Wabanikapaw, Joseph and Christina Kanawawasuw: M-9, Joseph Wabanikapaw married 10 October 1870 Christina Kanawawasuw, Witnesses: Charles Cardinal and Caroline Johnston, M. R. Remas priest o.m.i. (page 115-116)

Wabastow, Josephte: B-5, Josephte Wabastow, baptized 1 March 1869, age 70-80 years, Godfather: Martin Emard, M. R. Remas priest o.m.i. (page 99)

Wanipiteham, Felix: B-32, Felix Wanipiteham, bpatized 20 September 1880, age about 4 months, legitimate son of Joseph Wanipiteham and Therese, no godparents, E. Grouard priest o.m.i. (page 199)

Waniwewmanisis, Johny: B-2, Johny Waniwewmanisis, baptized 5 April 1873, age about 2 months, legitimate son of Waniwewmanisis and Bethsi Kanittawipaswayowisk, Godfather: Georges Bourque, Godmother: Agathe Ladouceur, Collignon o.m.i. (page 135)

Wapamikapaw, Basile: B-404, Basile Wapamikapaw, baptized 10 June 1867, age 5 months, son of Wapamikapaw and Kenawawasuw, Godmother: Therese Ladouceur, V. Vegreville, p.m.a.o.m.i. (page 81-82)

Wataskoupiway, Sebastien and Stanislas: B-21 and 21, Sebastien, age over two years, and Stanislas Wataskoupiway, age about 18 months,, baptized 19 January 1854, of the legitimate marriage of Charles Wataskoupiway and Therese, Godfather: Joseph Cardinal, M. R. Remas p.o.m.i. (page 4-5)

Watsikwan, Betsy: B-21, Betsy Watsikwan, baptized 10 April 1881, age about one year, daughter of Watsikwan and Misistikekwewiskwew, Godfather: Guillaume Villebrun, Collignon o.m.i. p. (page 206)

Watsikwan, Charlotte: B-32, Charlotte Watsikwan, baptized 24 September 1883, age about one month, daughter of Watsikwan and Oskipakaw, Godmother: Marguerite Tremblay, Collignon o.m.i.p. (page 231)

Watsikwan, Jules: B-20, Jules Watsikwan, baptized 10 April 1881, age about 4 years, son of Watsikwan and Misistikekwewiskwew, Godfather: Guillaume Villebrun, Collignon o.m.i. p. (page 206)

Waweyinam, Louis: B-7, Louis Waweyinam, baptized 13 April 1879 at Lac de Coeur, age about 3 months, legitimate son of Eugene Waweyinam and Eliza, Godfather: Louis Lavallee, Godmother: Scholastique Mustatip, E. Grouard priest o.m.i. (page 186)

Wawiyenam, Arsene: B-22, Arsene Wawiyenam, baptized 24 December 1874, age 3 weeks, of Eugene Wawiyenam and Elisa Cardinal, Godmother: Lisette Cardinal, J. V. Fourmond priest o.m.i. (page 147)

Wawiyenam, Eugene and Elisa Cardinal: M-63, Eugene Wawigenam, son of the deceased Kiyestinep and Kinweyimot, married 28 April 1868, Elisa Cardinal, minor daugher of Antoine Cardinal and Cecile Bouche, Present: Adam Ladouceur and Joseph Ladouceur, V. Vegreville p.m.a.o.m.i. (page 90)

Wawiyenam, Eugene: B-244, Eugene Wawiyenam, baptized 17 November 1861, age about 16 years, Godfather: Baptiste Kakikekamik, Tissot Jn. priest o.m.i. (page 45)

Lac la Biche Baptisms, Marriages and Burials 1853-1884

Wawiyenam, Mathilde: B-1, Mathilde Wawiyenam, baptized 3 April 1873, age 2 months, legitimate daughter of Eugene Wawiyenam and Elisa Cardinal, Godfather: Narcisse Boucher, Godmother: Mary Fraser, Collignon o.m.i. (page 135)

Wawiyenam, Norbert: B-40, Norbert Wawiyenam, baptized 24 December 1876, age about 2 months, legitimate son of Wawiyenam and Liza, Godfather: Charles Housse, Godmother: Silvie, Collignon o.m.i. (page 165)

Wawiyenam, Pierre: B-8, Pierre Wawiyenam, baptized 8 April 1871, born 30 March 1871, legitimate child of Eugene Wawiyenam and Elaiza Cardinal, Godmother: Cecile Boucher, M. R. Remas priest (page 120)

Wawiymam, Adele: B-27, Adele Wawiymam, baptized 20 August 1883, age 4 days, legitimate daughter of Eugene Wawiymam and Lisa Mustatip, Godfather: F. Mustatip, Godmother: Adele Mustatip, Collignon o.m.i.p. (page 229)

Wawiyonam, Peter: B-12, Peter Wawiyonam, baptized 24 February 1881, born 4 days, legitimate son of Eugene Wawiyonam and Liza Mustatip, Godmother: Lizette Mustatip, the priest served as godfather, Collignon o.m.i. p. (page 204)

Weskipasikn, Magdeleine: B-93, Magdeleine Weskipasikn, baptized 14 July 1856, age about 30 years, daughter of Eyatu Okanap, Godmother: Eugenie Ladouceur, Tissot Jn. priest o.m.i. (page 17-18)

Weskipaskn, Magdeleine; See Baptiste Kakikekamik and Magdeleine Weskipaskn

Wetokwan, Louis: B-169, Louis Wetokwan, baptized 2 December 1858, born 8 April 1858, of Wetokwan and Susanne Desjarlais, Godmother: Julie Auger, Tissot Jn. priest o.m.i. (page 31)

Wetokwan, Rosalie and Paul: B-16 and 17, Rosalie and Paul Wetokwan, children of Wetokwan and Suzanne Desjarlais, baptized 14 October 1853, Paul age a few months, Godfather: Theodore Decoing, Godmother: Catherine Ladouceur; and Rosalie age 3 years, Godmother: Lisette, R. M. Remas priest (page 4)

Wewesis, Marianne: B-77, Marianne Wewesis, baptized 8 September 1855, age over one month, daughter of Paul Wewesis and Euphrosine Cardinal, Godfather: Abraham Lariviere, Godmother: Marie, Tissot Jn. priest o.m.i. (page 14)

Whiteford, Samuel and Marie-Jeanne Pruden: M-7, Samuel Whiteford, adult son of Samuel Whiteford and Marie Whiteford of Victoria, married 21 December 1884, Marie-Jeanne Pruden, adult daughter of Patrice Pruden and Isabelle Bruneau, Present: Rev. P. Collignon (signed), Alexandre Hamelin (signed Alex Hamelin), and Edward Henderson (signed), + Henri, Ev. D'Anomour o.m.i. (page 244)

Windigo, Jean-Baptiste: B-421, Jean-Baptiste (dit Windigo), baptized 29 November 1867, age about 30 years, son of Baptiste and Wawekew, Godfather: Pierre Ladouceur, Godmother: Catherine Ladouceur, V. Vegreville p.m.a.o.m.i. (page 86)

Lac la Biche Baptisms, Marriages and Burials 1853-1884

Windigo, Jean-Baptiste: S-45, Jean-Baptiste (dit Windigo), buried 4 December 1867, died yesterday, age about 30 years, son of Baptiste and Wawekew, Present: Jean-Baptiste Cardinal and Johny Cardinal, V. Vegreville p.m.a.o.m.i. (page 86)

Wiskipakikus, Francoise: B-166, Francoise Wiskipakikus, baptized 26 October 1858, age 4 weeks, daughter of Wiskipakikus and Marie Desjarlais, Godfather: Joseph Ladouceur, Godmother: Isabelle Itwenkamikung, Maisonneuve A. priest o.m.i. (page 30-31)

Wiskipapamuttew, Rosalie: B-23, Rosalie Wiskipapamuttew, baptized 22 July 1876, age about 60 years, Godfather: Paul Cardinal, Godmother: Marie Landry (signed), M. R. Remas, priest o.m.i. (page 162)

Wiskipapamuttew, Rosalie; See Baptiste Petwiwitam and Rosalie Wiskipapamuttew

Witokwan, Susanne: B-111, Susanne Witokwan, baptized 18 January 1857, age one year, daughter of Witokwan and Susanne Desjarlais, Godmother: Susanne Nepissing, Maisonneuve A. priest o.m.i. (page 22)

Wiyasihupehusk, Marie: B-8, Marie Wiyasihupehusk, baptized 9 March 1875, age about 45 years, Godmother: Sister Tisseur (signed), H. Leduc priest o.m.i. (page 149)

Wiyaskakapawiw, Benjamin: B-386, Benjamin Wiyaskakapawiw, baptized 24 September 1866, age 15 days, son of Joseph Wiyaskakapawiw and Peswekanaapiw, Godmother: Catherine Cardinal, V. Vegreville o.m.i. (page 76)

Wiyaskakapawiw, Isabelle: B-385, Isabelle Wiyaskakapawiw, baptized 24 September 1866, age 3 years, daughter of Joseph Wiyaskakapawiw and Peswekanaapiew, Godmother: Catherine Cardinal, V. Vegreville o.m.i. (page 76)

Wiyaskiyakuhu, Alexis, B-254, Alexis Wiyaskiyakuhu, baptized 13 April 1862, age 6 months, son of Wiyaskiyakuhu and Mikunagus, Godmother: Angelique Desjarlais, Tissot Jn. priest o.m.i. (page 48)

Wiyasoskamukattew, Helene: B-29, Helene Wiyasoskamukattew, baptized 9 December 1872, age about 12 days, legitimate daughter of Schot Wiyasoskamukattew and Catherine Jacob, Godfather: Guilluame Vivier, Godmother: Flora Hope, Collignon o.m.i. (page 133)

Wiyotiniwatam, Moise: B-375, Moise Wiyotiniwatam, baptized 28 March 1866, age about 2 years, natural daughter of Wiyotiniwatam and Therese Tseyanats, Godmother: Rosalie Kakikekamik, Maisonneuve A. p. o.m.i. (page 73)

Woule, Lazare: B-14, Lazare Woule, baptized 4 June 1869, age 5 months, legitimate son of Thomas Woule and Adele Dibayase, Godfather: Louis Woule, Godmother: Marie Tsinnizegan, V. Vegreville p.m.a.o.m.i. (page 101)

Woule, Louis and Marie Tsinizegan: M-5, Louis Woule, adult son of the late Woule and Shamethe, married 5 June 1869, Marie Tsinizegan, widow of William Etecle, Present: Etienne Quintal and Pierre Quintal, V. Vegreville p.m.a.o.m.i. (page 101)

Lac la Biche Baptisms, Marriages and Burials 1853-1884

Yatuwatam, Catherine; See Jean-Baptiste Okkakew and Catherine Yatuwatam

Yeskatla, Andre and Marie Tsoulayze: M- 34, Andre Yeskatla married 5 September 1862 Marie Tsoulayze, Present: Charles Dekayers and Francois Ittetro, Tissot Jn. priest o.m.i. (page 49-50)

Yoskipis, Marie-Caroline: B-13, Marie-Caroline Yoskipis, baptized 8 June 1879, age about one month, legitimate daughter of Yoskipis and Emma (Lac Castor), Godmother: Caroline Ladouceur, Collignon o.m.i. (page 188)

www.ingramcontent.com/pod-product-compliance
Lightning Source LLC
Chambersburg PA
CBHW081222280526
45787CB00006B/2484